FREE THE PEOPLE TO FREE THE MONEY TO FREE THE PEOPLE

AN ORGANIZE THE RICH ANTHOLOGY

Edited by

Michael Gast, Marian Moore, and Alex T. Tom

Published by Organize the Rich

Designed by Dio Cramer

Printed by Smart Set in Minneapolis, MN

ISBN: 979-8-218-73534-0

We are able to bring this book to you through financial support from people and organizations. Want to fund future publications like this Anthology? Email funding@organizetherich.com

FREE THE PEOPLE TO FREE THE MONEY TO FREE THE PEOPLE

Edited by Michael Gast, Marian Moore, and Alex T. Tom

FOREWORD

ORIENTATION

LINEAGE

MOVEMENT ECONOMICS

STORIES FROM THE FIELD

FINDING A NEW WAY

ENDNOTES

JI MISAWAABANDAAMING

Winona LaDuke

Winona LaDuke is a Water Protector, farmer, economist and author. She has devoted her life to advocating for Indigenous Peoples' defense and caretaking of homelands and cultural practices. LaDuke is an enrolled member of the Mississippi Band of Anishinaabeg and lives on the White Earth Reservation in Minnesota.

"When enough seeds are awake, freed from fear and other negative aspects of the third and fourth level consciousness, the fifth level seeds will be able to sprout within humanity and form a whole."

Q'eros prophecies,[1] from the Andes

We live in the time of prophecies, and it is the time when we must dream and bring our future forward. We have a word in the Ojibwe or Anishinaabe language: *Ji misawaabandaaming*. That means something like, "Positive window shopping for your future."

That is what we do together. We are envisioning and creating a good future for our relatives, whether they have wings, fins, roots, paws or hands. That's our opportunity and responsibility. That is because we have agency and the ability to transform.

This is our covenant — that's what we would think of it as — the responsibility of humans. Or, in (my language) Anishinaabemowin, we understand that we are humans being. I like this concept, because it's an action, a verb — being, we as humans are in a process of being, and transforming. We are not a noun but a verb. This is

> We are envisioning and creating a good future for our relatives, whether they have wings, fins, roots, paws or hands.

---

1 The Q'eros are an Incan tribe that lives in the Andes mountains in what is currently known as Peru.

5

really our time. It is time to know who we are and understand our place in the world of prophecies, promises, chaos. It is our time to overcome fear and make that beautiful future.

Robin Wall Kimmerer, the Potawatomi scholar, writes in *Braiding Sweetgrass*: "We are all bound by a covenant of reciprocity: plant breath for animal breath, winter and summer, predator and prey, grass and fire, night and day, living and dying. Water knows this, clouds know this. Soil and rocks know they are dancing in a continuous giveaway of making, unmaking, and making again the earth. ... Flourishing is mutual. We need the berries and the berries need us. Their gifts multiply by our care for them, and dwindle from our neglect."

And so do we who are devoted to justice and caring for the earth need to understand that flourishing is mutual. Together, we join hands, no matter where we come from — across race, class, cultural difference — to do what is right, to nurture and help our relatives flourish.

I want you to read this book, so you can learn some of the history of people stepping beyond their owning-class allegiance to the broader covenant: the responsibility of humans being. I have been watching this movement grow for decades through friendships with people like Paul Haible and Marian Moore, and my now-deceased friend Jill Soffer. We have a shared history, and together, we are making a shared future. We make agreements on how to make this transformation together, and we create friendships and make long-term allies.

Where do I come from? Indoon jibaa omaa akiing. I come from here, right here on this land. This is where my roots are, on the land and the lakes of the North Country by the Great Lakes, or Akiing, the land to which the people belong. I am a patriot to a land, not a flag.

I come from people who lived simply, and well. I do not come from a lot of money, but I come from a life outdoors on the land, with those who created beautiful works of art honoring life and justice, and a people that embraced social justice as an intergenerational commitment. I come from people who saw change and decided to have the agency to be a part of it. That's

6

the fact: Change is inevitable; it's a question of who controls the change.

My father's people are Ojibwe from the north side of the White Earth Reservation, a place created to be a sanctuary for our people. But we are not from the reservation; we are from this land. We are from the lakes and land, and from a great story of people in epic times. Indeed, we are still a story. We came from the east, and we came from the north to this place. Uninterrupted, we lived well; we prayed here, harvested each gift of Mother Earth in succession and honored our covenant, or agreement, with Creation.

Then our world changed when the Wiindigo, or the Cannibal, came to our land and would not leave, no matter how we tried to vanquish them. Colonization is that process that consumes a people, a land and your dreams.

My grandfather and his brothers escaped from Carlisle Indian Industrial School, perhaps the most notorious of the Indian residential schools, and returned to the deep woods, *nopeming* (into the woods). So it is that we returned home. That is where I live. Despite much, my people remain here, in the woods. We are the people of the Great Lakes and wild rice.

My mother's parents were Jews from Poland. They fled a fearful world and became workers in New York City. My grandmother was a textile worker, a member of the International Ladies Garment Workers Union. My grandfather was a painter. My grandparents were active in movements for justice and joined with many other immigrant working families to create a place where they would be valued and nurtured.

Life is a lesson on returning home and on becoming yourself.

I come from people who have taken agency to transform — social movement people. People who understand that when you work together, you make a difference. My parents were active in the movements of farmworkers, the American Indian Movement, the Civil Rights and Antiwar Movements, and I grew up with a sense that you must do something if you can. And I was raised that it is best to do it together.

This remarkable mosaic of stories you are holding reveals both a history and possibilities for how we can do this together, across race, across class, across cultural difference. We all experience different kinds of privilege, and when brought together, we are most powerful and most whole.

I was born in social movements and know the power of people to make change. We all have our part. I went to Harvard at 17 years old in 1976. Harvard taught me a lot about privilege and power. I was one of a handful of Native students at the university, despite it being established for British *and* Native youths in the 1700s. I lived with and spent time with many students of color and many students of privileged financial backgrounds and, somehow in that, found many good friends and reaffirmed those human relationships and friendships between classes.

> **We all experience different kinds of privilege, and when brought together, we are most powerful and most whole.**

Harvard is not an institution of change. It's a bastion of the ivory tower, but I found a place there. One of my closest friends was Masilo Mabeta, a political exile from South Africa, and during my time at Harvard, we began organizing on South Africa divestment. I learned at Harvard about multiracial organizing and the work of allies. I remember a student approached us both one day at lunch at Adams House and said, "Masilo, why do you work so hard?" Masilo responded, "Because you refuse to work."

That's a pretty good lesson on solidarity work, for sure.

These are times that are complex, full of promise and full of fear. We must overcome the fear, which is intended to paralyze us, much like an abuser or a predator seeks to paralyze and immobilize their prey. Indeed, there's an orchestrated narrative of fear and pandering, hopelessness and doom. That narrative we must reject. And, in this time, remember that the Chinese character for chaos is also the same as the character for opportunity. In this destabilization, let us take our place.

The editors of this book want you to understand the history of when, where and how people with financial privilege have learned from communities who are fighting off the Wiindigo, the essence of greed, and are restoring the covenant. They want you to build on what has come before. We are reminded of our people's agency by understanding history, overcoming that American historical amnesia of not knowing the past and surrendering the future. Take it further. Envision, together, a new future — ji misawaabandaaming.

The editors of this book want you to understand the history of when, where and how people with financial privilege have learned from communities who are fighting off the Wiindigo, the essence of greed, and are restoring the covenant.

Amy Bowers Cordalis, attorney for the Yurok Tribe, talks about the deep understanding that came with the decommissioning of the Klamath River Dams, the largest dam removal in U.S. history: "I thought we were going to be the generation that witnessed the collapse and complete death of the river. ... But now we will be the generation that sees the rebirth and restoration of our ecosystem, our culture and lifeblood."[2]

Healing is possible; it takes our actions. And in this moment, it is upon us to summon up our best selves and call on our ancestors and our relatives to be — and, even more, to do. Humans being.

These are the times of prophecies. Ancestors before told of these times when the earth would change, when a web in the sky would create a new world and when there would be a choice between a green path and a scorched path. That is this time, and we are the ones who are here. I have been reading *Becoming Kin: An Indigenous Call to Unforgetting the Past and Reimagining Our Future*, by Patty Krawec. She writes: "Being a settler or a colonizer is not something you are; it is something you *do*. It describes your relationship to this land and the people in it. Remember that settlers come to impose a way of living on top of the existing people. Settler colonialism destroys in order to replace. If you are going to stop being a settler and start being kin, that's where we start." It is truly where you choose to stand.

There's no word in Anishinaabemowin for *reconciliation*.

---

2 Suzie Savoie, "Dam Removal a Success on the Klamath — Could Applegate Do the Same?" Ashland.news, February 19, 2025, https://ashland.news/dam-removal-a-success-on-the-klamath-could-applegate-do-the-same.

There's only the word *gwekizhichigemin,* which means "making it right," and that is what we must all do. We must make it right.

Money is one of the currencies that can help our movements grow. How that money comes to movements and the power dynamic in the flow of that money are important processes to get right. Read this book to soak in stories of people who have been trying to figure that out, while tending to their spirit.

My good friend John Trudell would talk about us being spirits in human form.[3] And he would remind us that this society eats your spirit. Protect and nurture your spirit; honor and uphold your part in the covenant.

We all have our basket to carry. In some societies, these are called Burden Baskets, and sometimes the basket is Cornucopia. What is in your basket? What can you share and help flourish with your basket? And, when you pass on, how is the basket — of not just money, but dreams, relationships, land and goodness — distributed?

We are relatives, and it is time to be seeds, to grow the future where our descendants will collectively reaffirm relationship.

The opportunity is one of perspective, but as we allow ourselves to transcend being nouns and become verbs, we can come into our place and path together. We are the people of the time of prophecies. I like very much the Zapatista saying, "They buried us; they forgot that we were seeds."

We are relatives, and it is time to be seeds, to grow the future where our descendants will collectively reaffirm relationship.

Winona LaDuke
Indakiingimin (the very land to which I belong) ▪

---

3 John Trudell was a Native American author, poet, actor, musician and political activist. He was the spokesperson for the Indians of All Tribes' takeover of Alcatraz beginning in 1969, broadcasting as *Radio Free Alcatraz.* During most of the 1970s, he served as the chairman of the American Indian Movement, based in Minneapolis, Minnesota. He died in 2015.

ORIENTATION

In this section we'll introduce ourselves, tell you why we put this together and share the big questions driving this anthology. You'll get an initial window into this world of organizing the rich, and the tone we're bringing to it all: honest, curious and lively. Consider this your preview of the mix of personal storytelling, strategic thinking, and "wait, did they really just compare class traitors to Star Wars rebels?" moments that lie ahead.

INTRODUCTION

Yes! Woohoo! In whatever way you made it here, we are delighted you found this anthology.

How this all started: This project originated out of Michael's two decades in this work, first as a person with wealth, involved with Resource Generation (RG),[1] and then as a staff leader at RG, a fundraiser and donor advisor. Over and over, he saw how little was known about the history and lineage of these efforts. He saw how shy and wary people were to talk openly about their hard-won lessons, successes and failures.

What started in 2022 as a book project has transformed into much more. Organize the Rich is now a multimedia writing, video and audio project, sharing interviews, stories and analyses about what it means to organize the rich as part of multiracial working-class-led movements. This anthology is its first printed work!

Who this is for: We had three particular groups in mind:

- Working-class leaders who are fundraising from wealthy people and building cross-class coalitions
- Middle-class professionals working with wealth holders to actualize their progressive values
- Wealthy people who are a part of or who want to join this growing movement to organize the rich

Whoever you are, whatever your work or background, we hope this is useful and sparks new thinking.

Meet your editors: In imagining this anthology, Michael aspired to have a team with a diverse set of experiences across generation,

---

1 Resource Generation (RG) is a national organization, founded in 1998, that organizes young people with wealth to be transformative leaders working toward the equitable distribution of wealth, land and power. More on RG in Michael's piece "What I Learned From RG ... and What You Can Too."

race, class and gender. In longtime colleague Marian Moore, he found an elder steeped in the work and world of organizing the rich, from a different but complementary lineage. In Alex T. Tom, he found a dear colleague with decades of experience organizing in working-class Asian American communities and building multiracial cross-class coalitions, and with a growing curiosity about organizing the rich. We've known each other for years now, through shared work and shared relationships, and have been delighted at the chance to collaborate more deeply.

Here's the crew:

Marian: Minneapolis-based elder, comes out of the lineage of the Threshold Foundation,[2] raised owning class, European Protestant ancestry

Alex: Oakland-based yelder (young elder), comes out of the lineage of the Chinese Progressive Association,[3] middle-class upbringing, Chinese heritage

Michael: Proudly middle-aged yelder-in-training, comes out of the lineage of Resource Generation, raised managerial/owning class, Oakland resident with Ashkenazi Jewish and European Catholic and Protestant heritage

One thing we have in common is that we've been personally transformed by talking openly about class and money in the context of the movements we're building. In addition to our mutual respect for and enjoyment of each other, we share a passion for understanding and uplifting who and what have come before us.

---

2 A philanthropic network founded in 1981. More on Threshold can be found in Marian Moore's piece "Through the Donut Door."

3 The Chinese Progressive Association (CPA) was founded in 1972 and organizes the low-income and working-class immigrant Chinese community in San Francisco for worker rights and better economic, racial and social justice for all. More on Alex's political journey, including his time with CPA, in his piece, "On Big Money and Movement Economics."

Our big questions:

> **How can we learn from previous efforts to organize the rich toward justice?**

> **How can we inspire and support cross-class alliance building by sharing stories from previous experiments?**

Much of what we share centers on organizing the rich, the heart of Marian and Michael's work for decades, while the second question shapes our broader vision, and has been at the core of Alex's work. We've all been part of efforts to answer these questions and are eager to share our stories and the stories of others.

While the three of us have different backgrounds, experiences and politics, the following ideas united us as we created this anthology:

Money

Our economic system needs to change. It has been an incredible engine of human innovation, while being fueled by exploitation, war, slavery, genocide and oppression — and it is creating a planet that is less and less livable for all people, including the rich. No one actually wins in our current economy.

"It is not their money." The money in the hands of the rich was made by everyone and from the earth we share. It belongs to all of us. We believe in the redistribution of wealth, land and power from the few to the many.

Liberation movements can and should be funded by everyone. It's imperative that the rich move their hoarded wealth toward movements for the collective good, contributing their fair share. At the same time, an overreliance on the financial support of the wealthy creates unhealthy dynamics. We must aim for financial self-determination and politically independent capital to build the power of poor and working-class-led people's movements.

HOW CAN WE LEARN
FROM PREVIOUS EFFORTS
TO ORGANIZE THE RICH
TOWARD JUSTICE?

HOW CAN WE INSPIRE
AND SUPPORT CROSS-
CLASS ALLIANCE-
BUILDING BY SHARING
STORIES FROM PREVIOUS
EXPERIMENTS?

People

Talking openly about money and class is a critical step to transforming our shared relationship to these powerful forces.

It will take a hugely diverse movement of humans, uniting together, to shift away from our current economic and social system and create a new one based on the needs all living beings. Everyone has a role to play, no matter their class background or current class position.

Liberation movements have always been cross-class. The poor and working class are the leading forces in any durable, lasting move toward an economy that works for everyone. And all types of people have been and will be important contributors.

In a recent conversation among the three of us, Alex offered, "Many poor, working- and middle-class people feel alienated when dealing with fundraising and issues of money, class, and power. While wealthy people have more material power and privilege, I've been surprised to learn that they also don't feel free. Through these untold stories of wealthy people's involvement in liberation movements, I've come to see that there are more of us who want to fundamentally change the system than I imagined. I hope reading this anthology will help make clear our shared interest in creating a more just world."

About the title: *Free the People to Free the Money to Free the People* evolved out of a conversation between former Peace Development Fund Executive Director Paul Haible and Marian Moore. He said he came to Threshold Foundation meetings "to liberate the money." Marian's rejoinder, "I came to liberate the people to liberate the money to liberate the people..."

This anthology began as an effort to illuminate an underreported history — the movement to organize the rich for social, economic and environmental justice. Our collaboration led us to a significant creative tension, reflected in the title. One approach to organizing the rich has been to advocate fiercely for material and structural change. Another emphasizes the need for personal and spiritual transformation. We see from this collected history that both are needed; to free the money, we need to free ourselves. We need to redistribute wealth *and* heal hearts and minds across the class spectrum. We believe these two strands of work need to be brought together, and we share examples that do that.

This anthology began as an effort to illuminate an underreported history — the movement to organize the rich for social, economic and environmental justice.

This is not a comprehensive history, guidebook or how-to manual, but one collection of stories that we chose to introduce a whole world from our unique perspective. We've focused much of this volume on the lineage of donor networks we know most intimately, from the Funding Exchange to Threshold, Resource Generation and Solidaire[4] alongside perspectives from cross-class collaborations and movement leaders. In future anthologies, we'd love to more fully explore other important lineages including the movement to raise taxes on the rich, progressive political giving, organizing in institutional philanthropy, and the world of social investing and business.

Why did we pick these contributors for the anthology? Mostly because of relationships. We know these stories and believe they need to be told and better understood.

We have organized the contents into sections. "Orientation" offers a taste of the analysis and storytelling that will be found in this anthology. We share a barn burner of an interview with Vini Bhansali, an introduction to this work from Michael, an engaging personal story from Iimay Ho and reflections from Braeden Lentz on how this project fits in a strategy to build working-class power.

"Lineage" provides a "family tree" and Michael's overview of the history we're sharing here.

"Movement Economics" contains personal interviews with beloved elders Linda Burnham and Max Elbaum on the shifting

---

4 We'll share details on all these groups in the many essays inside.

terrain of money and class in left movements. Nina Luo shares an incisive critique of social justice philanthropy and the current way left organizing is funded. Through personal stories and lessons from elders, Alex reflects on his growth as a middle-class leader and the challenges of movement economics in this moment.

With "Stories From the Field," Chuck Collins, Marian, Billy Wimsatt, Michael, Nigel Charles, Leah Hunt-Hendrix and Sharon Chen share an intimate and personal window into this work with nuance and complexity.

"Finding a New Way" includes interviews, analyses and reflections from leaders and practitioners of current-day efforts to free the people to free the money to free the people. In the closing piece, our dear colleague and friend Rajasvini Bhansali of Solidaire brings us home with thoughts on where we go from here.

With that, we will let the anthology tell you the rest.

Thank you to all the contributors whose work and writing made this book possible. Thank you for generously granting us permission to reprint previously published writing. Thank you for creating new work and for the pieces never before formally published as well.

Thank you to all of you who are part of this work and to those whose voices are not included in this first volume. And thanks to you, readers, for your curiosity.

Much love, respect and gratitude,
Michael, Marian and Alex

"ORGANIZING IS A SKILL LIKE ANYTHING ELSE. YOU CAN LEARN IT."

Interview With Rajasvini Bhansali

Rajasvini "Vini" Bhansali is the executive director of Solidaire, an intergenerational community of progressive wealthy people and foundations working toward a just and collective future. She is a multitalented leader who has a degree in astrophysics from University of California, Berkeley, was the executive director of an international public foundation that funds grassroots organizing in the Global South and has recently co-authored a book: *Leading With Joy: Practices for Uncertain Times*. She is a yoga instructor, a poet and one of the foremost leaders in organizing the rich toward justice in the world today.

This piece was originally published in August 2023 on the Organize the Rich Substack. This is the first of several interviews by Michael Gast in the anthology.

Mike: "Organizing" is a popular buzzword these days, with a lot of different definitions. I'm using it; many others are too. What does "organizing" and "organize the rich" mean to you?

Vini: Organizing is helping people believe in their own agency to change the world. Organizing works when people believe in their own capacity to be an actor, be a changemaker, and develop the skills they need to do it.

The opposite of organizing is when a rich person is like, "I'll write a check, but don't talk to me and don't ask me to talk to anyone else." A wealthy person with an organizing mindset says, "Yeah, of course, I'm going to bring my resources to this, but I'll also bring my friends and my uncle who's connected to this terrible hedge fund that we can help divest from the prison industry."

Organizing means looking at the whole of your life and all the resources at play and

> **Organizing means looking at the whole of your life and all the resources at play and bringing them to bear for a collective change agenda.**

bringing them to bear for a collective change agenda. I used to think of organizing the rich as a lot easier than it actually is. In the Global South movements I got to know at Thousand Currents,[1] everybody is seen as organizable all the time. I had that mindset. Now working more in the U.S., with entrenched wealth, and all the patterns of white supremacy and inequality, I'm understanding the immense challenge we face in a deeper way.

Organizing the rich is harder work than we give it credit for, which is why Solidaire is not going to be enough and Resource Generation is not going to be enough. We have to have an entire ecosystem of people that can speak to and organize different subsets of the wealthy. Donors of Color Network[2] can reach people Solidaire won't. Resource Generation reaches young wealthy people that Solidaire can develop further. We need all of us. And we all need to have a strategic division of labor, so we can organize a mass base.

There is so much disorganized wealth: wealthy people who are not connected to anything and don't want to be because they don't see the value in it. Somebody needs to get all these unorganized wealthy people to understand the value of being part of something bigger than themselves. We know that there are 725 or so billionaires in this country right now,[3] so 350 Solidaire members [their current number of members] is just a start.

> Somebody needs to get all these unorganized wealthy people to understand the value of being part of something bigger than themselves.

How many of these billionaires are part of something that we recognize as connected to progressive

---

1 Vini is the former executive director of Thousand Currents, formerly known as the International Development Exchange (IDEX). Thousand Currents was founded in 1985 and focuses on supporting grassroots organizations and movements in the Global South, particularly in Africa, Latin America and the Caribbean, and Asia and the Pacific.
2 Donors of Color Network is an organization founded in 2018 that brings together wealthy people of color to build community, share resources, and fund movements led by communities of color.
3 This number was as of 2023. The number of billionaires in the U.S. as of June 2025 is 902.

TO FREE THE MONEY

movements? Not many.

How many moderate billionaires get swept into the Right? Because the Right seems to create magnetic conditions of belonging?

Our task is huge and we have to be better at it.

Mike: How did you come to participate in organizing wealthy people for social justice?

Vini: I came to it from being a fundraiser. I spent a lot of years raising money from wealthy people and realized that there were many indignities, large and small, involved in the process. It all made me wonder what frontline organizers were going through to be able to get the resources they deserve for their work.

The earliest memory I have of fundraising indignities was when I used to volunteer for an organization called the Political Asylum Project of Austin. It was just impossible to talk to the wealthy donors about asylum and refugee seekers without falling into saviorism. It just didn't have an impact if we talked to our big donors about giving because it was the right thing to do or a movement that really deserved their solidarity.

The whole asylum, refugee, and immigrant rights movement learned to talk in a way that made the work about "the good immigrants" versus "the bad immigrants," the ones that had no choice in their circumstances versus those that chose to illegally migrate. There were all these polarities that were created mostly to raise money and speak to what organizations learned wealthy people wanted to hear.

I became the executive director at IDEX [now Thousand Currents] very young, at 31 years of age. I remember one meeting early on where I was sitting across from this white wealthy donor who said to me, "I like this work. I believe in this work, but for some reason, I can't trust you, so I am not going to renew my funding."

Even though I had done a lifetime of racial justice work, I remember being floored. I couldn't get out of bed for two days. I was so hurt and wounded by that. I understand that what he meant was that I was too brown, too young, too different — that somehow my accented English made it hard to believe me.

Coming out of that experience, I remember thinking, "If this is how we plan to raise resources for Global South solidarity, we are not going to be successful because our donors do not see themselves in this work."

Mike: What is your class background? How has it shaped your relationship to this work?

Vini: I have a mixed-class background. I grew up lower middle class, but with a lot of privileges because my dad worked in the civil service in India and rose up through the ranks. We had access to health, education, and housing benefits that weren't related to wealth, that were related to public service in India. When I came to the U.S., the idea that you have to twist yourself into a pretzel for what should be a public good was very new to me.

Now, I'm squarely upper middle class, both by way of my job, but also because my extended family's class position changed as my brothers made money working in finance. We now have these nuanced conversations within our family about what it means to have more than our relatives and what it means to support a larger extended community. All these questions about class and wealth have gone from being external to my experience to becoming internal to my family and life.

> All these questions about class and wealth have gone from being external to my experience to becoming internal to my family and life.

Mike: Who are your mentors in this work?

Vini: Two of my most important mentors have been Paul Strasburg and Mutombo M'Panya, the two co-founders of IDEX, now called Thousand Currents. They modeled values of deep humility and deep learning in relationship with whoever you consider your grantee partners, whoever you are in a position to resource financially. They embodied this understanding that you're not just donating out of a sense of charity, but you're really doing it for you.

This is the fundamental tenet of solidarity, especially between the Global North and Global South. You're not trying to help and save somebody else; you're actually doing this act of giving because it frees you and teaches you some other way of being with the resources in your control. The word that Mutombo always uses is being an "honest broker" between the North and the South. And it applies to solidarity in all situations. It's

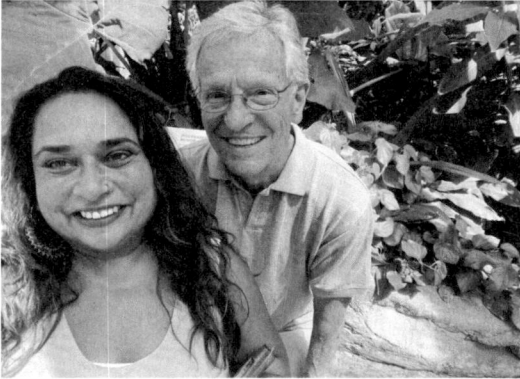

Vini with Paul Strasburg
(Courtesy of Rajasvini
Bhansali)

important to be honest about what we're learning and about how wealth accumulation is based on imperialism, exploitation, and more.

The other mentors I often think about are Jorge Santiago and María Estela Barco Huerta from DESMI in Chiapas.[4] I was at the launch of an experiment, the Buen Vivir Fund. We had brought

> You're not trying to help and save somebody else; you're actually doing this act of giving because it frees you and teaches you some other way of being with the resources in your control.

together all these impact investors with Global Southern leaders. At the meeting, Jorge said, "Let's get out of this dichotomy of investor and investee. The investors in this room, primarily white, primarily from the Global North, are bringing financial capital to the table. Those of us, quote unquote recipients, are bringing intellectual capital and political capital to the table. We will be far

---

4 DESMI (Desarrollo Económico y Social de los Mexicanos Indígenas) is an organization committed to the economic and social development of Indigenous Mexicans. Formed in Chiapas in 1969, it works to improve the livelihoods of rural populations and defend the rights of smallholder farmers.

more powerful together if we're in reciprocity, if we see each other as co-investors."

You can apply that to the idea of co-conspirators, of reciprocal lateral relationships, not this classic philanthropy "power over" dynamic. We are not just in a relationship where "you give me money; I'm subservient and subordinate to you," or "you get to enact your dreams for what you want in the world by making me your proxy; I get to come to you with the begging bowl." We need to be in an exchange and understand the different forms of "capital" in circulation.

Vini (*front row, center,* fist raised) at the 2016 Buen Vivir Member Assembly in Mexico City (Courtesy of Thousand Currents)

Lately, I have been blessed to learn so much from Solidaire's own Elder in Residence, Linda Burnham, and her massive strategic and power-building contributions to the field through the book *Power Concedes Nothing: How Grassroots Organizing Wins Elections* and the Project2050 report.[5] I have also been so fortunate lately to learn at the feet of Southern Cheyenne elder and scholar Dr. Henrietta Mann, who embodies the kind of principled brilliance and tenderhearted clarity that teaches me how to be utterly human at all times.

5 The report *Project2050: Toward the Development of a Shared Strategic Framework on the U.S. Left* is the product of a series of interviews with 80 key leaders of the left, with the goal of stimulating strategic thinking and alignment on the U.S. left and identifying the political goals that might be achievable over the next 25-30 years.

Vini with Dr. Henrietta Mann (*left*) and Vini with Linda Burnham (*right*)
(Courtesy of Rajasvini Bhansali)

My mentors have taught me how to do this work with a lot of joy and love, and a lot of centering, not on bitterness and hard political analysis, but on a deep belief in people's humanity and potential for transformation.

Mike: Are there particular ideas that you want future generations of leftists to know about organizing the rich that you hold or that you would like to lift up in this conversation?

Vini: There's so many. ... In Solidaire's new 10-year strategy, we write a lot about the protagonism of wealthy donors.[6] As a student of social movements and as a student of history, I strongly believe that people of all class backgrounds have to be involved in movement building.

What we often think of as a lack of protagonism from wealthy people in Left movements is often a kind of shadow protagonism. When wealthy people aren't explicitly engaged and given clear direction, they're often involved in sideways ways that cause more harm than good. That's why, where there is initiative from the rich towards

> What we often think of as a lack of protagonism from wealthy people in Left movements is often a kind of shadow protagonism.

6 As Vini recently wrote to me, "Protagonism = being active in shaping change; able to step up and lead when needed in accountability to others."

progressive social movements, where there is motivation, where there's inspiration, it makes sense to purposefully develop their leadership and give them clear roles and work to do.

I firmly believe that the protagonism of everyone, including rich folks, actually matters — it's not only about getting in line behind working-class movements, though that is vital. It's about each of us actually bringing our own influence, agency, power, and resources to the table. This full-bodied protagonism is what rich folks need to move from guilt- and shame-driven redistribution to a lasting role in systems change. U.S. capitalism, in my humble opinion, will not change without strategic action from the wealthy and those with access to wealth.

Another important notion that I hold dear is that organizing is a skill like anything else. You can learn it. It can be taught. What I feel progressives with access to wealth in this country don't get enough of are places to develop organizing skills, especially around the family systems and institutions that they can uniquely influence. Left and progressive donor networks are important because that's where they get to practice.

> **What I feel progressives with access to wealth in this country don't get enough of are places to develop organizing skills, especially around the family systems and institutions that they can uniquely influence.**

My wish may be that every one of our members arrives perfectly baked and does the exact right thing, but that feeling is actually just about control. That's not how real humans work. If we can create an alignment of values and an alignment of purpose, then wealthy people will also join the struggle for collective liberation. I've seen it with our own membership, where people come in really green, really fearful. They have never had to, given their wealthy background, work *with* people different from them.

Then they come into an organization like Solidaire, and over time, with practice and skill building and enough experiments, they begin to learn how to work *with* other people. Check their own ego, check their own assumptions, try to work on a project together, get their hands dirty, make some mistakes, learn hard lessons, and then try again.

That's how I became an organizer. I didn't go to college for it. I was deployed to door knock, to talk to people, to start initiatives, to bring others along. And with enough community work and enough feedback, we begin to get better at it. I mean, I'm still learning.

If you look at the history of philanthropy in particular, most trustees have been able to make decisions entirely in isolation, on their own, without any accountability. Wealthy people can have hundreds of staff that pretzel around just to try to give them the perfect case for support so they won't retract their funding. This is how mainstream philanthropy still operates. A trustee goes to a cocktail party, listens to an idea they like, and makes a new decision about their grantmaking. Suddenly, the flow of resources for their work, their foundation, their grantees changes overnight.

There's not enough movement- and values-aligned mechanisms for peer accountability, peer support, and peer learning at high levels of wealth. And without that, I don't see how we ever get out of these unhelpful and destructive patterns.

Mike: What is your 150-year vision of success?

Vini: That there are no rich. There's actually enough for everybody. We don't have the stratified, fragmented, disparate and desperate society we have now. The things that we are fighting so hard for, that seem so impossible, have become real. There is quality health care, housing, and food for all; there is clean air and water. These material conditions are understood to be basic rights. These social policies, that are radical now, become agreed upon and expected, like brushing your teeth before bed.

Mike: Any other thoughts you'd like to share today?

Vini: Whatever we do, I'd like us to be kinder and more understanding of ourselves and each other in the process.

We're really hard on ourselves in the U.S. Left. We're really, really hard on failures. We feel so much responsibility for getting it right. We feel so burdened. And I get it. I get why. We're up against authoritarianism. We're up against a Right that wants to

27

Whatever we do, I'd like us to be kinder and more understanding of ourselves and each other in the process.

take us out. We really feel beholden to our vision for human dignity and care and compassion. Sometimes what that means is if we fail, we just self-flagellate ourselves brutally.

Coming out of the pandemic, everybody is still in grief and exhausted. It's really hard to ask people to envision a world where things are better 10, 15, 20 years down the line when we're stuck in what feels like the muck right now.

Structurally speaking, a lot of our gains have been dismantled. We're dealing with movement-level heartbreak and sadness and grief while trying to keep up high levels of organizing. It's an intense time in the world. It's a big deal to ask people, in the midst of all of this, to keep imagining and trying and playing and collaborating — to ask people to set aside their egos and sense that it's all on them.

The structures that we're trying to change and dismantle in our work organizing the rich are about shifting the very nature of wealth as we know it. This is hard work, partly because, especially in the U.S., we don't know of and see alternative economic and social structures that are at scale. For many of us, we really have to build this thing — this cross-class multiracial movement, this solidarity economy, this just transition — and trust that it's going to be a thing without ever having seen it happen, without knowing it's possible. That's a lot to ask people who just survived a global pandemic and are just trying to live. It's the right ask and it's a big one. ∎

AN UNPRECEDENTED MOVEMENT OF THE RICH TOWARD JUSTICE? REAL TALK ABOUT THE RICH AND THE REST OF US

Michael Gast

Michael Gast has been engaging, fundraising and organizing the wealthy toward justice for over 20 years. He is the former director of Resource Generation (RG), where he spent 13 years as a member, leader and staff person. Since leaving RG in 2014, he's worked as a development director, fundraising consultant, donor educator and donor advisor with individual wealth holders and groups such as Movement Voter Project, Chinese Progressive Association, Showing Up for Racial Justice and Thousand Currents. These days, Michael directs a multimedia project called Organize the Rich. Born and raised in San Francisco, he currently lives in Oakland with his awesome wife and son.

There are so many ways to frame the different dimensions of this vast ecosystem, this is Michael's effort adapted from an August 2023 Organize the Rich Substack post.

From *White Lotus* to *The Real Housewives*, there's a lot of money being made off the stories of the rich and ridiculous. While sometimes funny, these stories can leave all of us — whatever our bank balance — collectively complacent and discouraged about our ability to do anything more than shake our heads at the late-stage capitalist death-coaster we're on.

With deep political unrest in the world, it may seem like dealing with the "idiot rich" should be the least of our concerns, but as has become clearer and clearer, corralling us effectively could make all the difference. As so many are painfully aware, our government, economy and society is run by and structured for the material benefit of the wealthy in many respects.

In this political moment, people of conscience *must* shift how we engage and organize "the rich." But who are the rich anyway? And who am I?

They are, we are, the owning class of the world. We are the ones who own the vast majority of the land and large businesses, stocks and bonds, debt and hedges. Unlike most people in capitalist economies, we generate significant income from our ownership and investment activities, rather than relying solely on income from our labor. This is the sector of society that owns the means of production and holds outsize economic power and influence over society. We are the ones who have profited for centuries from incredible human creativity and cruelty, from slavery to solar panels.

In this class are the oligarchs, like Elon Musk and Jeff Bezos, and many of the political leaders they work with, like Donald Trump and Vladimir Putin. It includes the heads of industry, the corporate and political elite, and their families.

As you are likely well aware, unprecedented levels of wealth have been carried out of the mines, fields and factories in poor countries over the last half century, and into bank accounts in the U.S. and Europe. This continued extraction of resources from the Global South to the Global North has led to extreme and growing inequality.

No longer is the owning class a few thousand kings, queens and rulers. These days, it's much bigger than that. According to the 2024 UBS Global Wealth Report,[1] 1.5% of adults in the world, about 58 million people, have $1 million or more in net assets. This is my group, the one my family is a part of, the people I know best and have spent my career organizing. This global 1.5% holds almost half of the world's wealth.

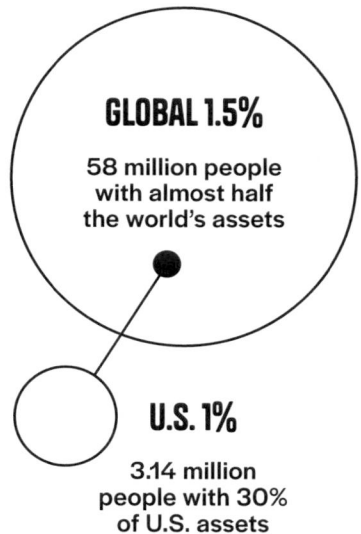

GLOBAL 1.5%

58 million people with almost half the world's assets

U.S. 1%

3.14 million people with 30% of U.S. assets

---

1 UBS, a global investment bank headquartered in Switzerland, has compiled a yearly report on wealth since 2009.

When we zoom in on the U.S., the epicenter of the owning class, with almost 40% of the world's millionaires and about a third of the world's billionaires, we see that the U.S. 1% is made up of around 3 million people. These are people with a minimum net worth of $13.7 million, who collectively own 30% of the total wealth in the country. The U.S. 1% includes the tippy top of the economic pyramid, i.e., the 902 U.S. billionaires[2] holding an astonishing $4.4 trillion dollars — more than the GDP of nations such as Brazil, Spain, Mexico and Switzerland.

To return to the global 1.5%, we are both CEOs *and* the well-paid professionals who work for them. In the U.S., we are largely on the receiving end of the $68 trillion about to be passed on by Baby Boomers in the greatest wealth transfer in human history. As of now, without significant changes to the U.S. tax code, this immense amount of money will stay within the country's wealthiest and primarily white families. This transfer of wealth represents a massive opportunity to redistribute economic power for generations to come.

For more than 20 years, I've been involved in the growing movement to organize the rich toward justice. Working with others, I've helped move hundreds of millions of dollars from thousands of wealthy people toward building the power of the multiracial working class, addressing the climate crisis, reclaiming our integrity and working for a healthy future for all.

I'm not writing to you about the glories (or horrors) of philanthropy or Wall Street, effective altruism or the benevolence and generosity of the righteous rich. I'm not talking about individual heroes or villains. I'm not talking about the charade of do-gooderism so well documented by Anand Giridharadas in his book *Winners Take All: The Elite Charade of Changing the World*. Though, let's be real, every one of the dynamics he names shows up in any organizing of the rich.

While the rich, as a whole, steadfastly defend their wealth and power, no matter the deadly repercussions, I am writing to you about the emergence of a small, yet significant, counterforce.

---

2 Out of the 3,000-plus billionaires worldwide, 902 are in the U.S., as of a summer 2025 count by *Forbes Magazine*.

As I've learned over the last decades, from Moses to Maud Younger, there have always been individual wealthy people participating in and supporting liberation movements.[3] What's new is their scale and institutional formation. Since the 1970s, there's been an upsurge in organized efforts to move wealthy people **collectively,** not just individually, toward a more fair and equitable society. And in the last decades, alongside extreme inequality, we've seen significant growth in interest from the rich in redistribution.

Wealthy people are advocating for higher taxes on the rich and for domestic worker rights, returning land and stolen wealth to Native and Black communities, turning private companies into worker-owned businesses, funding efforts to build the electoral power of the multiracial working class and using wealth inherited from oil fortunes to fund movements to address the climate crisis.

Does this signify an unprecedented movement of the rich toward justice?

My short answer is — yes!

What we're seeing is the largest movement of wealthy people in the history of class societies, attempting to work alongside poor, working-, and middle-class people for equity and justice.

What am I noticing?

Billionaires like MacKenzie Scott are adopting social justice philanthropy practices and pledging to give their wealth "back to the society that helped generate it."[4] Through groups like Movement Voter Project and Way to Win, wealthy individuals are moving hundreds of millions of dollars from their bank accounts to grassroots organizations in key states throughout the U.S. that

---

3 For more on the stories of individual class traitors, check out my piece "A Brief History of Organizing the Rich Toward Justice" later in this anthology. You can also find more of this history in *Traitors to Their Class*, by Peter Dreier and Chuck Collins (New Labor Forum 21, no. 1 [2012]: 86-91) and in Rachel Sherman's forthcoming book, *Class Traitors*.

4 In 2020, MacKenzie Scott announced, in a blog post on Medium, a new round of donations by writing, "Last year I pledged to give the majority of my wealth back to the society that helped generate it, to do it thoughtfully, to get started soon, and to keep at it until the safe is empty." "116 Organizations Driving Change," *Medium*, July 28, 2020.

are working to hold back the forces of authoritarianism, defend voting rights and protect the climate.

Wealthy families are making 10-year financial commitments to Black-led organizing groups such as the Movement for Black Lives (M4BL). Because of groups like M4BL and the Decolonizing Wealth Project, reparations are on the agenda at family meetings and being integrated into the giving strategies of family foundations. The #LandBack movement, supporting Indigenous liberation and Indigenous sovereignty, is growing in power, working with numerous wealthy individuals — as well as state, local and federal governments — to give back land and begin to repair the damage of genocide.

Wealthy investors are taking their money off Wall Street and moving it to worker-owned co-ops and the solidarity economy through loan funds like Seed Commons.[5] Shareholders are forcing oil companies such as Chevron and ExxonMobil to speed up their transition away from fossil fuels. Groups of wealthy individuals, like Patriotic Millionaires and Millionaires for Humanity, are advocating for higher taxes on the rich. Numerous inheritors are breaking the cycle of wealth hoarding, spending down their trust funds to resource frontline movements.[6] Thousands of wealthy people are becoming peer organizers through participation in groups like Resource Generation and Solidaire Network. Financial industry professionals are finding numerous wealthy clients interested in redistribution and reparations, deaccumulation and divestment.[7]

These are just a few notable examples highlighting how tens of thousands of wealthy people have been taking consistent, concerted, coordinated action, attempting to transform the system that gave them their wealth in the first place.

---

5 According to New Economy Coalition, the solidarity economy is a global movement to build a just and sustainable economy where we prioritize people and the planet over endless profit and growth.

6 Nancy Jo Sales, "The New Rules of Old Money," *Harper's Bazaar*, October 7, 2021.

7 Oliver Balch, "Revolutionising Wealth: Should the Rich Be 'Deaccumulating'?," *Raconteur*, June 27, 2023.

Who is part of this nascent movement?

I see this movement as living within three main areas in the U.S.: social justice philanthropy, electoral organizing and investing/ new economy.[8] Practices such as fundraising, and frameworks such as reparations, are used in all parts of this work.

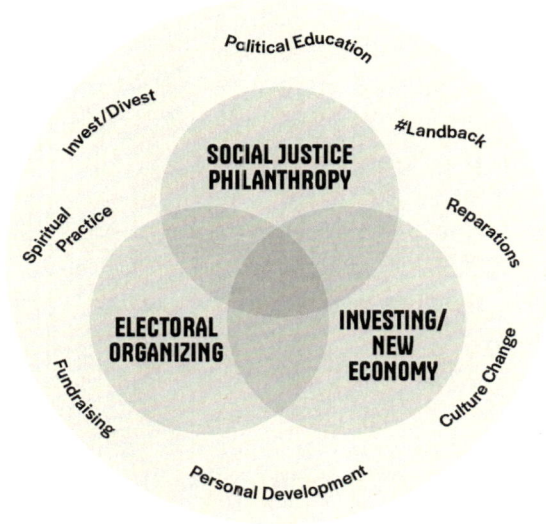

Here's an ecosystem map listing some of the groups involved in each area. My goal is definitely not to be comprehensive. My goal is to give you a high level picture of the nascent movement I'm referring to.[9]

---

8 "New economy" is one of the several terms used to describe an economy based on collective well-being for people and planet, rather than our current economy, based on extraction and exploitation. Other terms I've seen are "regenerative economy," "just economy" and "living economy." Some of these ideas are, at least in part, based on the "Just Transition" framework, as documented by Movement Generation: https://movementgeneration.org/justtransition.

9 DOCN = Donors of Color Network. WDN = Women Donors Network. MVP = Movement Voter Project. DA = Democracy Alliance. CHANGE Philanthropy, formerly known as Joint Affinity Groups, was founded in 1993 to unify identity-focused philanthropic affinity groups. It is a large coalition and meeting space for progressive to left philanthropy groups.

SOCIAL JUSTICE PHILANTHROPY

Thousand Currents

Social justice Public Foundations

Giving Project Network

CHANGE Philanthropy

ELECTORAL ORGANIZING

INVESTING/NEW ECONOMY

DOCN DA
Way to Win

NDN Collective

Hand in Hand

WDN

RG

Justice Funders

New Economy Coalition

Voices for Progress

MVP

Solidaire

Aligned investment funds

Center for Popular Democracy

New Media Ventures

Just Economy Institute

Working Families Party

Patriotic Millionaires

Aligned investment advisors

Committee on States

Center for Economic Democracy

In the endnotes of this anthology, you'll find a list of more of these groups, organized by decade and, despite our efforts, surely containing omissions. But it's a start. It includes the groups mentioned in this anthology and is designed to encourage your own exploration of the diverse contributions of each.

Who belongs on these maps and lists? What are the strengths and weaknesses of these efforts? What have we figured out and where have we struggled? These are the questions I want to wrestle with. Together.

This idea — of a movement in formation — is central to what this anthology is all about.

Why is it important that we talk about this movement of the rich?

1. It's vital that we end the power of the owning class over our economy, democracy and society. This ecosystem of groups represents a significant opportunity to do just that, by organizing a set of wealthy people into alignment with feminist, multiracial, working-class movements. This crack in the unity of the owning class should be documented and can be expanded.

2. Because recognizing our power is inspiring and exciting! If we want wealthy people, and our class system, to change, it's imperative to tell hopeful, honest stories of cross-class solidarity and the real work it entails. But even more than that, recognizing our power is key to effective organizing. If we want to engage a larger set of people, it's important to notice what we've accomplished so far and the power we already hold.

3. The more we notice our many successes in this work, the easier it will be to address our many challenges, limitations and mistakes.

4. In my experience, the groups in this ecosystem struggle to work together and have little sense of themselves as part of a broader movement to organize the rich. What could this set of folks pull off if they got to know each other and strategized together? What might be possible if these groups understood themselves as part of the same team?

5. I am a firm believer that we can ask wealthy people to do more in service of working-class liberation movements. From philanthropy to investments, reparations to advocacy, family organizing to electoral power building, these organizations represent an incredible menu of bold asks and demands to make of the managerial and owning class (the global 1.5%).

Ready to get started? Great! Here are a few things about organizing the rich that I've learned along the way.

1. This economic system isn't working for anyone, including the wealthy. We all have a mutual interest in ending classism and working toward a healthy world for all. Despite the real material benefits, being wealthy within an unjust society poisons our lives and relationships. Climbing the class ladder demands that we become increasingly competitive, individualistic and indifferent toward the suffering of others. We act out this harsh conditioning, not just on those with less wealth and power, but with our closest friends and family members. We treat each other as disposable. We are trained to have a "get mine at all costs" approach to life and relationships. Study after study shows that wealthy people are more isolated and unhappy than those with less income and assets. *This economic system isn't working for anyone, including us.*

2. We've been trained to be viciously ignorant thieves. We are no better or worse than anyone else... but we are systematically encouraged by our class-based society to be greedy, callous, entitled thieves. This is behavior we are conditioned and disciplined to take on and is true no matter one's political opinions or best intentions. We can't keep the money without justifying and ignoring the ways our wealth is extracted from people and the planet.

For people who become wealthy, climbing the class ladder demands complicity in the exploitation of others. Those who reach the owning class have been pushed to go along with the dominant culture of indifference and individualism that puts profit first and people and the planet last. Whether we shop at Bergdorf's or Goodwill, whether we drive a Porsche or a Prius, no matter how big our house is or how rabidly we rail against capitalism, if we're wealthy, we can't help but ingest and embody the classism in our society.

For people born into wealth, this training starts young. We are often raised in families and go to school in settings where competition is constant, image is everything and excellence is demanded. We are told we are lucky and privileged while being treated badly and loved conditionally. Over and over, we are led to believe we are smarter and more deserving than others. We live in segregated neighborhoods and gated communities, go to elite private schools and have little contact with people outside of our own class, except for those who are working for us. We often experience high amounts of separation and isolation. The "lonely rich kid" is an old story, and now there's a newly named phenomenon called "affluent neglect." [10]

Combine all that with the confusion about our self-worth that comes with neglect, isolation and conditional love. The results? Insecure adults pretending we know best, with little real information on how things work, and repeatedly acting out the indifference, competition and harshness we experienced as young people. Trump and Musk might be the poster boys, but this conditioning is also in the young trust fund kids at the Black Lives Matter protest, the well-meaning private school parents and me, too.

3. We are no better and no worse than anyone else. Unlike what we see on TV, wealthy people aren't the superheroes or supervillains we are made out to be. We have the same capacities for creativity, care, cooperation, cruelty and courage as anyone else. We thrive when treated with kindness and respect. Everything you know about the lovable and infuriating people you hang out with everyday applies to us. We are simply people who have more power than is good for us or the world.

Over and over, we are sold fake news that justifies our wealth and control. We are told that we're the job creators, that we deserve more because we're smarter and have worked harder. We're often trained to relate to social change work as charity and "helping those less fortunate." Instead of claiming our self-interest in a more equitable world, we are trained to become distant benefactors, at best, or committed opponents, at worst.

There's a different way. We can celebrate our contributions *and* hold ourselves responsible for our actions without denying our humanity or resorting to blame. We can insist on our own inherent dignity while owning up to our complicity in a rigged system. We can look at how we have profited from slavery, genocide and exploitation for centuries; commit to giving back what we've stolen; and help repair the damage. This both/and understanding

---

10 "Affluent neglect" is a recently coined term referring to the neglect experienced by children in wealthy families, where they are often raised by paid employees and where material possessions are used as a substitute for quality time and loving attention.

needs to be the foundation for any effective long-term organizing of the rich toward redistribution and repair.

4. We have a unique role to play and can be asked to do more. Wealthy people have a particular insider perspective on what is needed to change the dominant systems. We can help working-class movements understand where and how decisions are made within the owning class. We can be the translators, whistleblowers and organizers within wealthy communities, moving a slice of our people to the side of the multiracial, working-class majority.

And we can be asked to do much more. We can be trained to organize and lead our families, communities, workplaces and businesses toward the collective good rather than our personal comfort and narrow interests. We can learn how to tell our stories in ways that lift up campaigns, bring attention to important projects and shift power. We can disrupt business as usual, using our access to boardrooms and back rooms to change the conversation. If we can get clear, with help, that our best shot at true safety and security lies with people, relationships and solidarity, there is an endless amount we can do to strengthen movements for a healthy and just world.

We're creating an off-ramp for the rich, out of the world of wealth hoarding and the politics of domination that have been the norm for thousands of years. It's an incomplete exit route at this point. Exposed rebar, cavernous potholes, unfinished guardrails. We are building it at the same time as the roller coaster is veering more and more wildly out of control.

> **We're creating an off-ramp for the rich, out of the world of wealth hoarding and the politics of domination that have been the norm for thousands of years.**

Is it too late? Will these efforts make a difference? I think they have and they can, but it's up to all of us what happens next. ∎

WEALTHY CLASS TRAITORS BELONG IN THE REBELLION

Iimay Ho

Iimay Ho (they/them) is the former executive director of Resource Generation and the current managing director of people and operations for Local Progress, a group of local elected officials advancing a racial and economic justice agenda through all levels of local government.

This piece was written after Andor Season 1 was released in 2022. It was first published on the Organize the Rich Substack in April 2025.

Like many elder Millennials, watching the original *Star Wars* trilogy on tape is one of my cherished childhood memories. But these days instead of rewinding *A New Hope* while my mom calls me downstairs to set the table, I open the Disney+ app on my iPad to watch *Andor* after putting my toddler to bed.

Andor's nuanced character development, explicit anti-fascist message and depiction of a cross-class rebellion of ordinary people feels and looks a lot different than the *Star Wars* I grew up on. It blew me away.

One character in particular, Vel Sartha, caught me by surprise. She is a queer "rich girl running away from her family" who leads the successful heist against The Empire that ignites rebellions from prisons to planets. Vel leads among many in the fight for liberation while navigating what it means to be a rebel from a rich family, just like me. It wasn't until I was 36 that I'd see a character in mass media who held the complexities of identity that so closely mirrored my own.

> One thing Vel and I have in common is that we both hid (intentionally and unintentionally) our wealth from our fellow rebels.

One thing Vel and I have in common is that we both hid (intentionally and unintentionally) our wealth from our fellow rebels. Unlike her cousin Mon Mothma, who is a liberal in the

Imperial Senate, when it comes to supporting the Rebellion, Vel chooses not to embrace her connection to a wealthy and politically powerful family. Amongst all the complex character arcs and reveals in *Andor*, Vel's story hooked me the most, because in it, I see my own journey to understanding why honesty about wealth matters, especially when joining forces to take down an empire built on wealth inequality.

That journey begins back in the 90s in the bonus room of my suburban home, sprawled on the couch with my brothers, rewatching *A New Hope* for the umpteenth time. Not only did Luke's story introduce me to the idea of scrappy heroes risking it all for justice, it taught me that heroes are Chosen Ones and saviors. For a young queer Chinese kid growing up in the South, it was important to believe that maybe I too could be like Luke Skywalker and have a super-important destiny and special powers that would take me to a galaxy far far away from suburban North Carolina.

Iimay with their brothers, rocking their 90s outfits (Courtesy of Iimay Ho)

Growing up in a wealthy enclave in Cary, NC, as the child of immigrant parents was full of contradictions and feeling like an outsider in a place where my parents had fought to belong. My parents moved to Cary instead of one of the Asian immigrant hubs in California or New York because my dad found work there as an engineer. His job paid well enough for our upgrade to a new house in an elite neighborhood. So my house was bigger and nicer than most of my white friends at school, but that didn't stop other white kids from making racist jokes about my name and the shape of my eyes.

However, among the Asian community, I was treated with deference, since my mom was a well-respected figure who started an insurance business to help mostly working-class Chinese immigrants navigate American bureaucracy, get driver's licenses and purchase homes. As I grew older her clients became wealthier and

limay's parents in 1977, recently immigrated to the U.S. (Courtesy of limay Ho)

she started to insure investment homes instead of first cars, and my parents started to buy investment properties of their own.

I inherited my *Star Wars* fandom from my parents, who immigrated here from Taiwan as grad students in 1977. They came in hope of securing economic stability and as a backup/exit plan for the families they left behind in case war broke out between China and Taiwan. 1977 is also when *A New Hope* was released and it was their first introduction to an American blockbuster. For an American public reeling and exhausted from the Vietnam War and the impeachment of President Nixon, *A New Hope* was just the kind of popcorn entertainment they needed — they could once again see a young white American man be a hero, taking down The Empire instead of serving it.

To my parents, the movie that would become a quintessential part of American pop culture was derivative of Chinese martial arts epics, which often featured a band of scrappy heroes with hard-earned powers taking on the corrupt state and military. Luke Skywalker was the American version of the rebels and folk heroes they grew up admiring.

As for me, as a child I identified with Luke's restlessness, his sense that life was supposed to be different, bigger, more. As an adult, I roll my eyes at his whininess but also see echoes of my

TO FREE THE MONEY

parents in his resourceful pragmatism. Like them, he grew up working-class and needed to learn how to fend for himself early on. He knows how to haggle, fix his own droids, bullseye womp rats. He remains true to himself and doesn't sell out to The Empire.

Luke Skywalker seeped into my childhood psyche and informed what it means to be "a hero" — someone from humble beginnings, an underdog who, through his honor, skill and alliances, takes on and defeats enemies who are much more resourced and powerful than him.

During my high school years, I saw how The Empire doesn't just exist in the movies; the U.S. declared war against Iraq my senior year and I attended my first protest. This was my first experience of banding together with others around a shared cause, and as we chanted and marched I got a taste of what it might feel like to be part of the Rebellion — and wanted more.

> During my high school years, I saw how The Empire doesn't just exist in the movies.

I got involved in social change in college through coursework and student organizing and then moved to D.C. to pursue jobs at nonprofits focused on social justice. Like Luke, I wanted to be part of changing the world and a movement triumphing over the "bad guys." I wanted to take down The Empire.

I eagerly got involved in local social justice organizing: registering working-class Asian immigrants to vote, building community with other queer Asian Americans and starting a giving circle of donors who fundraised and gave small dollar grants to grassroots and community groups. I was feeling and living the possibility of social change, the possibility of racial and economic justice and making a difference in people's everyday lives.

In a way, it made me feel even prouder of my mom's business success as an Asian immigrant woman in an industry dominated by old white men. Her success despite all of the racism and sexism she faced was an example of what's possible when marginalized people have opportunities for self-determination.

But through my social justice work, I was also learning how

my family's small business empire wasn't just the result of my parents' hard work and determination. My dad had retired early and was building wealth through his stock portfolio, which he then funneled back into buying more rental properties and commercial real estate. Our family money relied on and benefited from the same structures that prop up U.S. empire — namely, racial capitalism and its requisite privatization of housing and real estate speculation.

Like their *Star Wars* fandom, my parents shared their wealth with me, too. It paid for college and for my unpaid D.C. internship, which landed me my first nonprofit job after I graduated. It subsidized my rent when I first moved to D.C. so that I could actually afford to take said job. I was 28 when I received my first inheritance check of $28,000 as a wedding gift.

I saw my commitment to social justice as choosing to "do good" with my privilege, but found myself feeling conflicted by my instinct to hide or omit details about my family's money, and by extension, my own. American culture both glorifies wealth and encourages secrecy about money as part of maintaining the myth of our "classless" society and "equal opportunity." Amidst all the mixed messages, it was easier to stay silent.

But working in nonprofits, money comes up *a lot*. Most, if not all, nonprofits rely on money from foundations and individuals to sustain their work. Back in my early 20s, I once found myself being congratulated for doing a successful fundraising pitch that raised $500 at a grassroots event — an amount I could have easily given myself. But I didn't mention this, nor did I match what was raised. At the time, I rationalized it as not wanting to call attention to myself or flaunt my wealth. Looking back, I can see I felt shame and guilt; I didn't know what to do about being able to give $500 at an event where giving $10 was a stretch for many.

As I continued my nonprofit and social change work, I kept experiencing the dissonance between asking for money a lot and talking about my personal access to money not at all, and the dynamic felt inauthentic and bordered on hypocritical.

I complained about this enough without doing anything about it that my not-wealthy partner finally handed me the book

Classified: How to Stop Hiding Privilege and Use It for Social Change. Flipping through the zine-style comics that illustrated common class privilege patterns, I felt both sheepish ("it's me") and relieved. I was not alone, other people shared my experience and wrestled with the same inner conflicts and I wanted to meet them IRL.

I kept experiencing the dissonance between asking for money a lot and talking about my personal access to money not at all, and the dynamic felt inauthentic and bordered on hypocritical.

The book was my entry point into Resource Generation, an organization that connected me with other young wealthy people committed to social justice. In chapter meetings, members normalized being honest about their and their family's access to wealth and how their money was connected to U.S. empire. These class traitors showed me that being transparent about their wealth and where it comes from was a critical first step to redistributing it in ways that addressed the racism and inequality that created it.

Supported by this community, I started to unpack my own family's wealth origins. I broke the "don't talk about money" taboo by telling my story, both in my personal relationships and publicly. I stopped hiding my access to money, which meant I had to be accountable to do something about it. So I took steps to increase my giving to 10% of my net assets,[1] tell my family's story in ways that debunk the model minority myth and participate in social change as a wealthy person, now bringing signs like "rich person for wealth redistribution" to rallies and marches.

As I was integrating my class identity into my activism, I also became more aware of how embedded class messages are in American pop culture and media, shaping how we understand good vs. evil.

Rewatching *A New Hope* before the *Star Wars* sequels came

[1] Iimay escalated their giving, in part, through inspiration and guidance from Resource Generation's redistribution guidelines, launched in 2019 to help increase the giving of the organization's constituents. More information can be found at https://resourcegeneration.org/redistribution-guidelines/.

45

out, I saw how the Rebels, with their blaster-scorched helmets and piece-of-junk ships, are contrasted with the Stormtroopers, in their gleaming uniforms and pristine Star Destroyers. Good guys don't get nice stuff; it's part of what makes their eventual victory so heroic. And bad guys have everything handed to them, which makes them arrogant jerks up to the second the Death Star blows up. But where are all the rich Rebels?

Cue *Andor*. Having been disappointed by the sequels' insistence on rehashing the same old Chosen One narrative, as I binge watched the show I experienced the unadulterated joy of a fan who sees a struggling franchise suddenly back in the championship league. Underdog, underfunded heroes are, of course, still fighting The Empire. But this time, there's a rich class traitor among them: Vel.

Of course, *Andor* works up to revealing Vel's family background. For the initial part of the series, Vel is only seen roughing it on The Empire-occupied planet Aldhani, and as she describes, "eating roots and sleeping on rocks for the Rebellion." However, her journey eventually brings her strolling, adorned with fancy sumptuous robes, into the inner sanctum of a mansion. She's meeting her cousin (a Senator, naturally) to discuss ways to continue funding the Rebellion.

I gasped at this reveal: *she's a secret rich kid!*

A dozen different thoughts flashed through my head: does she feel conflicted about hiding her wealth, like I did? Does she feel like she has something to prove? Does her old money family know she's a Rebel (and gay??)?

Was Vel hiding her wealth from others because she, like I did, thought she would be less credible or trustworthy if the other Rebels knew she was rich?

After all, we see her spending most of her time among the foot soldiers of the Rebellion, the majority of whom are enduring material scarcity of some sort while she has abundance at her fingertips. Cinta's (Vel's partner) scathing indictment of Vel as a "rich girl running away from her family" landed a little too close to home. As a younger person, I wanted to emphasize the parts of my activist identity that aligned with experiencing hardship

— miles walked and hours spent outdoors in harsh weather in actions and rallies — and not acknowledge how I got to return to my cushy home.

How often had I, like Vel, downplayed my access to wealth, emphasizing the hardships that my parents experienced as immigrants while neglecting to mention the multiple investment properties they own?

I imagine that Vel felt, like me, she needed to obscure (and therefore not fully leverage) wealth and privilege in order to belong, to be good, to be a hero.

But what I love about *Andor* is that there are no individual saviors. The "good" guys do terrible things and the "bad" guys aren't always terrible. The Rebellion is made up of smugglers, thieves, ex-Imperial officers, Senators and droids — surely it has room for Vel to be a rich revolutionary who *isn't* hiding her wealth.

After all, I found that I became more trustworthy when I was accountable and honest about my wealth, and less prone to saviorism or romanticizing poverty, which Vel seems to struggle with. But I also need a community of other rich class traitors to make sure I *stay* honest, and committed to fighting The Empire for the long haul, since for those of us with money, running away (to our second homes... on Mars??) is so much easier.

I hope in Season 2 Vel finds her cadre of class traitors to help her bring all of herself to the Rebellion, because saying "yes" to wealth transparency is in its own way an act of insurrection, both here and in a galaxy far far away. And as her comrade Nemik writes in his manifesto, "even the smallest act of insurrection pushes our lines forward." ∎

I found that I became more trustworthy when I was accountable and honest about my wealth, and less prone to saviorism or romanticizing poverty.

THE IMPERATIVE OF ORGANIZING THE RICH TO BUILD WORKING-CLASS POWER

Braeden Lentz

Braeden Lentz is the chief development officer of the Working Families Party. He was raised in a working-class white family in Syracuse, New York. He currently lives with his husband in New York City. Previously, he was on the board and staff of Resource Generation, and the staff of Solidaire — a network that nurtures relationships between social movements and funders. He is currently on the Advisory Team of Solidaire Action.

This piece is based on a conversation with Michael Gast in February 2025, soon after the presidential inauguration.

A government by, for and of the billionaires — with an authortarian edge — is already here. Millions of working-class people don't see themselves as part of the fight against authoritarianism, yet we need them to win. While most of our time and effort must be spent reaching working-class people of all races, we also have an opportunity to engage a subset of people who currently hold wealth in the project of building working-class power.

These are people who feel a deep dissonance across the wealth they have, the inequality they see in the world and their values based on wanting everyone to have enough. They crave authentic connection and feel in their bones the injustice of having excess. This hunger for a better world is an opening — and they deserve an invitation.

Those of us who seek to build a stronger democracy and an economy that serves the many — not billionaires — have an opportunity to learn from those who have experimented with organizing the rich for justice, democracy and working-class power over decades, building on a foundation of what's been tried before. This anthology offers their stories.

48

This effort to move a wedge of the owning class in support of working-class power isn't a silver bullet for solving the left's money problems — far from it. But I believe that a theory of change that doesn't include how the work is funded and who is moving the money — in the world as it is now and in the new world we seek to build — is an incomplete theory of change. How we fund our biggest, boldest aspirations from real people — across class — is essential to strategy at the Working Families Party.

The Rich are Already Being Organized

Anti-democratic forces and those seeking to consolidate wealth and power away from the working class in America are already organizing the rich.

The evidence was on full display at Trump's inauguration, where the richest people in the world — Meta CEO Mark Zuckerberg; Amazon founder Jeff Bezos; Google CEO Sundar Pichai; and Tesla, X and SpaceX owner Elon Musk — stood behind an anti-democratic president. Billionaires are forming a coalition with a white nationalist, faux-populist campaign to undermine the very foundation of a government and an economy that can actually work for working-class people.

> Anti-democratic forces and those seeking to consolidate wealth and power away from the working class in America are already organizing the rich.

We even saw the world's wealthiest person wielding a golden chainsaw — a gift from Argentina's reactionary president — onstage at a conservative American political event. As it's clear to so many of us, oligarchy has broken through globally.

If you doubted that rich people were being organized, you have your proof in those examples. That organizing is the result of the right's corporate interest, material self-interest and investment in the political development of rich and powerful people.

That's why those of us on the side of working people have an imperative to organize wealthy people too, and with precision — because when the rich are organized by the right, they become a powerful force for deepening inequality and nurturing authoritarianism. Only by organizing them for working-class power can we redirect their resources and influence to build a democracy that works for everyone.

Three Traps Associated with Organizing the Rich

For those of us who grew up working class, organizing the rich into working-class-led projects isn't easy — it comes with three big traps that can undermine the work if we're not careful.

I first started meeting ultra-high-net-worth people as a young grantmaking professional and member of the Resource Generation board. I remember listening to the money stories of wealthy people, hearing about the tens of millions in their control and thinking, "You have choices I've never had and never will. You could pay off my debts with one signature. You could transform the budget of every grassroots organization I've ever struggled to fundraise with."

Over and over, I've found it helpful to remind myself that this line of thinking — fixating on how individual wealthy people's cash could solve individual working-class people's and organization's problems — is the first trap in this work. Economic inequality, propped up by an uneven democracy, is not the fault of any one individual. It can't be solved by one individual. We are living in a self-perpetuating system of wealth inequality, to which individual members of the owning class and the working class are both subject.

The truth is that no amount of fundraising from one wealthy person is going to change our unequal *economic system*. The system of wealth inequality will continue to exist even if individual people with wealth choose to divest or spend down. The capture of our democracy by oligarchs will continue to deepen even if one organization has its budget fully funded. So I tell myself and others, "Yes, feel rage, feel grief, feel sadness. The system is not working for everyone. Let's use those feelings to motivate us to change it for everyone."

I've come to believe that organizing people with wealth as a constituency — grounded in strategy, reaching their peers, working at larger scales, extending beyond personal and organizational interests and toward working-class-led strategies for transforming the system — is our best shot at a path out of the cycle. We need a significant collective force of the rich, a surprise regiment, ready to throw their full support behind strategic, multiracial working-class movements that seek governing power.

A second trap: failing to state your goals clearly. To build relationships of integrity with wealthy people without sacrificing political independence, working-class organizations and leaders must start by being clear about their organizations' role and goal. Don't hide the ball.

As a working-class organizer, you're offering something valuable that wealthy people don't have: a plan to build something real, solid and world changing. Money, by itself, doesn't build anything. Money needs to be animated by leaders, visions and plans. When you're interacting with a rich person, you're giving them something they don't have — a way to change the world, along with a cross-class community.

Communicate your politics and goals clearly to people with wealth, so they can choose whether they can get behind it. One of the biggest mistakes I've seen, and made myself, is not being up-front because we're trying to get the money from a wealthy donor without believing they can actually get behind our mission.

If we figure out how to have a significant crew of wealthy people backing and flanking a multiracial working-class alignment of individuals and organizations like the Working Families Party, we can force a political realignment in America that disempowers the few and builds the power of the many.

A third trap: the perpetual-gap doom loop. I see wealthy progressive donors stuck in this loop of feeling like there are always going to be more gaps in organization budgets than they can fill, and more tears in our social safety net they can mend. Likewise, those of us who organize money are running on an annual fundraising hamster wheel. I've frequently heard some version of "No matter how much I give, it will never be enough." It can feel discouraging, but it's also true.

Philanthropy — the whims of willing wealthy people — will never be enough on its own. We need to change how democracy

WE NEED A SIGNIFICANT COLLECTIVE FORCE OF THE RICH, A SURPRISE REGIMENT, READY TO THROW THEIR FULL SUPPORT BEHIND STRATEGIC, MULTIRACIAL WORKING-CLASS MOVEMENTS THAT SEEK GOVERNING POWER.

Braeden Lentz

functions — ensuring that working-class participation doesn't rely on the rich — and how the economy functions so that everyone is taken care of. Anything short of a path out of the philanthropy-dependent woods is a trap.

The only way out of this third trap is to chart a path that makes philanthropy unnecessary. We need to set a vision for a future where the state delivers what people need and democracy is participatory — not shaped by billion-dollar ad campaigns — and then make a plan to get there.

Building a New World

Working-class voters are drifting away from the Democratic Party. Right-wing authoritarianism is gaining ground. But fighting authoritarianism is not the Democratic Party's job alone. That fight will require thinking beyond partisanship and old ways of doing things.

It's not enough to challenge corporate influence in the Democratic Party or defeat a MAGA-captured Republican Party. Failing working-class people has been a bipartisan effort. We must build vibrant political homes for working-class people of all races, in every part of the country. We can broaden the tent without compromising our ideals and stand firmly with working people of all backgrounds. At the Working Families Party, we believe there is a path to the healthy, vibrant democracy and society we all need.

There is a future where we can be in more equitable political and economic relationships. In that future, today's rich will have less in their bank accounts — but more connection, meaning and belonging in their hearts. There is room for everyone in the future the working class is designing — in the democracy we will build together over the coming decades. It's the job of those who organize the rich to extend that invitation.

Organizing the rich isn't just about fundraising for today's movements — it's about building the cross-class coalition we'll need to create a different world. Thank you for learning from the lessons of previous generations laid out so well in this anthology and taking on this important task. ∎

LINEAGE

Want an introduction to this lineage?
Including a family tree and a historical
overview? You've come to the right place.

AN (INCOMPLETE) ORGANIZE THE RICH FAMILY TREE

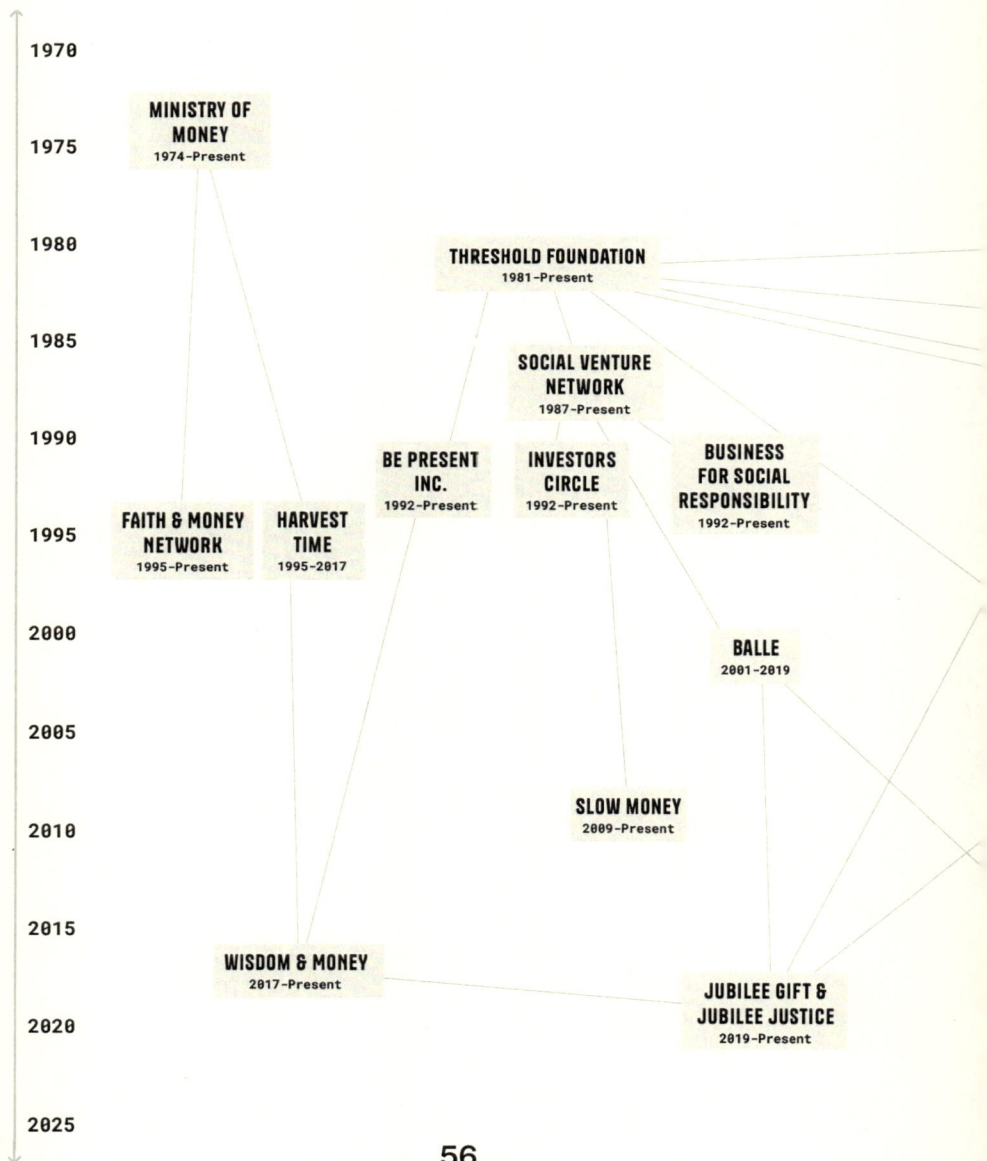

1970

1975 **MINISTRY OF MONEY**
1974–Present

1980 **THRESHOLD FOUNDATION**
1981–Present

1985

SOCIAL VENTURE NETWORK
1987–Present

1990

BE PRESENT INC.
1992–Present

INVESTORS CIRCLE
1992–Present

BUSINESS FOR SOCIAL RESPONSIBILITY
1992–Present

1995 **FAITH & MONEY NETWORK**
1995–Present

HARVEST TIME
1995–2017

2000 **BALLE**
2001–2019

2005

2010 **SLOW MONEY**
2009–Present

2015

WISDOM & MONEY
2017–Present

2020 **JUBILEE GIFT & JUBILEE JUSTICE**
2019–Present

2025

A BRIEF HISTORY OF ORGANIZING THE RICH TOWARD JUSTICE

Michael Gast

Here is my wildly incomplete history of organizing the rich for justice. I think this history is some of the good news that we need in the hard times that we're in.

This history reflects my particular experience in this work and my sense of its evolution. I've been involved in these efforts, as a person with wealth and as an organizer of other wealthy people, since I was a 23-year-old participant at my very first Making Money Make Change conference. I was a volunteer member and leader with Resource Generation for 5-plus years, on staff at Resource Generation for 5-plus years, and I have been a fundraiser, donor advisor and consultant wearing many hats over the last decade. In that time, I have talked to and connected with a wide range of people and organizations in this burgeoning ecosystem — and there are many versions of this story. I am telling only one piece from my particular location in the United States.

The goal of this brief history is to help us notice this growing movement, celebrate what we've accomplished and try bolder experiments that build off what's come before.

I am attempting to take these stories out of the realm of philanthropy, with its vague and evasive language of *donors* and *giving*. Instead, this story is focused on class, economics, power and movement building.

This story is focused on class, economics, power and movement building.

A few notes:

1. The story of wealthy people's involvement in social-justice movements has always been about seemingly contradictory trends coming together. There is no story of rich people for wealth redistribution without a story of rising inequality. There is no story of wealthy people advocating for higher taxes on the rich without a story of an increasingly unjust tax system. There is no story of land back without a story of land theft. We must hold all of it for the benefits and challenges of this growing movement to come into sharper focus. And, for this moment, I will tell one version of the liberatory part of this story, where the rich attempt to oppose the system that gave us our wealth in the first place.

2. This is not a simple story of individual heroes or villains. This is a story about lots of ordinary humans at a particularly dramatic moment in history. It's about people coming together to notice the system that has enriched them is unfair, unsustainable and needs to change.

The story of wealthy people's involvement in social justice movements has always been about seemingly contradictory trends coming together.

4,000 BCE to 1970: Individuals and Small Groups

Since the beginning of class societies, over 5,000 years ago, individuals and small groups of wealthy people have attempted to side with people's movements and to work for equity, justice and the collective good.

People like Moses, a classic rich kid, growing up in the palace of the Pharaoh. As a young man, he is awakened to the injustice around him, lashes out in anger and kills an Egyptian. He runs away from the palace, distances himself from his wealthy home and community, and becomes the black sheep of the family. He lives in the desert for 30 years, pretending he is simply a working-class goatherd, while marrying a woman very different from him

As it so often goes, he is called on by God/a burning bush/ an ayahuasca healing journey/a skilled therapist to return to his people and face the rich and powerful dad who raised him. He needs to figure out how to use his privilege and access to help oppressed people escape from bondage. He decides to use his voice to convince his dad to let his people go.

Moses isn't the only one. There's Buddha, otherwise known as Prince Siddhārtha Gautama. In another pretty stereotypical rich kid move, he forsakes his worldly possessions, including his wealth, family and royal status, to seek enlightenment after witnessing the suffering in the world. He renounces the luxuries of his childhood and becomes a monk.

These are ancient, world-changing stories of people who grew up with wealth and took radical action against the oppressive culture and social system that raised them. *These stories are hiding in plain sight if we look for them, and there are many more.*

These are ancient, world-changing stories of people who grew up with wealth and took radical action against the oppressive culture and social system that raised them.

Anasuya Sarabhai, a South Asian woman, was born into a wealthy family in Ahmedabad, India, in 1885. She would become a socialist and feminist labor organizer. She organized mill workers in opposition to the business association her uncle led. She would sit with workers at the negotiation table, helping them win better contracts. She helped found a textile workers union that would grow to have 150,000 members.

Madam C.J. Walker is in the book of Guinness World Records for being the first female millionaire. She was a Black woman who started a business in the 1910s and, as she made money, gave it to anti-lynching efforts and held civil rights and Black liberation meetings in her home.

There's my Jewish brother Julius Rosenwald, founder of Sears, Roebuck and Co., who started one of the earliest social justice foundations. His charitable foundation, among other efforts, gave fellowships to dozens of Black intellectuals and artists (including Langston Hughes, W.E.B. DuBois, Zora Neale Hurston and Marian Anderson) and supported the Highlander

Anasuya Sarabhai in England
(From the Sarabhai Archives)

Folk School, an interracial popular education institution founded in 1932 that became, and remains, central to struggles for Black liberation and labor rights. Unusual then and now, Rosenwald designated his foundation to spend its assets down, rather than attempt to last "in perpetuity" by investing principal and giving away only interest. The Julius Rosenwald Fund closed in 1948.

Madam C.J. Walker (Courtesy of Madam Walker Family Archives/A'Lelia Bundles)

And one of my favorite examples: the Mink Brigade. Great name, right? These were wealthy women, including J.P. Morgan's daughter, who would stand on picket lines with garment workers so they wouldn't get beaten up by the cops. In the early 1900s, these wealthy women helped cover food and rent for striking workers, bailed strikers out of jail and used their social capital to increase public support.

Julius Rosenwald (Source: Rosenwald Fund)

1970s: The Rich Kid Rebel Alliance

The 1970s is the first time that I know of that wealthy people started organizing themselves in significant numbers around a radical liberation and justice agenda. This is the period when the involvement of the wealthy shifted from individuals and small groups to larger groups and institutions, growing in scale from tens to hundreds and thousands. In this era, the first social justice public foundations and conferences for progressive inheritors were founded.

These new projects were generally initiated by young, white, wealthy inheritors connected to and inspired by the radical movements of the times.

Left to Right: 14 year old striker, Flora Dodge "Fola" La Follette (member of the Mink Brigade), and activist Rose Livingston during a garment strike in New York City in 1913 (Source: Flickr Commons project, 2011)

In Christopher Mogil and Anne Slepian's seminal book, *We Gave Away a Fortune*, there is a chapter on George Pillsbury, an heir to the Pillsbury baking fortune (and thus a "Dough-boy" in more ways than one). In it, he writes of a memory from 1968:

> When I was 18, I imagined organizing people of my class to use their money for progressive social change. This occurred to me one day after a debutante party that was particularly extreme in its display of wealth, held at the top of the RCA building in New York. I remember silver everywhere, because the father of the debutante had made all his money in South African minerals. I didn't know much about South Africa, but I knew it was bad.

> Before the party even started, I went into the bathroom and ripped the buckles off my Gucci shoes. That was really symbolic, because back in 1968 Gucci shoes were a status symbol for a rich person, and I was into clothes. When I came out of that party at 4am and hit the streets of New York, I

63

wanted to be out organizing a picket line against the party, rather than being part of it.

I felt troubled that some of the people at the party were my friends, and I didn't want to separate myself from them. I grew up so thoroughly upper class — all the right vacation places, the boarding schools — everything right out of a textbook. I don't have any ethnic identity; I'm not Jewish, or black, or gay, or a woman. The only group which I really feel a kinship is my class. That's why it came to me to try to organize people of my class — so I could continue to connect with the group that I grew up with. That is the basis for a lot of the organizing I have done with upper-class contributors to social change.

One of the first organizational forms this budding movement took was the Vanguard Public Foundation, started in San Francisco in 1972. It was founded by Obie Benz, a 23-year-old Middlebury graduate with inherited wealth, and a handful of other young wealthy inheritors, such as Christine Russell (from the Haas family, who started Levi Strauss), Daisy Paradis, Penny Gerbode, Maggie Roth (from the family who owned Matson shipping lines) and Peter Stern (another Middlebury graduate). The goal was to fund small grassroots community-organizing groups that weren't getting funding by the mainstream foundations. Vanguard initially decided to focus on women's rights, alternative media and prison reform and limited their grantmaking to groups in the San Francisco Bay Area. Every one of the founders was under 24 years old.

In 1973, Obie Benz would be introduced to George Pillsbury and Anne Hess, whose grandfather was Julius Rosenwald, the co-founder of Sears, Roebuck and Co., and one of the previously mentioned rich radicals. The three of them concocted the idea of organizing meetings for young inheritors from around the country who were interested in supporting grassroots organizing and progressive efforts. The first meeting, in 1974, lasted an afternoon and attracted five people. The second one, a few months later, had seven, and the third one, a few months after that, had 10.

Soon enough, they were organizing multiday retreats.[1]

The group gave itself nicknames like ARF (Amalgamated Rich Folks), YFC (Young Fat Cats) and BARF (Beautiful Amalgamated Rich Folks). These became gatherings of 30-50 young, white, wealthy inheritors talking about how to use their money, access and resources in alignment with their progressive values. After a year or two, it was renamed the classically opaque and generic sounding Conference on National Priorities (CNP).

The goal was to fund small grassroots community-organizing groups that weren't getting funding by the mainstream foundations.

Gathering of Progressive Donors, 1975 (Courtesy of Obie Benz)

These meetings — with their mix of personal storytelling, political education, and encouragement to action — became the prototype for every progressive rich person conference since. The attendees ranged from your everyday trust-fund kids to inheritors from some of the United States' wealthiest and best known families. There were Rockefellers and Roosevelts, as well as young people from the Haas family and the Dayton family, founders of Dayton-Hudson, the department store company that would become Target. As Obie Benz has written in his yet-to-be-published autobiography, "By the end of six years, we had organized eighteen meetings with over 120 people. The ripple effects were bearing fruit. Many individuals began giving for the first time based on what they had learned."

---

1 These details come from Obie Benz's forthcoming autobiography.

Photo from *Change Not Charity: The Story of the Funding Exchange* by Theodora Lurie

At the same time, the number of public social justice foundations started to grow. After George learned about Vanguard, he went home to Boston and helped found Haymarket Public Foundation. Soon after, Liberty Hill Foundation in Los Angeles was cofounded by George's sister Sarah. Then North Star Fund in New York and Bread and Roses in Philly.[2] Word was spreading. These ideas were catching hold. Between the CNP meetings and local efforts, a whole network of organizations and individuals was growing together, and by the end of the decade, the foundations involved became formalized into the Funding Exchange (FEX).

These foundations, and the FEX itself, took as their motto "Change, Not Charity." As Rachel Sherman[3] writes in her forthcoming book *Class Traitors*, they set themselves up as a radical alternative to mainstream philanthropy in several ways:

First, donations went to more progressive, political, and grassroots causes, rather than to the arts, educational and social service institutions that dominated traditional philanthropy (and still do). The idea was to "move money to the movement," in the words of one Haymarket activist. This typically meant giving grants to small, local organizations focused on radical activism. It also meant funding cutting

---

2 I've read conflicting reports: In some, Bread and Roses was first started in Philadelphia in 1971; in others, it started in 1977. I haven't figured out which is correct or what the story is.

3 Professor Rachel Sherman is author of *Uneasy Street: The Anxieties of Affluence* and the book, *Class Traitors*, coming soon from Princeton University Press.

edge causes. For example, Vanguard funded one of the first domestic violence shelters, in 1976, and an early brochure offering information on safe sex that was ultimately translated into 40 languages.

Second, donors did not control where the money went. These foundations created committees to make funding decisions, and the committees were either partially or entirely composed of community activists rather than wealthy people. This move was based, at least in part, on the idea that those most directly impacted should be the ones who get to set the agenda.

The foundations that made up the Funding Exchange were all experimenting with different versions of grantmaking that included leaders from the communities being funded as experts and decision makers. As one might expect, this type of cross-class power sharing was often difficult, leading to interpersonal and organizational conflict, as well as liberatory opportunities for everyone to step outside their class training and work together.[4]

By the mid 70s, some of the central leaders of these efforts: Sarah Pillsbury, Adam Hochschild[5], Obie Benz and Peter Stern envisioned publishing a pamphlet. It became *Robin Hood Was Right* (Vanguard Public Foundation, 1977), an important publicity, outreach and fundraising tool in the following years and decades.[6]

Another important part of this lineage, developing in this same period, was the women's philanthropy movement. Starting in the 70s, in the U.S. and Europe, young wealthy women joined with women from other class backgrounds to start a set of women's foundations. These actions became known as the Global Women's Funding Movement. The initial funds included the Astraea

---

4 What do I mean by "stepping outside of their class training"? I mean that the wealthy donors practiced sharing power and control, and the raised poor, working- and middle-class leaders involved practiced claiming their expertise and leading the way in decisions about large amounts of money.
5 Adam Hochschild is an American author, journalist, historian, lecturer and co-founder of Mother Jones Magazine.
6 It was edited and reprinted in 2000 by Chuck Collins, Joan P. Garner, and Pam Rogers.

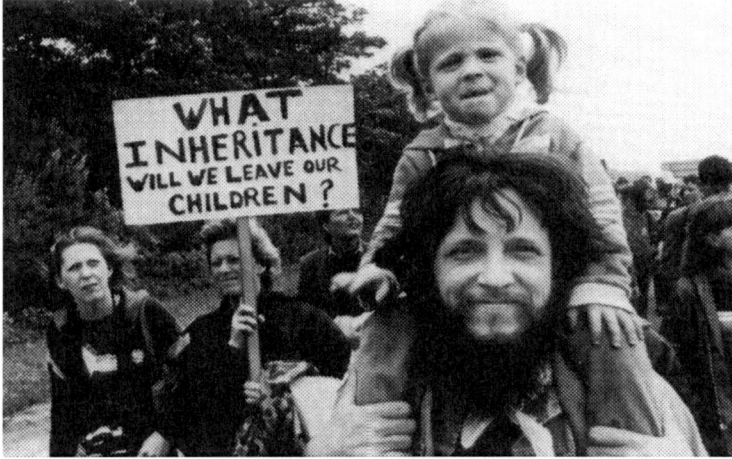

Photo from *Change Not Charity: The Story of the Funding Exchange* by Theodora Lurie

Lesbian Foundation for Justice, Ms. Foundation, Mama Cash and The Women's Foundation of California. Their efforts were part of the second wave of feminism and were inspired by the idea that "it will take a movement of women to raise the money required to fund women's equality."[7]

These projects were motivated in part by a report titled *Who's Funding the Women's Movement,* by Mary Jean Tully and published by NOW Legal Defense and Education Fund in 1975. "Key data points included that of the 30,000 foundations registered at the time, only 20 identified women's organizations as grantees. A total of $12 million of the $7 billion distributed could be identified as having gone to women's organizations and projects and only $2 million for women's movement and feminist projects such as addressing gender-based violence. ... Once the results of this survey were shared, feminist activists and philanthropic-minded women began organizing. Within five years of the survey, a dozen 'women's funds' had been established."[8]

Several prominent leaders in the women's philanthropy movement, such as Tracy Gary, co-founder of the Women's

---

7 Ndana Bofu-Tawamba et al., *Uprising: The Global Women's Funding Movement Emerges* (p. 6).
8 Ndana Bofu-Tawamba et al., *Uprising: The Global Women's Funding Movement Emerges* (p. 7).

Foundation of California, attended CNP meetings and were introduced to social justice philanthropy through the world of the FEX funds.

Neoliberalism and Rising Inequality

While these aspiring revolutionaries were setting up the women's funds and meeting as part of Conference for National Priorities, the corporate and conservative members of the owning class were developing their own plans and vision for the future.

In the 1970s, conservative funders and movement builders began a decades-long effort to rebuild the power and wealth of the owning class — pushing back on the radicalism of the 60s and attempting to roll back decades-old New Deal policies. These funders invested billions in a neoliberal agenda of tax cuts, deregulation and privatization, in alliance with a cultural campaign to promote conservative Christian values.

In the 1970s, conservative funders and movement builders began a decades-long effort to rebuild the power and wealth of the owning class.

Who were these conservative and libertarian funders, foundations and organizations? They were 30-something inheritors such as Charles and David Koch and Richard Mellon Scaife (heir to the Mellon banking and oil fortune), who worked alongside organizations such as the Heritage Foundation, the Cato Institute and the Business Roundtable. These individuals and groups made many of the initial investments in building political power for this neoliberal agenda.[9] Their financial support would begin to pay off with the election of Ronald Reagan and George Bush Sr., ushering in the "greed is good" and trickle-down economics era of the 80s while relentlessly attacking and diminishing the power of organized labor.

As the ascendancy of neoliberalism continued into the 1990s,

---

9 For more, read *Dark Money: The Hidden History of the Billionaires Behind the Rise of the Radical Right* by Jane Mayer.

with President Bill Clinton passing free trade agreements while scapegoating and criminalizing Black and Brown people, the U.S. government cut back on social spending. Nonprofits and private philanthropy were encouraged to step into the breach.

Starting in the 80s, the number of nonprofits in the U.S. skyrocketed, and they became the home base for much of progressive and left activism in the subsequent decades. The left fractured and the labor movement shrank. Progressive and left groups found themselves relying more and more on institutional philanthropy for the money to fight many of the same injustices that their funders relied on to amass their wealth in the first place.

While an organized set of the radical rich was growing to a scale never seen before, an alliance of conservative business leaders, politicians, academics and wealthy inheritors enacted a plan to regain their power and protect their money — and they were wildly successful.

In 1963, the wealthiest families in the U.S. had 36 times the wealth of families in the middle of the wealth distribution. By 2022, they had 71 times the wealth of families in the middle.[10] From 1970 to 2018, the share of aggregate income going to middle-class households fell from 62% to 43%. During the same period, the share held by upper-income households increased from 29% to 48%.[11]

The oppressive logic of class societies is always organizing the wealthy toward the status quo and the maintenance of owning-class power, and this period — from the 1970s to today — is no different.

In many ways, this history is a classic David vs. Goliath, Rebel Alliance vs. Death Star story. Every part of owning-class culture involves policing and pressuring old and new members of the club to sit on their wealth, justify and defend their power and accumulate more. As usual, the rebel alliance is outspent and outnumbered.

---

10 From *Nine Charts About Wealth Inequality in America*, part of the Urban Institute's Financial Well-Being Data Hub, https://apps.urban.org/features/wealth-inequality-charts/.
11 From Pew Research Center. "Trends in U.S. income and wealth inequality." January 9, 2020. https://www.pewresearch.org/social-trends/2020/01/09/trends-in-income-and-wealth-inequality/

In other ways, this is a familiar story that has played out at dinner tables across the class spectrum over the last 50 years. Young radicals arguing with more conservative, and often older, family members, both convinced of their righteousness. What could be more relatable?

The truth is always messier than any "good guys vs. bad guys" story. Every one of the righteous rich mentioned in this history has grappled daily with the contradictions of having wealth and caring about equity and justice. Every wealthy person, depending on the day, can be both generous and greedy, empathetic and entitled. Many of us both give more generously than those around us *and* continue to amass more wealth than we need. Many of us invest in the exact same companies that exacerbate the inequalities we are trying to fight.

The real issue has always been less about the individual ethics of the wealthy people involved and more about the larger vision that is winning hearts and minds. Since the 1970s, the vision of wealthy conservatives and libertarians has been ascendant, even as the owning-class rebel alliance gets in formation.

1980s: A Growing Range of Experiments

By the 1980s, the budding ecosystem that had started in the 70s began to blossom. Money moved. New experiments emerged. The initial set of convenings and groups, such as Conference on National Priorities and the Funding Exchange, inspired and motivated an increasing number of offshoots.

Threshold Foundation

One such example was a group that came out of the Funding Exchange world and became known as the Threshold Foundation, or the Dough-nuts (get it?). Founded in 1981, this group of young wealthy inheritors came together around their interest in spiritual and personal transformation. It was less activist oriented and more inward facing than the FEX funds. Since its founding, it has been a volunteer operation with a few paid support staff, run by and for progressive people with wealth. Out of the relationships built in

71

this community came many influential projects, such as Play BIG, Just Economy Institute, Rockwood Leadership Institute, Social Venture Network and other efforts toward socially responsible investing. For more about Threshold, read Marian Moore's piece, "Through the Donut Door," or the interview with Chuck Collins, "Soft Pillow vs. Marxist/Leninist," both featured later in this anthology.

The Phil Donahue Show, 1980. *Left to Right:* Patricia Silver, Leslie Brockelbank, Annie Hoffman, George Pillsbury. (Courtesy of George Pillsbury)

Movement for a New Society

The Movement for a New Society (MNS) in Philadelphia developed a generation of committed leaders working on class, classism and wealth inequality. MNS was started in the 1970s by a group of Quakers who were active in the movements of the 60s and wanted to pass along what they had learned.

MNS had strong connections to the Civil Rights Movement, antiwar movement and labor movement. It was deeply committed to nonviolent civil disobedience and feminism. Many of the members of the community were involved with and practiced Re-Evaluation Counseling, a type of peer counseling, developed in the '50s by a labor organizer named Harvey Jackins in Seattle, Washington.

During the 1970s and early 80s, Philadelphia was the base for MNS residential programs that trained U.S. and international activists in direct action organizing, group process, consensus decision-making and more. In Philly, MNS became a community of 20 homes housing around 120 people, mostly working- and middle-class white kids in their 20s and 30s. It was a laboratory for these young people to experiment with what a new society could and would look like.

Out of this community came leaders such as Chuck Collins, Betsy Leondar-Wright, Jerry Koch-Gonzalez, Felice Yeskel, Anne Slepian and Christopher Mogil (who would change their names to Anne and Christopher Ellinger).

Anne and Christopher would go on to popularize the term *donor organizing*, develop the practice of donor advising and found efforts such as *More than Money Journal* and Bolder Giving. Bolder Giving would eventually inspire the billionaire's Giving Pledge, which is both a victory for redistribution and exemplifies the vast limitations of a mostly values-neutral philanthropic strategy.[12] Christopher and Anne were active members in Threshold and leaders in the FEX funds, and played a bridge role between these communities and many others.

In the early 1990s, Chuck and Felice would go on to found United for a Fair Economy (UFE) and establish Responsible Wealth as a project of UFE. Responsible Wealth was one of the first groups of the recent era to organize wealthy people to lobby for tax hikes on the rich.

Betsy would cofound Class Action,[13] and she would write

---

12 In my view, the billionaire philanthropy inspired by the Giving Pledge has largely gone to projects and programs that do little to challenge the power of the rich or significantly decrease inequality. Like much of traditional philanthropy, the money moved often strengthens the legitimacy and reputation of the wealthy, serves as a money-saving tax break for the donor and does little to address the underlying systems that create poverty and injustice in the first place. While I am often supportive of the voluntary redistribution efforts of the rich, we need involuntary redistribution in the form of higher taxes on wealth to effectively create the healthy society I want. Projects like the Giving Pledge can serve as useful positive press for wealthy people fighting tooth and nail against tax policies that would reduce the need for their philanthropic dollars in the first place.
13 Class Action (2004-2022) was a national organization based in Western Massachusetts that ran political education programs and developed printed and online resources to raise awareness about class and inspire actions to end classism. They developed numerous trainings and materials on class, class cultures in activism, cross-class alliance building and led many different types of class caucusing activities.

IF WE WANT WEALTHY
PEOPLE, AND OUR
CLASS SYSTEM,
TO CHANGE, IT'S
IMPERATIVE TO TELL
HOPEFUL, HONEST
STORIES OF CROSS-
CLASS SOLIDARITY
AND THE REAL WORK IT
ENTAILS

seminal books, such as *Class Matters: Cross-Class Alliance Building for Middle Class Activists* and *The Color of Wealth: The Story Behind the U.S. Racial Wealth Divide.*

Jerry Koch-Gonzalez was on the board of United for a Fair Economy for many years, was a consultant and trainer with Class Action and helped develop and popularize a group decision-making process called sociocracy.

Chuck would go on to write numerous books, such as *Born on Third Base: A One Percenter Makes the Case for Tackling Inequality, Bringing Wealth Home, and Committing to the Common Good*, and found the Program on Inequality and the Common Good at the Institute for Policy Studies, focusing on policy interventions that reduce extreme inequality.

Donor Organizing

In the 1980s, the term *donor organizing* was coined and began to be developed as a practice by Christopher and Anne Ellinger and others in the FEX network. As Christopher and Anne recently shared with me:

> For years, we worked with the staff and donor activists of the Funding Exchange network to shift their thinking away from seeing donors simply as people who gave money, to seeing donors as people to fully engage as part of the community working for change. We termed the work "donor organizing."
>
> This was a significant reframe for most people — including the donors themselves. We challenged people to shift away from phrases like "targeting," "cultivation," "hit up" — which put people into dehumanizing roles and which actually made fundraising uncomfortable. Instead, we encouraged people to think of fundraising in a frame of inviting gift-exchange and partnership, and as just one part of empowering people with wealth to act on their love for the world.
>
> From our experience as organizers, interviewers and coaches, we believed that most people needed a package

of reinforcing, supportive practices. We wrote and shared principles and tools to support donor organizing leaders:

1. Hear the personal stories of role models (and, eventually, to share their own stories).

2. Join a network or support group with like-minded people supporting and challenging continued growth.

3. Receive ongoing support to thoughtfully prepare three important planning documents: (a) an estate plan, (b) a long-term giving plan (c) and a social investment plan.

4. Get personal coaching and/or professional support to address their individual needs.

We shared these ideas in a short piece we wrote and in meetings with staff in key networks like the National Network of Grantmakers, Tides Foundation, the Philanthropic Initiative, the Family Foundations program of the Council on Foundations, the Shefa Fund, the Ministry of Money [now the Faith and Money Network], the Funding Exchange, the Gill Foundation and others.

From the beginning, the term donor organizing was both a useful shift toward a more relational style of fundraising and a humanistic approach to the wealthy, while also being a class-evasive code word for organizing the rich.[14]

Many Flowers Bloom: Springtime in Rich-People-Organizing Land

Throughout the decade, organizations and networks continued

---

14 I have always had trouble with the term *donor organizing* when it is used as a code word for organizing or fundraising the rich. I like how it can help fundraisers and resource mobilizers see themselves as organizers, responsible for more than just shifting dollars. At the same time, it has significant downsides. The term can lead us to forget that 1) The majority of donors and the most generous donors, as a percentage of their total income and assets, are poor, working- and middle-class people. 2) We have a much bigger vision for the rich than just becoming "good donors" (though that is always a fine place to start). 3) It's not only possible but also important to talk to wealthy people directly about their class position. "Donor organizing" is an understandable starting place but I'm concerned about how it can limit and confuse our efforts.

to bloom, far too many to name here. Drummond Pike, who had worked for a foundation of an early member of Conference on National Priorities, started the Tides Foundation; Josh Mailman, a founder of Threshold, cocreated the Social Venture Network.

The women's foundations, started in the 70s, began to organize into larger formations. Tracy Gary and many others established the Women's Funding Network and the Women Donors Network. The National Network of Grantmakers, an important home base for the upstart social justice philanthropy movement since its founding in the 70s, continued to grow. It helped launch Funders for LGBTQ Issues, among other identity-and issue-specific efforts.[15]

1990s and 2000s: New Projects Emerge

This is the period when Resource Generation (RG) was founded. The young rich kids who started out as radicals in the 1970s were suddenly middle aged, like I am now. They had built a whole slew of foundations and supported many nonprofits and political candidates, but they also knew, "We need another generation of young, wealthy people to help fund these movements!" In 1995, a group of organizations and individual wealth holders, mainly from the Boston area, came together and started RG — first known as Comfort Zone.[16]

"We need another generation of young, wealthy people to help fund these movements!"

RG brought together the community building and focus on personal transformation of the Threshold Foundation with the cross-class, multiracial movement-building focus of FEX. It was also significantly influenced by popular political tendencies on the left during that time, such as women-of-color feminism,

---

15 This paragraph is based on the research and writing work of Professor Rachel Sherman, author of *Uneasy Street: The Anxieties of Affluence and Class Traitors*, forthcoming from Princeton University Press.
16 Boston has been and remains a central hub and hotbed of work on class, money, wealth and cross-class alliance building. Important groups like Haymarket Foundation, Resource Generation and New Economy Coalition were all founded in the area. Leaders like George Pillsbury, Chuck Collins, Betsy Leondar-Wright and many others have called it home.

intersectionality, anti-racism, transformative organizing and Freiren popular education[17].[18]

Other notable groups and important trends to mention from these decades include:

1. The Democracy Alliance (DA), founded in 2004 as an attempt to organize wealthy liberals to invest in a long-term plan to win progressive power. The DA was modeled, in some ways, on what right-wing wealthy people had successfully pulled off starting in the 70s. In 2007, Democracy Alliance helped to start Voices for Progress and the Committee on States, a network of progressive state-based donor alliances such as California Donor Table, Michigan Donor Alliance and the Missouri Wins Investor Network[19].

2. The field of socially responsible investing started to take off, with the support of many wealth holders involved in the progressive donor networks of the time.

3. The 80s and early 90s saw the establishment of international social-justice funders like Grassroots International and IDEX (now Thousand Currents), along with Funders Network on Trade and Globalization.

4. A host of philanthropic intermediaries like Hispanics in Philanthropy and Association of Black Foundation Executives

---

17 Paolo Freire (1921-1997) was a Brazilian educator and philosopher. He is best known for his book *Pedagogy of the Oppressed*, in which he reimagines teaching as a collaborative act of liberation rather than transmission.
18 This analysis is in part based on Laura Wernick's 2009 dissertation, "How Young Progressives With Wealth Are Leveraging Their Power and Privilege to Support Social Justice: A Case Study of Social Justice Philanthropy and Young Donor Organizing" (Ph.D. diss., University of Michigan, 2009).
19 For more on the founding of the Democracy Alliance, read Gara LaMarche's essay on pages 70-73 in the book *George Soros: A Life in Full* (Harvard Business Review Press, 2022) and *Rob Stein's Liberal Legacy* by Micah Sifry on his Substack, The Connector from 2022.

came together in 1993 as the Joint Affinity Groups (now CHANGE Philanthropy), supporting and educating foundation staff and trustees toward justice.

5. Outgiving is founded in 1993 by Hosie Baskin, Phillip Rush and David Becker as the first-ever gathering of progressive LGBTQ donors. The first event is held in Cummington, Massachusetts with 12-15 attendees. In 1996, software engineer and tech entrepreneur Tim Gill received permission to use the name Outgiving, and hosted the first conference under his leadership in Aspen, Colorado.

The 2008 Financial Crisis and Occupy: Neoliberalism in Crisis

In 2008, the neoliberal consensus began to crumble. A stock market crash that started on Wall Street rippled around the world. A series of uprisings, like the Arab Spring, arose to challenge entrenched power.

In 2011, during the Occupy Movement, RG members like Farhad Ebrahimi and Elspeth Gilmore went viral by holding up signs saying, "I am the 1%. I stand with the 99%."[20] This message turned into a powerful media campaign using the slogan "We are the 1%. We stand with the 99%."

For the first time in my life, I witnessed a broad questioning of capitalism. So many were articulating the sentiment, "This current system does not work, and we need something different." The populist movements of Barack Obama and Trump, outsider candidates promising change, emerged with their own answers to this outcry.

We're still in this populist moment. So many are noticing, "Things are broken. What we thought was stable is falling apart. We need something different. But what?"

---

20 Farhad Ebrahimi is a wealthy inheritor, organizer and strategist who was a member and leader in Resource Generation and is co-founder of Solidaire. Most recently, Farhad was the founder and president of the spend-down Chorus Foundation. He currently, in 2025, works at Solidaire as an organizer. Elspeth is a wealthy inheritor, longtime leader in this work and former executive director of Resource Generation. She is the co-founder of the Trust Web, profiled later in this anthology.

79

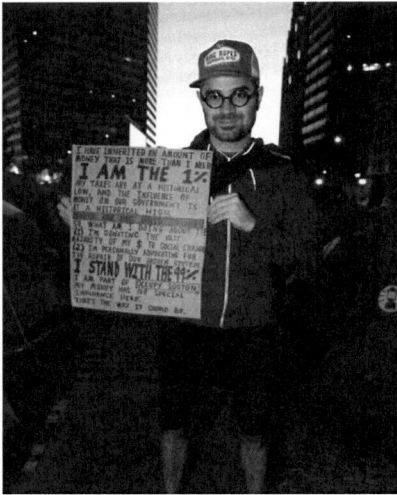

2011 photos of Farhad Ebrahimi (*left*) and Elspeth Gilmore (*right*) (Courtesy of Farhad and Elspeth)

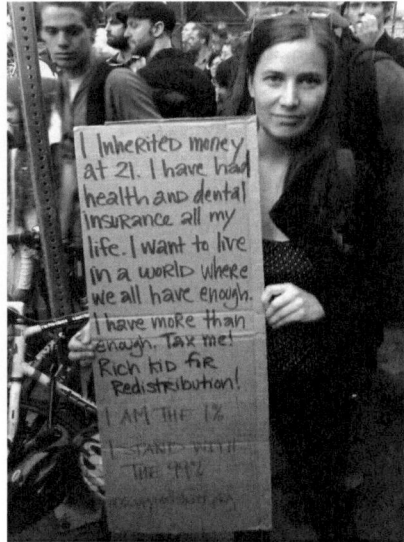

2010s to Today: Boom Times

Since 2010, as inequality soared, the work of organizing the rich toward justice has taken off.

For the first time in my life, I witnessed a broad questioning of capitalism.

In 2010, Patriotic Millionaires was founded as a public relations and lobbying group, leveraging the stories of its wealthy members to organize for higher taxes on the rich, increasing the minimum wage and campaign finance reform. It supported its members, like Abigail Disney, to be more visible and effective spokespeople, pushing back on the anti-tax, anti-government messages of the Right.[21]

In 2013, Solidaire was founded by a crew of young people with wealth and several social-justice leaders from other class

---

21 One of the things I love about PM is that it has mobilized a set of older men, many of them raised working or middle class, who became wealthy in their lifetime. This is a constituency largely missing from many of the social justice philanthropy groups I've been involved with, which are majority female and inheritors. For more on Patriotic Millionaires, check out their book *Tax the Rich! How Lies, Loopholes,* and *Lobbyists Make the Rich Even Richer* (2021), by Morris Pearl, Erica Payne and the Patriotic Millionaires.

80

backgrounds as a rapid-response-funding vehicle for progressive movements.[22] Over time it turned into an intergenerational, cross-class political home for social-justice donor organizers.

Progressive electoral funding groups like Movement Voter Project (MVP) and Way to Win were launched before and after the 2016 election.[23] They were responding to the growing understanding that winning elections requires consistent and increased financial support for grassroots organizing in local communities. By the 2020 election, MVP and Way to Win were each separately moving over $100 million per cycle to a swath of electoral organizing efforts in swing states. These funders provided the financial support that helped swing Georgia and Arizona to Biden in 2020, and remain an important piece of the pro-democracy movement.

In 2016, Donors of Color Network was founded as the first donor network specifically for people of color with wealth. Their efforts led to campaigns like the Climate Funders Justice Pledge and began to make real the decades long vision of a truly multiracial movement of the rich.

Other growing parts of the ecosystem have included efforts related to land return, Indigenous sovereignty, reparations, social-justice investing, the ethical business movement and an increasing number of sister organizations outside of the U.S., in Canada, the UK, continental Europe and Australia.

We've Always Been Led By...

It's important for me to note that throughout this history, from Moses to the Movement Voter Project, from Anasuya Sarabhai to Solidaire, young wealthy people have been at the forefront. Young people with wealth have been bravely naming and acting upon what they know in their heart — that this class-based society is

22 Many of the young people with wealth involved were a part of or connected through Resource Generation.
23 Another small world fun fact: Billy Wimsatt, founder of Movement Voter Project, and Leah Hunt Hendrix, one of the co-founders of Way to Win, were two of the co-founders of Solidaire. They were motivated, in part, to launch both groups because of conversations they had while in Solidaire.

unfair and needs to change.

This nascent movement has always been disproportionately led by people with some experience of marginalization: young people, women, LGBTQ people, Jews, Indigenous people and people of color. These leaders have often been the most ready to take the leap to oppose and act against the class system as a whole.

Yet, even this brief history makes it clear that the movement has had leadership from people of all class and racial backgrounds, including many white men of Christian heritage, such as George Pillsbury, Obie Benz and Chuck Collins.

Lastly, this work has always been moved forward through cross-class relationships and multiracial teams. There is no movement of the rich toward justice without the leadership, hard work, perspective and strategic thinking of poor, working- and middle-class leaders — often leaders of color. These leaders have too often faced ongoing classism, racism, and sexism in their

Young people with wealth have been bravely naming and acting upon what they know in their heart — that this class-based society is unfair and needs to change.

efforts to work with the radical rich. There is nothing acceptable about the toll this work has taken on those involved in our well-meaning but often confused attempts. These relationships have almost always been messy and meaningful—full of conflict as well as opportunities for partnership and solidarity.

Photo from Vanguard Public Foundation 1980-1981 Annual Report. Caption on photo reads "Staff members Beatriz Rosales, Paul Haible, Betsy Weedon and Evelyn Shapiro."

Photo from Vanguard Public Foundation 1980-1981 Annual Report. Caption on photo reads, "Community Board members Maya Escudero, Leo Robinson, Yolanda Alcantar, Janice Mirikitani and Steve Owyang."

The truth is we don't yet know how to build the powerful cross-class movements we need to enable the liberated society that works for us all. But scattered through these experiments, across five decades and five millennia, are the seeds of a new way — germinating answers to almost any question or challenge we now face.

What Do I Take From This Brief History of Organizing the Rich?

When I read over this history, I can more easily see that this budding movement is historic — but wildly insufficient on its own. Looking back to the beginning of class societies, we saw that wealthy people have always had the capacity to work against our class interests and alongside movements for justice. In the 1970s and 80s, we learned that wealthy people can be organized to be donors *and* peer organizers. In the 1990s and 2000s, the variety of ways the wealthy can advocate alongside working class movements expanded into areas such as electoral organizing, investing, tax policy, and international solidarity. In the 2010s, a powerful force of the rich for wealth redistribution was not only possible, it was forming up before our eyes.

83

Where do we find ourselves today?

As best as I can see it, neoliberalism is teetering as an economic logic. Right-wing populism is ascendant. Crises abound. The dominant system is collapsing.

This movement of the rich toward justice has reached an initial level of maturity as a practice with a developing theory and growing base of the wealthy that numbers in the thousands. There's an opportunity here to grow a team and widen a crack within the owning class at a scale we have never seen before. There's an opportunity to unlock billions of dollars for social-justice movements — but for whom and behind what strategies? And what will it take to scale our numbers from the thousands to the tens of thousands, even as systems-collapse brings fear and conservatism?

These questions can only be worked out in practice. The efforts of today owe much to the legacy of the last 50 years. Let us celebrate how far we have come in building true cross-class alliances while acknowledging how far we still need to go. ▪

MOVEMENT ECONOMICS

To learn how to build powerful cross-class coalitions, it's important to understand how left and progressive movements have been funded over time. This section includes excerpts from interviews with Linda Burnham and Max Elbaum, an article by Nina Luo, and a never-before-published piece by Alex Tom. Together, they help paint a picture of the economics of left social movements over the past 50+ years while sharing some of the central questions and challenges we face today.

"THE ASSUMPTION WAS EVERYBODY WORKS AND THEN DOES THEIR POLITICAL WORK ON THE SIDE"

Interview With Linda Burnham

Linda Burnham at around 25 years old in a photo from the Third World Women's Alliance *(left)* and a more recent photo of Linda *(right)* (Courtesy of Linda Burnham)

Linda Burnham has been a Black feminist leader, activist, writer, researcher and strategist for over 50 years. She is a co-editor of, and a contributor to, *Power Concedes Nothing: How Grassroots Organizing Wins Elections*. Burnham served as national research director and senior advisor at the National Domestic Workers Alliance for nearly a decade. She cofounded, with Miriam Ching Louie, the Women of Color Resource Center and served as the organization's executive director for 18 years. Burnham has published numerous articles on African American women, African American politics and feminist theory in a wide range of periodicals and anthologies.

This is an excerpt from Michael Gast's interview with Burnham, published on the Organize the Rich Substack in November 2024.

Mike: What's your class background?

Linda: I would describe my background as stable working class. My parents were both organizers and political. They were first-generation college students, educated. My mom was a biologist who worked in labs while we were growing up, then later became a community college teacher at Empire State. My dad was an organizer his whole life and the editor of a newspaper called *Freedom*.

We weren't hungry and didn't suffer financially, but we also weren't going on European vacations. We wore hand-me-downs. That was pretty typical for our broader family — teachers, city workers, that kind of thing.

Mike: How did you get connected and involved in social movements?

Linda: I got connected because I was raised by Black communists. Politics was a big thing around the dinner table, and I got involved really young. My first independent demonstration was a ban-the-bomb peace demonstration in Union Square. In high school, we organized around Ebinger's Bakery, which had "no colored folk" at the front of the house. We boycotted the bakery.

Politics was a big thing around the dinner table, and I got involved really young.

I was born in '48, so my high school years were '61 to '64. Then there was early anti-Vietnam stuff — I remember hearing about U.S. incursions into Vietnam in junior high school.

I got politicized pretty early. I went to public school in New York — Erasmus, this huge high school. Then my first year of college was at Bennett, a historically Black college in Greensboro, North Carolina. I left Bennett because it was very socially conservative, more than I could handle as someone who grew up pretty free-ranging. It was a lockdown situation, so I needed out. I went to Reed College in Portland, Oregon — the polar opposite of Bennett.

I ended up in the Bay Area in 1969 and quickly got involved in Black feminist organizing. At that point, any five people could create an organization — I was in one called Black Sisters United. Then the Third World Women's Alliance, and onward from there.

Mike: You were on the forefront of developing these conversations about intersectionality. How much was cross-class alliance building, cross-class unity, and work around people's class background a part of that mix?

Linda: That's a great question. We didn't think about class enough, actually. I'm glad you're thinking about it now. We came more from a vantage point of "the ruling class is all the enemy — why even bother trying to sort it out?" We weren't particularly thinking about cross-class alliances beyond maybe the upper middle class. We just didn't go there. Looking back, I'd say we had a pretty crude analysis of what we were trying to do.

This was also before the whole nonprofit industrial complex. Everything we did was based on dues — people were expected to pay somewhat proportional to their income, though you never exactly knew what that meant for different people. There was no assumption that some wealthy person in the wings was going to fund the whole thing. There are strengths and weaknesses to that kind of organizing. I've been thinking about it a lot recently as I look at some of the dysfunction in the nonprofit world.

Mike: Ooh. I'd love to hear more. What do you see as the strengths and weaknesses of that model?

Linda: In Black Sisters United, Third World Women's Alliance, the Alliance Against Women's Oppression, none of that was funded by outside folks. There was no staff. Eventually, in Line of March, a Marxist formation — not a great name, but whatever — there were maybe a couple people on staff. There were some folks working on the newspaper and journal. But everybody else had full-time jobs. It's not like you had a staff of dozens or hundreds — that just wasn't a thing. The assumption was everybody works and then does their political work on the side.

Late 1970s photo from the Third World Women's Alliance, celebrating the wedding of the couple in the very bottom front. Linda is in the lower middle, with the white-collared shirt and blue patterned dress. Her daughter is the young child in overalls in the front. (Courtesy of Linda Burnham)

In the Third World Women's Alliance, we did bake sales, sold cupcakes for 25 cents — I mean literally — and tried to figure out how to raise enough money to get a newsletter out. The advantage of that is that everybody who's in it is in it because they actually really want to do the work. There's nobody there because they've got this much politics [holding fingers closely together] and need a job, so they're on staff at some non-profit but unwilling to do whatever's needed. You get people who are truly dedicated to the mission, who are mission-driven and willing to give up a lot.

The assumption was everybody works and then does their political work on the side.

I was talking to my daughter a couple months ago, and I said, "Yeah, you grew up pretty poor because we were." And she said, "I know, Mom."

It wasn't news to her, but we didn't *feel* particularly poor to me. There are some reasons for that. One is that housing costs were nowhere near as crazy as they are now. Plus, people were willing to live with housemates and all that — though that only works until you're a certain age, and for some people, it doesn't work at all.

It also means that some people can't work in that way. As you get older, you have responsibilities towards kids or aging parents. I had the advantage that I was healthy; my family was healthy. I wasn't called on by a whole bunch of other family-related stuff, so I could exist on a part-time job and a limited income and be okay with that, and do all my political work on the side. But that only takes you so far.

Mike: What you're saying paints a picture of a very different movement economics before neoliberalism ratcheted everything up. There was a stable working class that existed in a way it doesn't now, and there was a bit of a stable middle class that could allow people to take financial risks without feeling like they'd be underwater or in debt forever, which is so common today.

Linda: Yeah, that's true. That was a different period — my parents owned their house; my grandparents owned their houses. The neighborhood my daughter grew up in, there's no way we could be there now. The neighborhood I'm in now, I wouldn't be able to be in it had I not gotten lucky. The economics were really, really different.

I think the disadvantage now in the nonprofit world is that it's so profoundly dependent on big money and philanthropy that people really can't imagine crossing the street without $150,000 in hand. That's a real problem. The ways we're structured now... I have a really hard time figuring out how you get from where we are now to a more mass formation when everybody's looking for a salary. I actually don't get it.

Mike: These questions you've raised are so important: How do we build a mass movement when we can't pay everybody to be involved? How can we have a cross-class united front, led by the working class, with the rich backing it, when so quickly it becomes the opposite? [i.e., the rich leading the way]

Linda: Corruption creeps into the movement because people doing the work start to look at the money. Before you can even work through strategy, it becomes about "how do we get the money?" It encourages corrupt actors and can have a corrupting

90

influence on people who maybe didn't start that way.

Folks come into movement now and expect that the movement owes them an upper-middle-class life. There's no fucking social justice movement that owes you an upper-middle class life!

Before you can even work through strategy, it becomes about "how do we get the money?" It encourages corrupt actors and can have a corrupting influence on people who maybe didn't start that way.

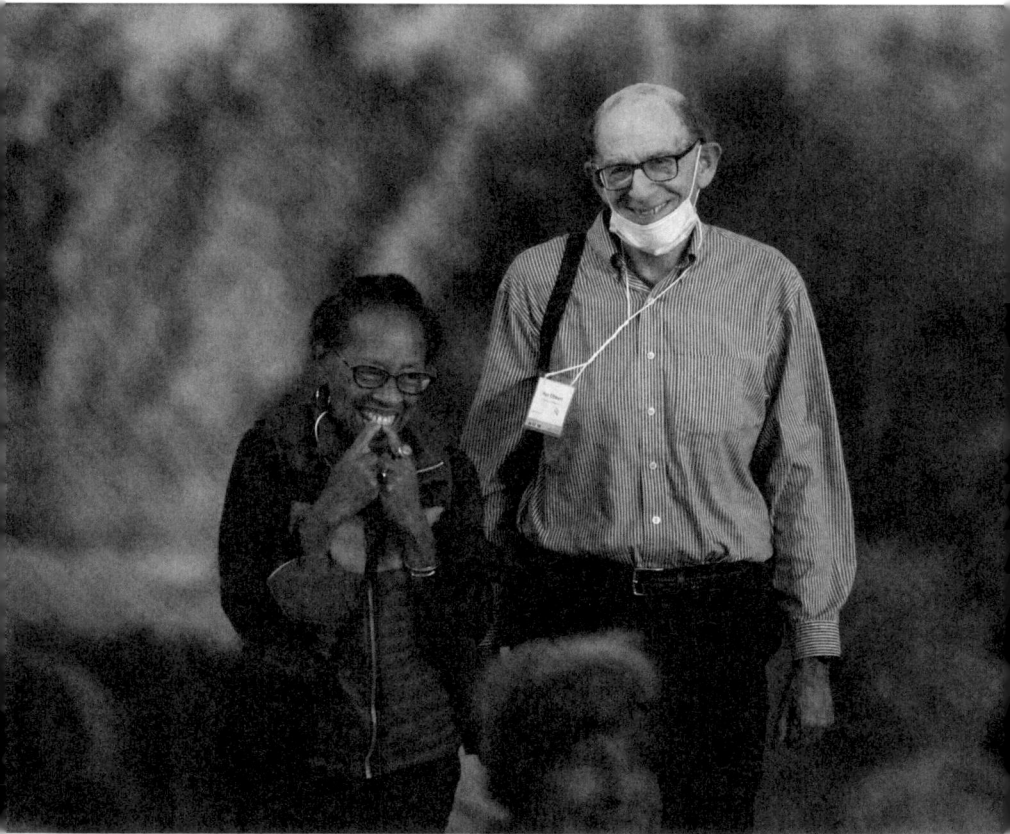

Linda Burnham and Max Elbaum walking together at Solidaire's 2023 Unity and Power Retreat. Max and Linda are long-time friends and comrades (Courtesy of Solidaire)

HOW HAVE LIBERATION MOVEMENTS BEEN FUNDED OVER TIME?

WHAT WOULD A 'MOVEMENT ECONOMICS' LOOK LIKE THAT BUILDS THE POWER OF POOR AND WORKING-CLASS PEOPLE'S MOVEMENTS?

"MOVEMENT TOWARD WHAT?"

Interview With Max Elbaum

Max Elbaum is a longtime left movement leader and writer. He was a member of Students for a Democratic Society in the 60s and a group called Line of March in the 70s, 80s and 90s. He wrote a book on the new communist movement, *Revolution in the Air: Sixties Radicals Turn to Lenin, Mao and Che*; co-edited an anthology, *Power Concedes Nothing: How Grassroots Organizing Wins Elections*; and currently writes for and is on the editorial board of *Convergence Magazine*.

This interview took place in Michael Gast's kitchen in December 2023, almost a year before Trump's reelection the following November. It was published in two parts on the Organize the Rich Substack in February 2025. This is an excerpt from the longer interview.

Max: I grew up middle class. My father owned a small business. My mother was a librarian. Our family followed a common trajectory for Eastern European Jews who emigrated to the U.S. in the early 1900s: my grandparents, first generation immigrants, worked in the garment industry. The second generation climbed up the class ladder a notch to become teachers, social workers, and small-business owners. And the third generation was supposed to go on to become doctors or lawyers —

Mike: Or Communist organizers? *[laughs]*

Max: Yeah, I got off that train [of upward mobility] and went in a different direction.

My parents said, "You want to be a communist!? Can't you be a communist doctor or a communist lawyer or a communist college professor?" They didn't like communism particularly much, but what they really didn't like was me not climbing the professional ladder.

Mike: *[Laughing]* I love that story.

Max: We tussled about it for a while but eventually they learned to live with my choice. I was a student activist but did graduate college, then joined many other radicals in my generation in getting a working-class job and living in a working-class community in order to organize workers for the revolution.

I was a student activist but did graduate college, then joined many other radicals in my generation in getting a working class job and living in a working-class community in order to organize workers for the revolution.

In the mid-1970s I was pressed to become part of a full-time "internal" cadre doing mostly writing and editing. I did that kind of work for the next 20 years, for the first 15 years earning subsistence wages as part of a communist organization, the last five earning a bit more — I think I got up to $20K a year — editing a more ecumenical radical publication.

In 1995 I left that role so a younger person could take the paid position at the magazine I worked for at the time. I got an office job in the records management department of a company that leased railroad cars and airplanes and went back to my roots in doing my political activism as a volunteer in my non-working hours. I retired in 2019 just before the pandemic.

Mike: As far as I've found, formalized efforts to organize the progressive rich started in earnest in the 1970s with projects like the Vanguard Public Foundation, Haymarket People's Fund, and the Conference on National Priorities.

What are some of the broader trends in the left in the 70s that are important to understand, so I can put those efforts into context? Both around the left's strategy and your experience of its relationship to wealthy progressives.

Max: In the early to mid-1970s, the mass upsurge that had been a feature of U.S. politics since 1955 turned toward an ebb. The initiative was starting to shift from the movements for social justice to the right-wing backlash which by the end of that decade brought Ronald Reagan to the White House.

As this process unfolded, some individuals and groups who had participated in the protests and direct actions of the radical

60s shifted their strategies. With the Voting Rights Act still in force and a large base of people who had progressive sentiments ready to vote, if not to go into the streets, there were openings for social justice advocates to get elected at the local, state and even national level. Policy expertise and skills at working the legislative system took on greater importance in the fight for specific reforms.

There was a general need for projects and institutions that functioned with a larger proportion of staff to volunteer energy than had been the case when there was energy welling up from below. And there were people who had the resources to support those kinds of institutions. A layer of people, who had been radicalized in the 1960s, and who had access to family money, had come into being. This was the context in which those community funds, starting with initiatives like the Vanguard Public Foundation, took shape.

There was a general need for projects and institutions that functioned with a larger proportion of staff to volunteer energy than had been the case when there was energy welling up from below. And there were people who had the resources to support those kinds of institutions.

The current on the left I was a part of recognized that we were going into an ebb period. But we felt it would be relatively short-lived. We thought that more and more countries in what we then called the Third World and now is generally termed the Global South would break free of the U.S.-led world capitalist system. We believed that the U.S. ruling class would face a serious profit squeeze, and that the resulting attacks on the U.S. working-class' standard of living would produce another upsurge that would be both more radical than the 1960s and more rooted in the multi-racial working class.

We saw our task as embedding ourselves in the working class and building the kind of combative political party that would be able to exercise leadership in a period of intense, perhaps even insurrectionary, class struggle.

95

We saw our task as embedding ourselves in the working class and building the kind of combative political party that would be able to exercise leadership in a period of intense, perhaps even insurrectionary, class struggle. It was an ultra-left assessment, but it seemed plausible to a lot of us at the time.

So a lot of young folks from middle-class backgrounds moved to working-class neighborhoods; mostly to get jobs in factories, hospitals, sweatshops and so on, with some focused on non-workplace organizing of youth or bringing their politics to existing community organizations. A lot of young people from working-class backgrounds took this course too.

The 60s were the first time large numbers of working-class youth and youth of color went to college, and many were radicalized and decided to return to organize the communities from which they sprang. There were rich kids doing this too; not a large number, but some. This "organize the working class" trend was taken up under one or another ideological banner within Marxism or Marxism-Leninism.

The economy at the time made taking this course easier than it is for young people today. It was before de-industrialization and it was possible to get a blue-collar job. Union density was higher so you could get a job in a unionized workplace. And the cost of living, especially of housing, was much less than today. Salaries went a lot further then, and twenty-somethings without kids could live cheaply, or crash on couches like SNCC [Student Nonviolent Coordinating Committee] and SDS [Students for a Democratic Society] activists before us. A couple of folks working full-time could support someone organizing full-time, and also pay substantial dues to whatever radical group they were members of. Like churches, the groups that aspired to become a revolutionary party expected members to tithe — anywhere from five to twenty percent of their income. The economics were totally different back then.

Our wing of the left never considered focusing on rich people and I don't know of any other current in the radical left of the time that did either. When wealthy folks joined us, we integrated them [into our project of organizing the working class] — some became

Poster for a concert to aid sit-in movements and the Martin Luther King Defense, 1960 (Courtesy Smithsonian Institution)

dedicated cadre. Many kept their wealth quiet, maybe telling leadership privately. We'd handle their financial contributions differently but otherwise treat them like anyone else.

Mike: In your experience, how was left organizing funded before the rise of nonprofits and institutional philanthropy in the 70s and 80s?

Max: From what I know, there were four funding sources:

1. Dues-paying and donating working- and middle-class members.
2. Income from the sale of subscriptions to the newspaper and political journal, and from the sale of individual copies of various pamphlets and books published by the organization.
3. Special fundraising often through artist-led benefits. In the 60s, especially during the civil-rights movement, many artists and entertainers gave personal funds, but more often did benefits. Harry Belafonte is the classic example, but you also had Barbara Dane, Holly Near, Jane Fonda's

97

FTA [Fuck the Army] tour. Even Bob Dylan did a benefit or two. These cultural workers served two goals: popularizing left ideas — and fundraising.
4. Financial angels. These were individuals like those described above who had more resources and were willing to make substantial donations to the organization.

But for all of those groups by far the main source of income was the first three categories noted above, especially the first category, member dues. This was the same for the Communist Party and other groups of the "Old Left." Each one had a few wealthy supporters, but the overwhelming source of income was dues from working-class (and some middle-class) members who went to work, organized at their job or in the community, and supported the party financially.

Mike: Thank you for that. It's a helpful breakdown. ... Do you have thoughts on the strengths and challenges of how the left currently engages wealthy people?

Max: I take your question to be referring mainly to that part of the left that is organized into 501(c)(3)s, heavily reliant on philanthropy for its income, is organized on the Governing Board/Empowered Executive Director (or Co-Directors) model, with most work done by paid staff.[1]

What I see in these groups is a tendency to write grants to match what they perceive to be funders' interests, then try to work around the constraints. Some of those groups have a coherent theory of change and political strategy; others don't. But what I

---

1 I love that Max distinguishes between the different organizational forms that left organizing can take. Whether an organization is a foundation-dependent 501(c)(3) or a dues-funded labor union or a mid to large donor-funded 501(c)(4) makes a big difference to the culture, tendencies and power that they have.

don't see enough is even groups that have a clear strategy putting that forward to the funders in the same way they talk about it internally or with those they are trying to organize. I don't see keeping quiet about a group's strategy as an approach that can win over the long haul.

Avoiding deep political discussions with rich supporters for fear of losing funding is shortsighted. If there's a real disconnect, it'll surface eventually — might as well get it out in the open. Sure, you need to consider each person's situation, but start by treating them like any other serious political person. Try to convince them of your politics, just like you would anyone else.

Avoiding deep political discussions with rich supporters for fear of losing funding is shortsighted.

I was lucky that I came up in a time when large numbers of people with very diverse views were opposing the Vietnam War, fighting racism, and searching for a path to deep-going change. I was forced to learn how to function in coalitions and spaces where there were many political disagreements.

I learned that you don't give a speech with your entire political outlook every time you open your mouth. But if you're in a setting where someone really wants to know what you think; if someone is open to becoming a supporter of your work or taking some of the work on themselves, you have to treat them strategically. You tell them what you think, what you have firm opinions about and what you don't. No dissembling.

Mike: You make it sound so simple!

Max: The framework is simple. Carrying it out in the rough and tumble of the real world is not. And I get it that folks who don't have or come from money and are in projects that need money can feel awkward, stressed or just plain uncomfortable when talking to people who have resources.

* * *

Mike: Can you continue talking about the broader trends in the left in the 70s and 80s, and particularly how groups related to electoral politics?

Max: The part of the left that I was involved with in the late 1960s and early 1970s was not ideologically anti-electoral.

But we had an assessment — a wrong one as we discovered within a few years — that a very large part of the population had moved past seeing the electoral arena as a viable route for change.

> We had an assessment — a wrong one as we discovered within a few years — that a very large part of the population had moved past seeing the electoral arena as a viable route for change.

Generally, the Marxist view is that masses of people who want political change will first try to accomplish their goals through the options most readily available. In a society like the U.S., that means first via elections. Only when that option is pushed to its limits do most people decide they need to pursue tougher and riskier routes. While some people will be convinced that elections have limits in making change, majorities will only come to that conclusion via learning from their experience.

In the late 1960s, the "new communist" part of the left that I was in believed that the aftermath of Mississippi Summer showed many the limits of electoral action.[2] And that the urban uprisings of the mid- to late 1960s, and the assassinations of Malcolm X and Martin Luther King, and then Robert Kennedy, underscored that lesson.

So from 1968 through most of the 1970s, we mostly avoided electoral work. There were some exceptions, but they were few and far between. But as important sections of the constituencies we regarded as key to radical change — the African-American community in the first place — got more and more into fighting electoral battles, we began to shift. The Harold Washington campaign in Chicago in 1983, the efforts to elect Black mayors in many major cities, and the election of Ronald Reagan in 1980 were major developments that affected our thinking.

Especially significant was Jesse Jackson announcing in 1983

2 Mississippi Summer refers to when the Democratic Party refused to seat the Mississippi Freedom Democratic Party (MFDP) rather than the "official" party delegation, which had been chosen in a segregated election, offering the MFDP two seats.

that he would seek the Democratic Party nomination for president in 1984 on a peace, jobs, and justice platform. Jesse's campaign sparked an outpouring of support and he took steps to form a new umbrella organization, the Rainbow Coalition, that would engage in electoral and non-electoral work linked to his presidential run. At this point, most of the new communist movement, as well as many other radicals who had come out of the 1960s, shifted their assessment decisively and threw themselves into the Rainbow.

Only the people who really were ideologically anti-electoral — like, don't have anything to do with it — or third-party only stayed out. People who decided that we had been wrong in our assessment of where the masses were politically [like Max himself] shifted gears.

Mike: You're saying, parts of the left you were in said, "Let's do it. Let's join the Rainbow Coalition. Let's get involved in a big tent electoral project."

Max: Yes. One of the good things about electoral politics is it forces you to think about winning, which means you've got to get a majority. If you're not doing elections and you're just doing demonstrations, well, you can have 1,100 people. That's great. But you don't have a measuring stick of where you are in relation to power in the country.

Between the demise of the Rainbow Coalition in 1988-1990 and 2015-2016, the left was a protest movement. That's what we were doing.

There were a few groups that had some kind of power-building strategy, but basically there wasn't much of an opening. There was no practical way for political power to be at the center of the agenda. I mean, you could vote for Obama, which was good. I voted for Obama. I was in Times Square in 2008 when they called the election for Obama. It was totally emotional. We [the left] could, and did, make contributions to important movements — for global justice, for lesbian/gay rights, against the so-called "War on Terror" and so on. But important as this activity was, it was protest, not politics.

But in 2015-2016, with Trump and Bernie and Hillary, all of a sudden everybody wakes up to the fact that it actually matters who's in office. All of the questions of political power come flooding onto the agenda. And the whole conversation on the left shifts. So now everybody's talking about power-building strategy, coordinating electoral and non-electoral work, obtaining governing power. Those conversations did not exist in that way before 2015.

Old communists like me basically got trained on the idea that politics is the fight for state power. That's number one. That's what being a revolutionary means. Many of us passed through a stage of thinking that only storming barricades, only some form of insurrectionary action, was truly revolutionary. But somewhere in the 70s or 80s, pretty much most of the people who believe in the importance of state power figured out that in an advanced industrial country, a country with an established electoral system, you can't circumvent that system if you want to take a path to power. You have to go through it. You have to get a share of governing power through the system.

Like Maurice Mitchell, executive director of Working Families Party, says, you have to get enough power within a rigged system to unrig it. I think for most of the revolutionaries of my generation who are still active in left politics, that kind of perspective has become integral to our strategic thinking. It resonates with our training and what we've learned about political change in this country in the decades we've traversed. That's become our lodestar.

* * *

Today the population of the U.S. is more than double what it was in the 1930s and 40s. We need to be thinking of creating a broad coalition for deep-going change that is on an even greater scale, one that is rooted in a host of different constituencies and that gives people who step forward avenues to shape the coalition's strategy.

A vibrant, radical and flexible left will be needed to forge that kind of coalition and take on the tough tasks of keeping it united and combative in the face of an authoritarian MAGA movement that isn't going to disappear just because of one or two electoral defeats. ▪

YOU HAVE TO GET ENOUGH POWER WITHIN A RIGGED SYSTEM TO UNRIG IT

Maurice Mitchell

LEFT ORGANIZING IS IN CRISIS. PHILANTHROPY IS A MAJOR REASON WHY.

Nina Luo

Nina Luo is an organizer and political strategist with 13 years of experience organizing and leading dozens of campaigns of all kinds. She was raised in an immigrant family that accumulated wealth over time and is currently a senior strategist at the Working Families Party, building a new philanthropic model and community. Previously, she was Representative Alexandria Ocasio-Cortez's political director.

Editor's Note (MG): Nina shares one of the most clear and compelling critiques of current approaches to social justice philanthropy that I've seen. I think it's important that we engage with and consider what Nina has to share. Below is an excerpt from her January 2025 article in The Nation magazine. © 2025 The Nation Company. All rights reserved. Used under license.

In the wake of Trump's reelection, many of us on the progressive left are reevaluating our work. We're taking a hard look at the campaigns and movements we've given our lives to and asking ourselves, where did we go wrong? I've especially seen this humility from the leaders who have delivered some of the few wins we've had over the last decade — the formation of new unions, federal climate investments, student debt forgiveness, and the expansion of social safety nets in blue states. This is because — unlike, apparently, many Democratic consultants and campaign advisers — we know we're in much bigger trouble than just a messaging misstep or a weak presidential candidate.

> We're taking a hard look at the campaigns and movements we've given our lives to and asking ourselves, where did we go wrong?

In the last few decades, globalization and a shift in economic investment from manufacturing to knowledge sectors resulted in job loss and stagnant wages for most workers. Meanwhile, neoliberal policy destroyed the state-based social safety net those same workers once relied on. For the vast majority of people in this country, the bottom fell out. The purchasing power of the average hourly wage last peaked in 1978 (after adjusting for inflation). Since just last year, American homelessness has increased by 18 percent. Kamala Harris's campaign offered some proposals aimed at the working class, but failed to make economic insecurity (and people's anger at the establishment) the number-one priority in its communications. An analysis performed by *Jacobin* of Harris's speeches, rallies, press gaggles, and interview scripts found that the campaign "pivoted away from the economy starting around mid-September ... moving away from an adversarial stance toward elites."

Unsurprisingly, on Election Day we saw working-class voters continue to move to the Republican Party.

Unsurprisingly, on Election Day we saw working-class voters continue to move to the Republican Party. According to NBC News exit polls, non-college-educated voters were evenly split between the Republican and Democratic candidate "as recently as 2012," as Alex Seitz-Wald observed for NBC, but in this cycle, "they broke 2-to-1 for Trump over Harris."

Rather than grappling seriously with how Democrats should respond to this macroeconomic crisis in the electorate, many pundits have blamed progressive nonprofit advocacy groups for pushing the Democratic Party too far to the left on identity politics, as Matthew Yglesias did in his postelection analysis. Yglesias is wrong, though, about "the groups" being the decision-makers on this. More often than not, Democratic operatives themselves, in their attempt to hold a heterogenous voter coalition together, were appealing to identity politics or non-economic issues — seemingly so that they could avoid giving into populist economic demands and keep their big donors happy.

However, Yglesias did get something right: "The groups" he refers to do have a "demonstrated inability to actually drive votes or deliver constituencies." And that is what progressive leaders must now reckon with. Many of our "groups" do not represent the multiracial working class, and besides labor, it's not clear who on the left still does. Both political scientist Theda Skocpol and the late labor leader Jane McAlevey have documented the erosion of organized bases that are truly active. National organizations may claim memberships of hundreds of thousands or millions, but in reality include online petition signatures in that count. Local grassroots organizations may claim to represent the working people of a city or county, but struggle to turn out more than 30 people to an action. A "member" once was someone who attended weekly political education sessions and regularly canvassed their entire apartment building; now what counts as "membership" is hollow.

In that sense, the progressive left is to blame for Trump's reelection, because, no matter how hard the center or right make the conditions, it is still up to the left to organize and build the power of the working class and prevent the rise of fascism. Both the labor movement of the 1930s and the civil rights movement of the 1960s succeeded in building militant mass bases. How did we get to a 21st-century left that is basically divorced from that project? Several historical factors explain why, but a big one is the evolution of funding.

Union dues resourced the industrial labor movement of the 1930s and 1940s, while a mix of Black churches, dues, and modestly sized but radical foundations funded the civil rights movement.[1] Today, the majority of progressive nonprofits rely on institutional philanthropy (foundations and large-dollar donors) for their budgets.[2] Whether we like it or not, funding is the primary incentive structure that

Whether we like it or not, funding is the primary incentive structure that makes and remakes the current American left ecosystem today, what determines which work gets funded (or defunded), how, where, to what scale, on what timeline.

---

1 This history is shared in the report *Freedom Funders: Philanthropy and the Civil Rights Movement, 1955-1965*, written by Sean Dobson, commissioned by National Committee for Responsive Philanthropy and published in June 2014.
2 For more on this dynamic, read Robert Kuttner, "The Left's Fragile Foundations," *The American Prospect*, July 30, 2024.

makes and remakes the current American left ecosystem today, what determines which work gets funded (or defunded), how, where, to what scale, on what timeline. If the money backing that work is unstrategic, the work itself will also be unstrategic.

The corrosive impact is much broader than the obvious case, e.g., when an organization ends a strategic program because a funder stops backing it. I've seen organizations prop up out-of-touch, losing issues or bills for years because they're funded to do so; duplicative coalitions that fight with each other for the same reason; organizations forced to, for the worse, reshape 501c4 (electioneering) work into 501c3 (non-election-related) work; organizations unable to take on ambitious or experimental projects because they're too overwhelmed working on existing but ineffective funded projects; and zombie "base-building" organizations that should have sunsetted decades ago continue to lumber along without purpose. For each of these problems, there is a funder directive behind it: The funder is narrowly invested in a siloed issue or bill; the funder wants to donate c3 money and not c4 money for tax reasons; the funder can't tell which organization or coalition is best positioned to take on a project, so it funds competing or even contradictory efforts; the "zombie" organization's founder is a funder darling even though everyone on the ground knows that the organization doesn't do what it says it does anymore. Back when I was an issue campaigner, we often suffered from the fact that many of our organizations' executive directors had "funder brain," a phenomenon where an ED spends so much time packaging and spinning their work to funders that they could no longer be the disciplined, strategic leaders we needed them to be.

The left has a fundamentally different and harder problem than the right.

The right's own nonprofit ecosystem is also backed by big donors — and groups such as the Federalist Society and Americans for Prosperity are successful despite being largely philanthropy-funded. But the left has a fundamentally different and harder problem than the right. First, the material interests of the right's donors are aligned with their agenda. Second, the right has a culture of ruthlessness,[3] a total non-ambivalence about doing whatever it takes to win power, that the left lacks. Third, and most importantly, the right-wing project is to further entrench power and wealth in the hands of the few rather than the many. The right can win by using a primarily top-down approach, funding political, ideological, and media projects that capture institutions and shape people's worldviews. The left must not only do that, but also build mass movements that strengthen people's capacity to act together so they can take power back from the few. We are running uphill rather than downhill.

Since we are the underdog, strategy is particularly important, because strategy allows us to discover the stronger opponent's few weak points and apply our strengths to their weaknesses. This is a concept known as "strategic leverage." Good strategy is not a vision or an inspiring speech, a list of all the activities we wish we could do, and not a template we fill out. Good strategy primarily relies on an accurate diagnosis of a problem that can simplify a complex landscape down into a few factors that can be leveraged. And when the left does this, we know we can win. The electoral left used good strategy when they ran candidates of color against white incumbents in majority-minority districts (such as when Representative Alexandria Ocasio-Cortez pulled off an upset victory in 2018). Organizations such as IfNotNow used good strategy when they mobilized Jewish communities to public action after October 7, relying on the growing generational divide within Jewish communities on the issue of Israel-Palestine. New labor formations such as Starbucks Workers United used good strategy when they took issue stances that matched their workers' and consumers' sentiments better than Starbucks did.

Unfortunately, complex structural change is hard. There are many myths about how change actually happens, including the

---

3 For more on right-wing funders and their multidecade strategy to win power, read Jane Mayer, *Dark Money: The Hidden History of the Billionaires Behind the Rise of the Radical Right* (Doubleday, 2016).

liberal belief, the "monolithic myth,"[4] that great men in history (politicians and business leaders) have sole decision-making authority and change happens only by pressuring them into or out of policies. But the left also has its own myths. Too many of us believe in "magic bullet" theories of change, in which a specific narrow tactic — just worker co-ops or just progressive primaries, for instance — will save us. In reality, change is a process of successfully building an entire ecosystem, not just one thing, to compete with and replace the entire existing ecosystem. In this approach,[5] we would not only win elections but also resource our elected officials with the communications and political infrastructure they need to pass bills; we would not only expand the state-based social safety net but also invest in economic alternatives such as community banks and land trusts; we would not only build new unions but also rebuild third spaces where people can form meaningful relationships with each other that we can then organize. How to fund and build this ecosystem strategically is the question.

Normally, the warring camps of philanthropy are quite entrenched in defending their practices. In this moment when the organizing side of the progressive movement is open to honesty and self-reflection, I wonder if those of us on the funder side — myself included — could be more open to reevaluating existing philanthropic approaches as well. We must grapple with the reality that the current models we have for philanthropy are not up to the task of incubating, developing and supporting strategy

4 For more on this myth, read Mark Engler and Paul Engler, "The 'Make Me Do It' Myth," *Dissent Magazine*, February 26, 2021.
5 For more about this ecosystem understanding, check out the Ayni Institute and their work on Movement Ecology.

on the left.

There are a few prominent models within left-wing philanthropy. Effective Altruism uses utilitarian calculations that seek to maximize the efficiency of capital in returning greater quality of life. What it claims to be its strength — being ideology-neutral — is actually its weakness, because it fails to recognize the fundamentally political nature of problems and thus overly focuses on addressing symptoms, rather than causes, of power imbalance. While EA often funds left causes, many EA philanthropists have also supported right-wing politicians, thinking they were making savvy deals. In doing so they were actually propping up on the front end the exact system whose symptoms they were trying to remedy on the backend. This is an example of how EA was never designed to produce good strategy: There is no strategic leverage in Band-Aid solutions.

We must grapple with the reality that the current models we have for philanthropy are not up to the task of incubating, developing and supporting strategy on the left.

In another dominant model, Strategic Philanthropy, funders set goals, create plans, and measure outcomes with metrics and benchmarks. In theory, this sounds good — funders are trying to apply a consistent logic to their giving and evaluate its success. However, in practice, the power dynamic between funders and grantees means grantees have a structural incentive to obfuscate the nature and results of their work. Frank sharing of information is critical to good strategy. A second danger lies in mistaking a process for strategy, as one of the founders of this giving framework, Hal Harvey, later admitted. Harvey laments philanthropists who "conjure best practices, metrics, milestones, key performance indicators, reporting requirements, and more. Each item may make sense on its own, but in total it's nonsense. And in any event, doing all of this is still no substitute for a real strategy."

Finally, Trust-Based Philanthropy, which attempts to bring funders and grantees into deeper relationships through long-term grants, fewer grant restrictions, and fewer reporting burdens, is a vast improvement on some of the failings of previous models. However, especially in its most rudimentary forms, TBP still does not produce the conditions necessary for good strategy. TBP often makes funders feel good by having people of color, current/former movement leaders and various people with impacted identities serve as advisers, senior staff, board members, and decision-makers. We agree that people don't have good strategy just because of an elite education or fancy job; similarly, people don't have good strategy just because of an identity or past nonprofit job. The hyperfocus on representation of identities in TBP serves as a release valve for white guilt but does not automatically translate to work that actually changes power relations or material conditions for people. In *Elite Capture* academic Olúfẹ́mi Táíwò explains three challenges with this "politics of deference," as often practiced in TBP. First, deference can be a form of abdication of responsibility. Second, deferring continuously, rather than struggling through principled disagreement, is actually antithetical to the kind of coalition-building politics we need to win. And finally, and most importantly, it misidentifies the problem as who gets to speak inside a room when the problem is what's happening to the vast majority of people outside that room. Our ultimate duty is to build multiracial working-class power so we can win a world where philanthropy is no longer needed, not to make the institution of philanthropy somewhat more equitable. TBP helps us do the latter, but unfortunately, doing the latter in no way guarantees the former.

All three camps struggle with the same basic problem: good strategy is really hard. Swapping algorithms (EA), metrics and best practices (Strategic Philanthropy), and one set of people for another in decision-making roles (TBP) — none of these things sufficiently create the conditions for a strategic left. Nor is it as simple as deriding the nonprofit industrial complex and renouncing philanthropy as a source of funding altogether. We need money to win. Some of that can and should come from alternative revenue models, such as membership dues or selling a popular product at scale, as activist and entrepreneur Peter

Murray described.[6] But philanthropy isn't going anywhere, and the left shouldn't leave power on the table by rejecting it altogether.

Trump's reelection should be a wake-up call. My challenge to my fellow funders is this: You, more than anyone else, shape the left ecosystem that is supposed to be strong enough to win over the right. All of us who have the power to move or influence the moving of money must reexamine our assumptions.

So if what we're doing isn't working, what would? ▪

All of us who have the power to move or influence the moving of money must reexamine our assumptions.

---

6 Peter Murray, "The Secret of Scale," *Stanford Social Innovation Review* (Fall 2013).

ON BIG MONEY AND MOVEMENT ECONOMICS

Alex T. Tom

Alex T. Tom is a second-generation Chinese American born and raised in San Francisco and the Bay Area. He is the former executive director of the Chinese Progressive Association in San Francisco and is currently the executive director of the Center for Empowered Politics, a movement capacity-building center that aims to train and develop leaders and grow movement infrastructure at the intersection of racial justice, organizing and power building. Alex is also a proud baba (father) of an awesome and autistic son and blogs regularly on parenting and politics on Diary of a Baba. In this chapter, Alex writes about his multi-decade journey and transformation as a middle-class Asian American organizer and his quest to understand the economics of past movements, how they sustained themselves and how we adapt these lessons to our conditions today.

Introduction

I've been participating in social justice work for more than 30 years now, with youth programs, left collectives and organizations, as well as paid organizing and electoral work. A majority of my time and paid work has been in the progressive 501(c)(3) nonprofit sector. In particular, for 15 years in San Francisco, I was on staff at Chinese Progressive Association (CPA), where I helped to build multiple regional, state and national formations.

I feel fortunate to have been part of social justice movements since I was 15 years old. At nearly 50 years old, I am a proud yelder (young elder) — a bridge between generations.

Ever since I was a baby organizer, I've been an avid learner in pursuit of these critical questions: *How did activists, organizers and organizations sustain themselves in past movements? How do we adapt lessons from the past to our current context of rising authoritarianism?*

Many in my generation came up in the 80's and 90's during the decimation of the left and the rise of neoliberalism and

113

globalization. This period also included the growth of the 501(c)(3) social justice sector. On the one hand, social justice nonprofits created economic opportunities and leadership development for working-class people, especially organizers who came out of the youth and student sector. It allowed us to build infrastructure, sustain grassroots organizing, experiment and scale our impact in new ways.

On the other hand, the nonprofit structure created a challenge: Our political work was tied to employment, when such work was previously largely unpaid. While the 501(c)(3) is still an important and necessary tool, I now see an overreliance on the 501(c)(3) infrastructure. The nonprofit model has become more limiting and restrictive,[1] especially in these times. In the face of multiple and overlapping economic, political, social and environmental crises, and rising authoritarianism and fascism, I believe we need a new "movement economy" to sustain our work in the long run, one that has nimble and strategic infrastructure for people, organizations, "movement of movements"[2] and money. Rather than just relying on the 501(c)(3) infrastructure, we need to leverage it towards a clearer long-term strategy.

This essay is grounded in my journey and transformation in this work. I have been writing for many years through my "Diary of a Baba" blog and for various anthologies about Asian American organizing. However, this is by far the most personal and political.

I've always felt like I needed to be ideologically pure and almost a martyr to be in social justice movements. After a while, I realized that *many* people don't feel "down enough" to be in "the movement" (even people who are actively involved already!). In particular, I saw a lot of middle-class activists and organizers (like me) either denying their class privilege and putting out some of the most radical views to prove themselves or overcompensating by making many conversations focus on how to deal with their

---

1 Large donors and foundations impose many restrictions on how nonprofits use funding, limiting their work.
2 Coined by Naomi Klein, a "movement of movements" is a movement that brings movements, organizations and activists from different issues, sectors and communities into a shared struggle against the intersecting systems that produce injustice and inequality.

privilege. Both approaches failed to result in positive personal transformation, material changes in anyone's day-to-day lives or advancements in our collective liberation.

I, too, perpetuated this self-destructive attitude at a young age. For example, I still remember in high school, instead of engaging and meeting people where they were at, I would lecture and call out my peers for wearing Nike because of sweatshop labor. I later saw how this led to the exclusion of others and my own burnout.

Nowadays, this behavior is called cancel culture. Although this culture has shifted over the decades, it still shows up. Eventually, I learned to *embrace* my privilege and *leverage* it strategically for my community and the broader movement. This shift took years of self-work and building a community of friends and peers who could support and challenge me including a squad of people

To win, we need to win the hearts and minds of millions, not just the people who already agree with us.

I've worked with for decades. In this process, I learned that to win, we need to win the hearts and minds of millions, not just the people who already agree with us.

To be clear, my struggles with ideological purity, martyrdom and cancel culture that keeps our social justice movements small and marginal are more than a personal issue; they reflect a structural challenge social justice movements need to face head-on. For our collective liberation, we need to fundamentally transform the movement economy and the system of U.S. racial capitalism.

As a yelder, I feel a responsibility to pass on the lessons and stories I've received from movement elders, friends, comrades and everyday people over the decades. All the brilliant ideas I share in this piece should be credited to them, and any misrepresentation, misunderstandings and/or romanticization are my fault alone. I am not an expert in economics; I am a longtime movement leader, a comrade, friend, partner and baba (father) who wants collective liberation for everyone.

One more note: I am able to write this essay because of the strength and courage I've gained from my participation in the

Trust Web, a wealth distribution experiment covered in detail by Marian Moore later on in this anthology (See "The Trust Web: Money Like Water"). I have not experienced any other space where I could talk about and process so openly my judgments, triggers and privileges associated with money. It has helped me see the humanity in all people. Thank you to members of the Trust Web for your encouragement, deep compassion and love.

"Big Money"

My family got their start in the United States in San Francisco ("Old Gold Mountain") Chinatown in the early 1960s. Those were some hard times. They had just finished a difficult journey. My grandfather came first and then sent for my grandmother, my dad and a few of his siblings. They left China during the Civil War and went to Hong Kong, then to Taiwan.

They were one of the few families that came to the U.S. before the 1965 Immigration and Nationality Act, on an artist visa. After many years, they opened their first jewelry store in Chinatown. My grandfather was a master ("sifu") in Chinatown who trained and mentored many of the other jewelers there. I did not know how well respected he was until I started working in Chinatown decades later in life. To this day, I attribute much of my ability to be nimble, creative and entrepreneurial to my family and upbringing.

After the business became successful, my mom and dad were matched by a mutual family friend in Taiwan. My mom moved to the U.S. in the mid-1970s and had me two years later. Soon after, we moved to the Sunset District, which is a more suburban area in San Francisco. My brother came two years after I was born. We were truly there for each other growing up. I consider him one of my closest friends today.

I became the oldest grandson of a Chinese patriarch with 14 grandkids. I was born in 1976, the Year of the Dragon. I also came out very big and round and looked like a little Buddha. With the trifecta of me being a large baby, a dragon and the oldest grandson, they named me Big Money (大元 in Chinese and "Tai-Yuen" in English), which became my middle name. They named me Alexander after Alexander the Great. No pressure right? It took me many years to embrace and transform my own name and identity as Alex T. Tom or Alex "Big Money" Tom.

The idea of "money" has followed me my whole life. In a culture of expectation, obligation and excellence, it was not enough to make money; I needed to be the best. Instead, I grew up pretty awkward, chunky, quite nerdy (not book smart!) and not very athletic. I always felt like an underdog and was constantly bullied and picked on well into high school. When they found out I was colorblind, my parents were worried that I would never find a "real" job. In the 1980s becoming a programmer or engineer in Silicon Valley would be a decent sign of success, but somehow being colorblind seemed a barrier to entry.

> In a culture of expectation, obligation and excellence, it was not enough to make money; I needed to be the best.

My parents lost faith in me being on the stereotypical Asian American "model minority" path, so I charted my own course. Thinking back, they really encouraged me to work many kinds of jobs. From a paper route and working in fast food to selling knives door-to-door and various business ventures with my mom, I learned to do a lot of things hands-on. Still, I grew up very middle class and was truly privileged not to worry about money day to day. Instead, I worried more about fulfilling my life purpose of being "Big Money." Every part of my family's story and my early training around money, race and class has made a profound impact on my role in the movement.

"Big Money" Meets Social Justice

We moved to Fremont, a suburb near Silicon Valley, in the mid-1980s, during a rise in xenophobia and white nationalism. As a major car manufacturing hub, the General Motors Fremont Assembly experienced major layoffs in the early 1980s, due to outsourcing. At the same time, Fremont became a new suburb for Silicon Valley workers, including many Asian immigrants. (The population of Asian immigrants grew more than three times, from 2,823 in 1970 to 9,611 in 1980.) These changes meant that the primarily white working class in Fremont were losing their jobs at the same time as middle-class Asian Americans, like me, were moving in.

I still remember when someone sprayed KKK on our house, our car and on the sidewalk. I was constantly called "chink," "jap" or "gook." I was, at best, confused, but most of the time, I was angry and resentful.

When I was 15, I went to a national six-week summer camp called the Encampment for Citizenship. EFC was started by Eleanor Roosevelt in the 1940s after World War II to fight fascism, antisemitism and oppression. It truly transformed my life. It was the first time I met and lived together with poor and working-class queer, Native, Puerto Rican, Latinx, Black and White people. Through interactive workshops, discussion groups and experiential learning in the community, I learned about systems of oppression and my own internalized oppression for the first time.

By the end of that summer, the Bay Area youth from the camp formed Empowering Youth Educating Society (EYES). I was finding my voice and political identity. Senior year of high school I narrowly won the election to become student body president. For Black History Month, I invited my friends from EYES to lead a Malcolm X and Martin Luther King Jr. Unity Day school assembly. It was intense. They presented a history of the 500 years of resistance from the genocide of Native people and enslavement of African Americans to the Civil Rights and Black Power movements.[3] Most people had never heard this history nor seen or heard from that many Black and Latinx people in their lives.

Shortly after the assembly, I became very popular but for the wrong reason. This seemingly nice Chinese American boy they elected as their student body president no longer fit the stereotypical "model minority" of being quiet, easygoing and subservient. I became too "radical" and was attacked and taunted.

---

3 The 500 Years of Resistance curriculum was developed by UC Berkeley students in the early 1990s. Some EYES members were part of Roots Against War, which was a Bay Area coalition formed during the first Gulf War.

That is when I started to understand what it meant to be Asian American. Asians, and especially East Asians, are often the wedge pitted against other communities of color or can be a critical force for uniting with other communities of color to tear down white supremacy. Twenty years later, I found out from EYES members that they were banned from ever coming back to our high school to present.

By the time I went to college at University of California San Diego in the 1990s, California was experiencing one of its worst

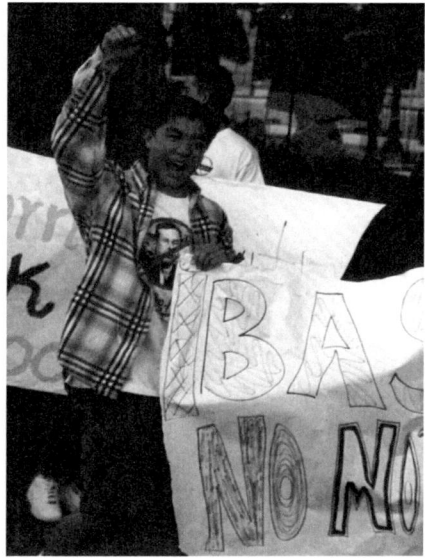

1995 photo of Alex protesting outside of UC Regent Davies office for supporting the elimination of affirmative action. This was the first rally Alex can remember attending in college. (Courtesy of Alex Tom)

economic recessions, due to job losses of more than 720,000.[4] State political leadership, such as Governor Pete Wilson, responded by passing a slew of nativist and reactionary ballot propositions, including Proposition 184 (harsher sentencing laws), Proposition 187 (banned services to undocumented immigrants), Proposition 209 (elimination of affirmative action), Proposition 21 (targeting and criminalizing youth of color) and Proposition 22 (targeting the LGBTQ community). In 2003, the Patriot Act helped launch a new chapter of xenophobia and surveillance, especially in border regions like San Diego.

I was full of self-righteous rage. Since I was one of the few East Asians at UC San Diego who publicly defended affirmative action, I was truly seen as an odd "angry Asian." I remember being told by other Chinese Americans that I was not "Chinese enough" because of my "radical" politics. Others would ask me, "Why

4 According to the California Legislative Analyst's Office, the majority of job losses in the 1990s were in aerospace manufacturing, finance, insurance and construction.

1999 photo of Alex with long hair pulled back doing a workshop on Proposition 21 at a youth conference (Courtesy of Alex Tom)

are you so angry?" I felt deep isolation and like I didn't belong–imposter syndrome ran deep. I'm indebted to all the mentors who guided me along the way, especially queer women and women of color.[5] They called me in to not just be angry and righteous but to move people, bring people along and, most importantly, *organize*, especially people in the Asian American community.

After college, in 1999, during the height of a new youth movement that was born out of the fight against Proposition 21,[6] I got a once-in-a-lifetime opportunity to incubate and build an organizer training program — called Students for Economic Justice (housed at the Center on Policy Initiatives [CPI] in San Diego) — and built a network across San Diego. At the same time, my nonpaid political work involved co-leading the San Diego chapter of Youth Organizing Communities, a statewide network of young people formed to oppose Proposition 21 and to end the school-to-prison pipeline. I understood my more radical volunteer work was distinct from my paid social justice work, but they were not mutually exclusive. The executive director of CPI, Donald Cohen, encouraged me to use the resources available to me through my work at CPI to support my youth organizing — and I totally did. We had our weekly meetings at the CPI office, which became our headquarters. This planted the seeds for

5 I was University of California San Diego's campus organizing director and trained by the University of California Student Association, which was led by Kimi Lee and Sabrina Smith.
6 Proposition 21 in California criminalized youth of color by lowering the age to prosecute youth as adults to 14 years old.

learning how to leverage the power and resources of institutions.

Although San Diego was very diverse, it had a stronghold of conservatism due to the military bases and U.S.-Mexico border region. There was very little progressive nonprofit infrastructure, which taught me to work with a broad range of community activists, unions and service agencies. This time period, in the late 90's, was the beginning of youth "online digital organizing." I remember trying to call youth, but there were no cell phones. Most were easier to reach on AOL (America Online), which was an internet service provider and web portal in the 1990s. Many of us were still using pagers. I learned how to build a youth and student base. I began to learn what it would take to build a long-term, bottom-up, local-to-regional, statewide power.[7] San Diego is truly where I first cut my teeth in organizing.

After nearly a decade in San Diego, I decided to return to the Bay Area. I remember telling the young people I was organizing, mostly Latinx youth, that I needed to study and improve my Mandarin and Cantonese language skills. They were confused. I said, "You know I'm Chinese, right?" They said, "You are too down to be Chinese!" At that moment, I knew. I needed to return to my people. I decided to confront my feelings that I was not Chinese enough and too middle class, and go organize in my own community: San Francisco Chinatown.

Coming Full Circle: San Francisco Chinatown

I worked in the working-class Chinese immigrant community for more than 15 years at the Chinese Progressive Association in San

---

7 Through CPI, I was fortunate to be in STEP (the Strategic Trainings Education Program) from 2020-2021, which was co-led and co-designed by Anthony Thigpenn and Deepak Pateriya of AGENDA/SCOPE and Sandra Hinson and Richard Healey of the Grassroots Policy Project (GPP). This phase focused on California organizations and developed a shared analysis and common framework for power. It was a catalyst to forming California Calls, a grassroots statewide power building alliance.

Francisco. CPA had been a historic progressive anchor within the Chinese immigrant community and the broader movement for decades. CPA was core to my development as an organizer, leader and the person I am today. Most importantly, it let me evolve and practice my organizing craft, and find my people and my purpose.

I was truly coming full circle. I'm grateful for the community of organizers, members, leaders and movement elders who guided me along the way. There are so many leaders and comrades to thank, but I am especially grateful for Pam Tau Lee, a co-founder of CPA and our board chair during my tenure.

My time at CPA was not without heartache, loneliness and deep introspection. Even though I had roots in Chinatown and was active in the movement already, I was "new" to the Bay Area left. Although CPA was more than 30 years old, there were past divisions and a new generation in leadership as it became a more formalized nonprofit organization. Also within Chinatown, the progressive organizations did not work together because of past conflicts. My leadership was often perceived as too idealistic and slow moving. Within the broader Bay Area left, there were ongoing ideological splits and interpersonal dynamics that hindered the broad-based united front needed to build power. I'm proud that with my leadership and a new generation of organizers, CPA moved through these tensions and eventually grew to become a movement-building hub in the Bay Area and beyond.

After being at CPA for 15 years, I found my purpose and my way of living into my birth name: "Big Money." Instead of shying

1999 photo of Alex with SEIU janitors at his first civil disobedience arrest (Courtesy of Alex Tom)

2004 photo of Alex at his first CPA Worker Organizing Center Committee Meeting (Courtesy of Alex Tom)

away or hiding from my privilege, I learned to lean in, embrace and, most importantly, leverage my privilege.

I knew that CPA lacked power and needed to build a united front strategically. One of the first things I did when I became the director of CPA was to meet with Rose Pak, a prominent community leader and the head of the Chinese Chamber of Commerce. Often seen as CPA's rival, I wanted her to know that I had deep roots in Chinatown, in the small business community, particularly. Although CPA represented the interests of the working class, I believed we had a shared interest in improving Chinatown for everyone. She was shocked and somewhat amused when she realized who my grandfather was; he was an elder and trailblazer in the Chinese small business community and I, on the other hand, was organizing Chinatown workers. She said, "This is poetic justice." Over the years, we developed a mutual understanding and respect, even if we were on different sides of issues.

> Instead of shying away or hiding from my privilege, I learned to lean in, embrace and, most importantly, leverage my privilege.

CPA and the working-class community embraced me and my leadership, while I embedded myself in the community. My time with CPA transformed me. As a young organizer, I quickly learned that having the right ideas was not actually organizing. I remember long conversations with members and leaders about workplace campaigns against Chinese bosses, Black and Asian tensions, the emergence of the Chinese American right wing, globalization and our strategy to build power to scale.

I distinctly remember sitting down for hours with Qi Wan Pan, who passed away in 2017 at the age of 96. She had been a member of CPA since the 1980s and was among the first generation of revolutionaries in China in 1949. She would push me to think more dialectically,[8] and she would often say, "It is never black or white, the truth is between." She taught me that the ability to listen and shift a perspective is not being conciliatory; instead, it is sharpening our collective analysis toward the long-term vision.

> **I quickly learned that having the right ideas was not actually organizing.**

I learned early on that the key to building a resilient and durable culture was to be intergenerational and to have a leaderful team. I learned that the basis of organizing is work across generations with an understanding of the complexities of issues and identities. We did not need to agree on everything but could struggle alongside people. My time at CPA was truly a humbling journey. I made my fair share of mistakes along the way and could not have done any of it alone. I feel fortunate that I found a squad of leaders who continue to work together decades later but in different roles.

Over and over, during my time at CPA and since, I have come back to these questions that I shared earlier: *How did activists, organizers and organizations sustain themselves in past movements? How do we adapt lessons from past movements for the current context of rising authoritarianism and fascism?*

Movement Economics: Wisdom From Movement Elders

Here are three stories that developed my thinking around the

---

8 A process of analyzing that involves embracing seemingly opposing ideas that can both be true to create a more comprehensive understanding.

first of these questions — the question of "movement economics." To me, movement economics is recognizing the need to build a nimble and strategic infrastructure to support and sustain people, to build organization(s) and resource ourselves toward our longer-term vision. This account represents my best recollection of three transformative conversations with movement elders. For confidentiality, some names will not be shared.

* * *

In 2014, CPA was still small and scrappy but had bold ideas. During a five-year strategic planning unveiling at the Center for Political Education in San Francisco, we presented plans for becoming a national Asian American Movement and capacity-building hub, expanding our organizing and civic engagement work beyond San Francisco and expanding CPA's constituency. There was music, food and a fancy PowerPoint. The room was filled with 40-50 mostly young Asian Americans. We had just launched Seeding Change, a national training program for Asian Americans, and AAPI FORCE (AAPIs for Civic Empowerment), a new statewide partnership with the Asian Pacific Environmental Network and Korean Resource Center. Folks were excited and inspired.

Toward the end of the event, Francis Wong,[9] a former board member and longtime community leader, pulled me aside. He said, "This bold vision is great. It is amazing to have people who believe in this vision. They don't need to be here; they can find many other jobs, even high paying ones, but they are here because of you and the rest of the leadership."

I had a gut feeling that he had some hard truths for me. What he said next made my heart sink. He said, "Don't let people walk off the cliff." In the 1970s, he had seen people ready to do whatever it took in the name of the struggle. The movement relied on incredible sacrifice in the belief that the "revolution was around the corner."

He asked, "What kind of movement economy are you trying

---

9 Francis Wong started Asian Improv Arts, a nonprofit, in 1987 to raise money for and support social justice artists in the movement. After nearly 40 years, this work has expanded among an impressive national network of Asian American and other BIPOC artists, scholars, organizations and community leaders.

to build? Is it one that keeps the people moving along in the ecosystem, supported and resourced and headed towards our vision?"

I still remember so vividly he said, "Remember to take care of them."

It was a bit of a buzzkill. I was puzzled. Maybe I was a bit defensive, too. I shared all the things we were doing to train, mentor and coach young people. I asked, "Is that what you mean?"

He said, "Yes, but there is more. No matter what, make sure people have health care and other benefits to take care of themselves and their families."

He was right, and I needed to hear it. Although we had bold ideas, CPA had been running a deficit for years. To be clear, he was not talking about building the nonprofit industrial complex. His wisdom was more radical and provocative: building a movement economy based on the principle that even when there is no money, you will take care of each other.

His story taught me how critical it is to ground and center love, care and material support for each other on the journey and path to justice. This is what inspired me to begin thinking and writing about a movement workforce development approach that can support and steward leadership wherever they are in the movement as a paid organizer or a worker leader. To do this, we need to build a "movement economy" that can sustain people and organizations over multiple generations.

* * *

After leaving San Diego, I found my way back to the Bay Area in 2003. I was a young activist and organizer. I did spoken word, wore baggy pants and had long hair to my waist. I fit the profile of a self-righteous radical. I was on a flight from San Francisco to Washington, D.C., and I had laid out a stack of books on Black Power, including *Revolutionary Suicide,* by Huey P. Newton; *Black Power: The Politics of Liberation,* by Kwame Ture (formerly Stokely Carmichael) and Charles V. Hamilton; and *The Making of Black Revolutionaries,* by James Forman. I somehow thought I was going to read them all on one flight. I never did.

All of a sudden, I heard a deep sigh next to me, coming from

TO FREE THE MONEY

an older Black woman who looked either confused or frustrated. She took off her glasses, gave me a look and asked, "What do you know about Black Power?"

I was shocked because usually the books were a way to prove my politics and intimidate the people around me, not to actually engage in a conversation! I turned around like I was called out (or called in). That was the beginning of a profound and grounding conversation that altered my perspective about how to build movement organizations and ecosystems. It turns out that I was sitting next to one of the foundational SNCC leaders![10]

As a good elder, she gave me some real talk and tough love. She told me that those books will not tell me how those organizations were run, how the money worked and who did the behind-the-scenes work. I remember her saying, "Operations is political." It requires politically aligned people whose responsibility is to hold the organization, the resources and the political security. SNCC leaders were mentored and influenced by Ella Baker. There was a lot of invisible labor by majority Black women that held SNCC together.

> I remember her saying, "Operations is political."

We talked about the Freedom Summer of 1964. How it was organized, who organized it, who funded it. For example, the budget for the Freedom Summer was $800,000, which is roughly $6.5 million today.[11] This was raised primarily from and by wealthy performers, artists and musicians. Holding and moving these resources required a nimble infrastructure and operations team that could manage the logistics for travel, accommodations and political security for more than 2,000 youth (Black and White) and adult allies involved in the Freedom Summer.

SNCC operated as an unincorporated nonprofit organization, although it never had 501(c)(3) status. They briefly received

---

10 SNCC stands for the Student Nonviolent Coordinating Committee. SNCC was a pivotal organization in the American Civil Rights Movement and was founded in 1960 by young people who emerged from the sit-in movement. SNCC played a key role in grassroots organizing, voter registration and direct action campaigns, particularly in the Deep South.

11 SNCC digital archive (https://snccdigital.org/inside-sncc/sncc-national-office/fund-raising-new-york-office/)

foundation grants that became restrictive and refused most grants they were offered thereafter. However, they moved resources through other institutions. By 1965, SNCC's annual budget was $1,153,000 ($11,552,000 in today's dollars).

We talked the entire flight, and by the end, I had even more questions, but more than anything, I understood what it actually takes — people, organization and money — to build movements that win. SNCC built up people, raised resources from numerous sources, navigated various organizational forms and constructed an early example of multi-entity infrastructure. Most importantly, their operations team was critical to creating the movement economics needed to enable their long-term vision and goals.

* * *

The Bay Area is a special place. I felt grateful for the multiple intergenerational spaces, formal and informal, that I was able to be a part of. It was common to be in political space with former Black Panthers and other movement elders who were still trying to figure out what our generation was up to. Some were grumpy and not the best at mentoring, but there were many who truly wanted to be in dialogue and share their reflections and lessons. I especially remember one conversation in the 2000s with a Panther who helped to raise money for the free breakfast programs.[12]

"We also used the master's tools against the system; we invested in U.S. Steel stock to pay for our programs!"

We talked about many things. How the Panthers were not just about being armed for self defense, but about knowing their rights and self-determination. He said that no one will write about how they funded their programs, but he was determined to school me.

He asked me, "Do you know how we funded the breakfast programs?" I knew they sold *The Red Book* on college campuses and had a newspaper called *Seize the Time*. But it sounded like

---

12 The Black Panther Party implemented numerous community programs, known as "survival programs," to address systemic issues in Black communities and challenge existing power structures. These programs focused on self-determination and services that were often not provided or inadequately provided by mainstream institutions.

a trick question. I said, "Donations? I thought you all 'liberated food.'" He gave me that look and rolled his eyes. "Yes, that was one way," but he said "liberating food" takes a lot of work, especially if you are trying to serve 20,000 kids every day! He said, "We also used the master's tools against the system; we invested in U.S. Steel stock to pay for our programs!"

Through the years, other Panther elders shared with me how they sustained themselves using multiple forms.[13] For example, the breakfast programs and other health initiatives were volunteer run and resourced through various entities, including churches, businesses, cooperatives and community organizations. They had the support of wealthy activists and actresses like Jane Fonda. Although all the proceeds from her popular and groundbreaking workout tape went to the Campaign for Economic Democracy, a political action committee for progressive candidates, she personally donated and raised hundreds of thousands of dollars to bail out Panthers who were political prisoners. In a recent email exchange, Jane remembered calling Elizabeth Taylor one night. Taylor was at a party when she took the call,

They were not stuck in the contradiction of having "clean money" under capitalism; instead, it was more important to have a clear vision and purpose and then build self-determined and independent resources toward that aim.

but when Jane asked for bail fund money, she gave $10,000 on the spot.

What I learned from listening to these stories is that no matter where the resources came from, the Panthers learned to use them toward their long-term vision. They were not stuck in the contradiction of having "clean money" under capitalism; instead, it was more important to have a clear vision and purpose and then build self-determined and independent resources toward

---

13 Some functions were centralized from local chapters to the national level. However, they were mindful of political security; therefore, some of these efforts were also decentralized and autonomous.

that aim.[14]

* * *

These three stories from movement elders, braided together, inspire me to this day; however, I tell them not out of nostalgia or to romanticize the past. With multiple and overlapping crises, and rising fascism and authoritarianism in the U.S. and globally, it is crucial to understand that movements have always been agile in navigating the conditions and contradictions of the political moment. Past movements have almost always been intergenerational and cross class, and leveraged multiple resources to sustain themselves.

> **We need to remember that our 501(c)(3) infrastructure is and has always been just one part of a much broader movement — it is not the entire movement.**

Adapting These Lessons

There is much we can learn from the past, but we must also acknowledge the unique contradictions in our current context.

For example, while most movement work in the past has been unpaid, these days, it largely resides in nonprofit organizations — the 501(c)(3)s. In particular, in the last 20 years, social justice and progressive-oriented nonprofits have punched above their weight and become more robust and powerful. Many in my generation helped to build and grow this infrastructure. It is no surprise that the right wing is repressing and attacking this vital movement infrastructure.

While the growth of nonprofits has been an opportunity for social justice movements to grow their capacity, it has also led to an overreliance on this form. We need to remember that our 501(c)(3) infrastructure is and has always been just one part of a much broader movement — it is not the entire movement.

---

14 As Linda Burnham and Max Elbaum write in this anthology, before the rise of nonprofits in the 80s and 90s, there were revolutionary organizations which were primarily resourced by dues. In addition, there was a lower cost of living and more robust safety net in the US in the 60s and 70s, conditions fought for and won by social justice movements in the past. This made it more possible for thousands to sacrifice their time and money for the cause.

This dynamic of nonprofits being *the* movement has also caused generational differences in expectations. Beyond employment, some have treated social justice nonprofits as a space to heal and develop their personal politics. This is understandable and has led to significant challenges as well. As Maurice Mitchell writes in his seminal piece, "Building Resilient Organizations," social justice nonprofits often struggle with a tendency towards "unanchored care," where "the onus is on the organization to deal with the harm, burnout, or psychological stress one may experience through the work. ... Additionally, the scope of care a movement space, organization, or group is responsible for is sprawling — potentially addressing all or most personal triggers and traumas experienced in and outside the work."[15] Relatedly, there is another harmful dynamic of "unanchored politics," where the organization is expected to be the place for every staff person to express their personal politics and to prioritize their political development rather than a political home base for community members. Furthermore, as Vanessa Daniels writes in *Unrig the Game: What Women of Color Can Teach Everyone About Winning*, women-of-color leaders often bear the brunt of these harmful dynamics with little to no support.

In the *Project2050*,[16] a report launched in 2020 to spark strategic thinking and greater alignment of the U.S. Left, 80 key organizational leaders and thought leaders were interviewed. They identified key limitations of the 501(c)(3) structure: For example: Many nonprofits fall into a pattern of reacting to the whims of philanthropy and wealthy donors. This means they are funded based on a specific constituency and a short-term single issue campaign instead of the long-term vision. This kind of work fosters unhealthy competition and fragmentation across the sector. There is also an overreliance on paid staff instead of utilizing a base of volunteers and members. (See Linda Burnham's interview in this anthology for more on this topic.)

---

15 Maurice Mitchell, "Building Resilient Organizations: Toward Joy and Durable Power in a Time of Crisis," *Nonprofit Quarterly*, November 29, 2022.

16 Project2050: Toward the Development of a Shared Strategic Framework on the U.S. Left (Solidaire, 2023).

These limitations have often been criticized as the "nonprofit industrial complex." This concept is a helpful starting point. However, this critical posture and understanding is inadequate in application and doesn't offer much useful guidance in addressing the dramatic shift in conditions over the last 50+ years. As initiated by the Powell memo[17], the neoliberal project of the last 50 years has been quite disciplined and effective. It has: 1) decimated the left and social movements, 2) stripped major gains in the labor movement, 3) and deteriorated the public safety net through privatization. All this has created greater instability and enabled the conditions for the rise of fascism and authoritarianism. However, I'm often reminded by movement elders that past repression did *not* end social movements; the work always continued in a new context.

I believe we need to learn to leverage the 501(c)(3) infrastructure toward a clearer strategy and movement needs based on the political conditions, not abandon it.

Furthermore, I believe we need to learn to leverage the 501(c)(3) infrastructure toward a clearer strategy and movement needs based on the political conditions, not abandon it. Some movement elders have shared that, back in the '90s, organizations like CPA needed to shift our strategy and transition to a more formalized 501(c)(3) structure to survive. With the emergence of globalization and the neoliberal order in the 1990s, it became clear to leftists and radicals that revolution was *not* around the corner. This shift required a different approach and protracted period of resistance. Moving to the nonprofit form was an important way for our movements to survive.

In these uncertain political times, we, too, will need to prepare and envision what our next iteration will look like as the right wing makes concerted attacks on 501(c)(3) organizations. How do our movements survive this new period of struggle? We need to be more nimble and less rigid and prescriptive as we assess our next moves.

---

17 The Powell memo, entitled "Attack on American Free Enterprise System" was written by Jerome Powell in 1971, before he became a Supreme Court Justice. It has been described as a catalyst for the neoconservative movement.

The Path Ahead

What do I make of all these stories and experiences? What do I think is needed now?

It has become increasingly clear that there is a very small window to make a concerted intervention to prevent the full consolidation of authoritarianism for an entire generation. Here are some key interventions to begin to make this pivot, some of which have already been in motion.

We need a mass movement of millions. This political moment has made clear that we need a broad cross-class strategy, movement of many movements and a movement of millions. We need a big tent with as many people as possible, including "anti-Trump generals to street-fighting anarchists"[18] united against fascism and authoritarianism. Within that, we also need a clear and compelling long-term vision. We also need to shift from our traditional protests to strategic mass disruptions, leverage openings to delegitimize the administration, and split and organize defections from the MAGA coalition. For example, at the time of this writing, while Elon Musk and Donald Trump are publicly feuding, are there segments of the center right that we can neutralize or organize into the big tent?

We need a vibrant movement ecosystem to sustain and resource our people. As Francis Wong said,[19] we need to take care of our people. We need to shift to a movement workforce development approach within a movement economy where we identify, cultivate and support leaders beyond one role or organization throughout their time in the movement. We need to create more roles for elders, yelders and experienced organizers to laterally support new organizers across the movement ecosystem. We need more strategic intergenerational spaces to reflect and share key lessons learned. To be clear, this is not just limited to paid organizers. If and when we govern, there are many roles in the ecosystem that need

18 Quote from Linda Burnham.
19 Francis Wong, mentioned earlier in this chapter, is a movement elder who was CPA's former board chair and is a longtime supporter and community activist.

to be included: caretakers, doctors, storytellers, cultural workers, social workers, service workers, economists, chefs, healers, teachers, engineers, farmers, spiritual and religious leaders, activists and organizers. We also need all kinds of organizations. We ultimately will need a vibrant and radical movement ecosystem, including neighborhood and civic organizations to political and left organizations beyond just 501(c)(3)s, that will weather the storm and advance our long-term vision. And let's not forget that we also need a government that can provide care and a safety net for society. We need it all.

We ultimately will need a vibrant and radical movement ecosystem, including neighborhood and civic organizations to political and left organizations beyond just 501(c)(3)s, that will weather the storm and advance our long-term vision.

We need nimble multi-entity shared infrastructure and movement operations. We are not building infrastructure just to defend and protect but to win and build power. We need to support and grow nimble multi-entity infrastructure and movement operations across various types of entities — including 501(c)(3)s, 501(c)(4)s, 501(c)(5)s, limited liability companies (LLCs) and political action committees (PACs) — and more informal unincorporated organizations,[20] to have multiple political spaces and homes to absorb millions of everyday people into the movement. We need to practice retrofitting, repurposing and deploying the incredible infrastructure we built the last few decades. Most importantly, we need to be honest about each of our organization's highest and best uses and learn to sharpen functions and purpose rather than getting stuck on building and maintaining our institutions and organizational forms. As one movement elder told me point-blank when I was asking him how to navigate the contradictions of the

---

20 Multi-entity infrastructure means that movements use the different organizational forms available to them, as needed, to build and win power, including 501(c)(3)s, 501(c)(4)s, PACs, super PACs, LLCs and more. Some organizations have also built back-office infrastructure, which provides nimble and flexible operation services to multiple projects and organizations.

nonprofit industrial complex: "We've never had the resources to train, organize and manage staff and grassroots working-class leaders at this scale. We can't help you. This is your generation's contradiction to figure out!" He was right. Too often we look to elders for answers when we're really looking for lessons. As a yelder, in this current moment, we are an important bridge across multiple generations. We have access to lessons from past movements, and we also were part of the experiment to build a social justice 501(c)(3) nonprofit infrastructure. Our task is to draw from past lessons, adapt, innovate and experiment with new kinds of movement infrastructure and operations beyond just 501(c)(3)s toward our long-term vision and strategy.

We need to free the money to free the people! In late-stage capitalism, as Dimple Abichandani writes in her new book *A New Era of Philanthropy: Ten Practices to Transform Wealth Into a More Just and Sustainable Future* — How We Fund in Times of Crisis and Opportunity, we are on the cusp of the greatest wealth transfer in history — with $84 trillion moving between generations in the next 20 years. These resources are meant to be leveraged and transformed beyond just 501(c)(3) dollars. We need diverse and flexible revenue streams so that we can innovate, experiment and put more people into motion. These dollars can be invested in new mass organizing and experiments like movement-led political consultancy firms and canvas firms. Donors and funders should be encouraged to give more 501(c)(4) and/or PAC dollars, especially given the greater scrutiny and restrictions on the field. Also, let us never forget, we need to tax the rich!

In the last five years, I've been most moved and transformed by the Trust Web, a cross-class wealth-distribution experiment centered on trust, relationships and liberation. While on this powerful journey to redistribute her money, Elspeth Gilmore (an owning-class inheritor) would constantly say as a reminder, "This is not my money." It took me years to fully absorb this. I realized that it took Elspeth decades to unlearn practices she was taught — years to heal, transform and liberate her inheritance. The Trust Web has broken siloes to create a new type of cross-class space and practice. This has allowed me to transform my relationship to money and capital as well. I now see how the system is relentless. It continues to divide us from each other and our humanity. I now believe in my agency to take collective action to build powerful cross-class relationships and movements.

This approach with the Trust Web embodies our movement's legacy of cross-class strategies, as shared by many in this anthology. In the end, it is not the owning class and middle class *versus* the poor and working class. It is not about the rich just "getting out of the way" and relinquishing the "means of production." Instead, it is about all of us transforming to fundamentally change the system. We need to build a broad, cross-class movement that will be undeniable and unstoppable, but it takes time and practice. We need many more experiments like the Trust Web that are both about our personal transformation and liberating resources toward a more equitable and just multiracial democracy.

This can all feel very daunting, and it is hard to know how to begin. As we have seen the targeting and disappearing of activists, mass deportations and new wars, I started hearing dangerous narratives like "We are not ready" or "Our organizations are not built for this moment." I, too, have said these things and have felt stuck. While it is good to be humble and clear-eyed, we should not unintentionally convince ourselves that there is no path ahead. That is exactly what the powers that be want. There is an unhelpful binary to either overcorrect and start anew or be in denial and stay the course. Our elders often remind us that in these times and ruptures, there are vultures that will prey on us and pit us against each other. But these are also moments of opportunity. The system of globalization and U.S. racial capitalism is highly unstable and the MAGA coalition is fragile.

We are not starting from zero. From past movements in the U.S. and internationally, to the Black radical tradition of the

South, to Native and Indigenous communities who have been self-governing as sovereign nations for thousands of years, we need to lean into our movement muscle memory. Our immigrant and refugee communities have survived wars, authoritarianism and fascism abroad. I'm constantly reminded that some regions, like the South, have already lived under fascistic conditions; they are more prepared than ever for this current moment. Finally, many of us have learned and grown from the collective uprisings of the last 20 years. Through 9/11, Occupy, Standing Rock, Black Lives Matter, Trump 1.0, the COVID pandemic, the murder of George Floyd, immigrant rights and climate justice movement, our generation has built this muscle of mass resistance, movement building and mutual aid. We should remember these lessons and build from them.

2023 photo of Alex with co-founders of CPA at an intergenerational dialogue during CPA's 50th anniversary celebration (Courtesy of Alex Tom)

The greatest antidote to the paralysis we might feel is self-work and collective action. Under U.S. racial capitalism, we are living in generations of trauma. From silent meditation and therapy to generative somatics and puppy love, I've done it all. Do what you need to do to take care of yourself and to reflect, grow and find your purpose. And we can always remember: Our collective liberation is bigger than any one of us. Let's stay in motion, take collective action and not get stuck in purism or perfectionism.

With a critical mass and a concerted intervention, we can change course just enough to stop the authoritarian consolidation and reach the next horizon. Still, it will take decades to repair the harms from Trumpism and the systems of oppression in place long before Trump — and generations for us to truly advance our vision.

Closing Words from an Elder

I want to end by sharing a story that has kept me going in these hard times. Once, Ben Lee, a co-founder of CPA, shared how the movement elders (also known as the "Lo Wah Que" in Chinese) approached the younger generation in Chinatown to form CPA in the 1970s. Ben explained that many of these elders organized within the Chinese Worker Mutual Aid Association (CWMAA) in the 1930s, and many had weathered intense repression during the 1950s McCarthy era.

In the early 1970s, they met young radicals inspired by Black Liberation and the Asian American movements. Ben was one of these young radicals. He worked as a field assistant as part of Asian Studies at UC Berkeley, a program that came out of the Third World Liberation Front. At first, the elders considered restarting CWMAA but decided that it would be better to build CPA together *with* the next generation. Rather than a traditional mentorship, it was an accompaniment, where they worked with and guided Ben and many others to found CPA. With this strong intergenerational foundation, CPA has gone on to survive and thrive over decades.

This story is my everyday reminder that from the 1930s to now, the spirit of the struggle lives on. Social justice movements didn't end in the 1950s; they just continued in a new way and form. Ben's story is a reminder that it takes all of us, across generations, to hold the long arc of struggle; this is in our collective DNA.

Next year, I turn 50, and I know my "Big Money" purpose is to bring forward more of the stories and lessons I've learned and take greater leadership with the younger generation. Our future depends on it. Let's get to work. ∎

STORIES FROM THE FIELD

This section offers intimate, first-person accounts from practitioners who have spent decades organizing wealthy people toward justice. These stories reveal what this work actually looks like—the relationships, experiments, victories and failures that happen when people commit to facing their financial privilege and redistributing wealth and power. From Threshold Foundation to Resource Generation, Solidaire, Women Donors Network, Donors of Color Network, and Way to Win, these pieces share an insiders' perspectives on just what it means to free the people to free the money to free the people.

SOFT PILLOW VS. MARXIST/LENINIST

Interview With Chuck Collins

This interview with Chuck Collins, by Michael Gast, was originally published on the Organize the Rich Substack in September 2023.

Chuck Collins is a warm, big-hearted white protestant guy from the wealthy family who started Oscar Mayer. He gave away his $500,000 inheritance as a young man and has spent the rest of his life organizing against wealth inequality and for the collective good. He's done this as a prolific author, speaker, advocate, and organizer. He's been involved in many different efforts over the last 50 years to move wealthy people towards progressive movements and a more just and fair economy, including cofounding United for a Fair Economy and Patriotic Millionaires.

He's a mentor of mine and one of the people supporting me to write this book. During one of our early meetings he mentioned an idea that I love and want to share with you.

According to Chuck, since the more formalized versions of organizing the rich began in earnest in the '70s, there have been two competing approaches. One he calls "Soft Pillow," the other "Marxist/Leninist." They are useful labels for different tendencies in this work.

The Soft Pillow approach prioritizes the physical and emotional comfort of wealthy people; there will be few conversations or actions pushing them to increase their giving or share their power.

> According to Chuck, since the more formalized versions of organizing the rich began in earnest in the '70s, there have been two competing approaches. One he calls "Soft Pillow," the other "Marxist/Leninist."

Marxists/Leninist[1] is the name he gives for the approach that firmly directs the rich to hand over both money and control to poor and working-class activists and organizers, and get out of the way. This tendency, in its dramatized form, has a harsh tone and cares little about the emotional well-being of the wealthy people involved.

When Chuck shared this with me, I nodded my head, snapped my fingers, pointed at him across the Zoom screen, and yelled, "Yes!!" I knew just what he was talking about. In my 20+ years in this work, I've experienced over and over this tendency to swing between a liberal, coddling attitude towards the rich and a harsh, "put you in your place and tell you what to do and how to do it" approach. We constantly move between these two poles, struggling to be both supportive and challenging, caring and agitational, direct and kind, loving and rigorous.

Chuck went on to describe how he saw these tendencies play out in the '70s and '80s, when he was a young man and in his first decade or two of involvement and leadership in progressive efforts to engage the wealthy. He talked about how the Soft Pillow approach was embodied by Threshold Foundation and the Marxist/Leninist approach showed up in Funding Exchange conferences.

Here's an excerpt from our conversation in 2022.

Mike: Tell me about these two trends you just named, the Soft Pillow versus the Marxist/Leninist. What's the story there?

Chuck: Well, the first thing to understand is that a whole set of social justice public foundations were founded around the country in the late '70s. Subsequently, these public foundations came together as the Funding Exchange (FEX) Funds.

FEX started having these national conferences for wealthy progressive donors, where I met some really interesting people. We had meetings and interactions with poor, working- and

---

1 If it wasn't clear, Chuck's name for this trend is *not* based on a direct analysis of the words or theory of Marx or Lenin.

middle-class activists, and activist-led field trips. It was a uniquely cross-class space.

We had a lot of fun at these Funding Exchange gatherings — at least at the start. Over the years, they became a lot less enjoyable.

In the early '80s, there was a new-age subgroup at these conferences that said, "This is just a little too political." It wasn't really meeting their needs. So they started the Doughnuts. They tried to keep the name out of circulation, but part of what I remember, which is embodied in the name, is that they always had a sense of humor about themselves. There was an embedded ability to laugh at themselves.

The Funding Exchange people often had this attitude like, "Wealthy people are holding on to their privilege. Our job as donors is to turn the power over to activists who are going to make better decisions." "Wealthy people have nothing to offer to the strategy discussions. You are faucets." And the Doughnuts were like, "We're holding on to the decision-making power and we don't want to be challenged about that." That was very simplistically how it broke out.

The Doughnuts became the Threshold Foundation and adopted its own culture. It had its own language and it had a lot of new-age rituals. Josh Mailman was one of the founders and leaders. [Mailman also cofounded Social Venture Network in 1987 and Business for Social Responsibility in 1992.] Their network met twice a year. They usually met in really nice places with hot springs. They would meet for a week. It became people's family. The personal connections created during those meetings were quite strong because they were doing personal work and there was often a heart connection. There was more intention about building personal relationships and a culture that didn't want to make people feel bad, unlike the Funding Exchange. They had an attitude of "Let's not make people feel guilty."

I remember going and giving a presentation at a Threshold meeting and feeling like I was a little bit considered on the "making people feel bad" end of the spectrum, you know? So I wasn't going to get invited back. Just the fact that I had given away my wealth made people feel bad. But occasionally I still get invited to speak at one of their gatherings. So I have a little window into the group.

They did a lot more nurturing of themselves and others, and lo and behold, they still exist.

Relationships matter. They last.

While Threshold was growing and building their community, the Funding Exchange continued to do these annual conferences. Over time, they got smaller and smaller. People didn't mesh and didn't come back year after year.

At some point, around the '90s, FEX noticed they weren't getting many more young wealthy people and decided to do something about it. They invested in the writing of *Robin Hood Was Right: A Guide to Giving Your Money for Social Change* (written by Chuck Collins, Pam Rogers and Joan P. Garner) and the early proto version of Resource Generation [RG]. Several networks funded the early reconnaissance work by people like Christopher and Anne Ellinger, which led to RG.

In many ways, Resource Generation was a coming together of these two trends, the Soft Pillow and Marxist/Leninist. It took the best from all these different donor networks into its DNA. Having a mix of personal and political offerings. Creating safe space while also setting a radical intention for what people can do with their wealth. Being welcoming and accepting, while also pushing people to move money and shift power. It's a tricky balance, and I am for every effort and project that bring lessons from both tendencies. ▪

WE CONSTANTLY MOVE BETWEEN TWO POLES, HARSH AND PRESCRIPTIVE OR CODDLING AND PERMISSIVE. HOW CAN WE BE BOTH SUPPORTIVE AND CHALLENGING, CARING AND AGITATIONAL, LOVING AND RIGOROUS IN HOW WE ENGAGE THE RICH?

THROUGH THE DONUT DOOR

Marian Moore

Marian came to the work of convening, facilitating, coaching and organizing wealthy people through her experience in the Threshold Community, aka Donuts, which she joined in 1990. She co-founded and co-led Play BIG, Lead with Land, Just Economy Institute, the Trust Web, Jubilee Gift, and Jubilee Justice's Our Ancestral Journey, some of which are still in play.

Her ancestors were colonizers who arrived here between the 1600s and 1800s. Many accumulated massive wealth and land, some of which she inherited. Her parents changed the trajectory of that lineage through their social justice activism. Marian's work emphasizes the need to shift consciousness to change patterns of wealth and land accumulation and activate redistribution and repair.

Introduction

It is 1988, and I am standing in the kitchen of Nina and Eric Utne, new friends who live just a mile from me in Minneapolis. Eric knows that I have inherited money. Across the kitchen counter, he asks, "How much money do you have?" In the 11 years since I'd gotten my inheritance, no one had ever asked me that question. I think I had told a past boyfriend, and I'd told my new husband before we married. But other than that, I kept numbers to myself. Even the fact that I had money beyond what I was earning — a fact certainly known among my friend group ("How could she afford that new Toyota Celica? That big apartment?") — was never discussed. I remember that moment, looking eye-to-eye with Eric, and saying, "Seven hundred thousand, and I am due to inherit some more in three years when I turn 35."

"We could have lots of fun with you at Donuts!" he said in the kitchen that day.

Cut to 2025. I am in another kitchen. This one is in a home in what is now Alabama, belonging to a small community of Maskoke people who have returned to the homeland of their ancestors. These people are the descendants of the survivors of a genocide brought upon their ancestors between 1813 and 1837. Some of their forebears were pushed west to Oklahoma, and some had been pushed south to Florida. These survivors' descendants have returned to their homelands to create an eco-village called Ekvn-Yefolecv (pronounced "ee-gun yee-full-lee-juh" — Maskoke for "returning to our homelands") so that they may live full time as Maskoke people, to enable their language and its teachings to live on for generations to come.

I am cutting parsley for tonight's meal. We are chatting about the last three days of hosting the first of what became three annual gatherings of Indigenous communities also devoted to land-based culture and language revitalization. Earlier in the day, I was one of two non-Indigenous people present as six different communities — Dakota, Diné, Mohawk, Monacan, Winnemem Wintu, Yuchi — shared the histories of their people and visions for their future.

In the large ceremonial roundhouse made from the earth and trees of this land, Marcus Briggs-Cloud, the founding visionary of the village, invites me to share my story. Sitting on the hard wooden bench in the company of 40 Indigenous people, I take a deep breath, heart beating fast, and speak into the mic.

"My parents were products of generational wealth made through extractive capitalism, many of their ancestors having arrived in the 1600s. But my parents were civil rights activists who raised me to take a different path; my dad was an Episcopal bishop, my mom a writer." I say that I am devoted to "reckoning and repair," that I am honored to be with them and intend to help heal the damage wrought by my ancestors. "One way I am doing that is to invite funds for Indigenous people to buy back land, as with Ekvn-Yefolecv."

146

I give the mic back to Marcus, who adds that through his relationship with me, he has been introduced to a different kind of fundraising. He shares multiple anecdotes describing a series of magical synchronicities we have followed together that seem spiritually orchestrated and that, in nine months, helped Ekvn-Yefolecv pay off a $2.2 million loan for more than 500 acres of land. (In subsequent years, they have purchased over 5,000 acres more.) He explains to the group, "This is not traditional fundraising." A Diné elder named Pat McCabe whispers loudly, "Or maybe it *is* traditional fundraising" to a chuckle that ripples through the roundhouse.

What happened in those 35-plus years between kitchens? I've had the gift of so much learning and growth as I have followed the thread of this work — too much to recount in one essay. I want to offer the story of the beginning of this evolution that traces some of my personal experience of the Threshold Foundation community, also known as Donuts, in the years from 1990 to 2020, when I reckoned with my inheritance, built leadership skills and grew in perspective and understanding through collaboration with an ever-widening circle that eventually led to experiences like the one in the Maskoke roundhouse. I went from learning with and from mostly rich, white people to being part of a vast cross-class, cross-race and cross-cultural network of activists and wisdom carriers. I have had the deep honor to help create and lead Play BIG (2005-2018), Lead with Land (2016-2019), Just Economy Institute (2017-present), the Trust Web (2017-present), Jubilee Gift (2019-present) and the Our Ancestral Journey program of Jubilee Justice (2019-present).

I would not have found my way to this multitude of wildly inspiring and transformative assignments if not for having walked through the Donut door. What a magical portal it was for me. Yet, there were many times over those decades of deep engagement that I felt uncomfortable within myself at Donuts, thinking, "This is very weird being with only rich, white people. How is this different from a country club?" Some days I would answer, "Not so different." Some days I would reassure myself that being in what my Donut friend Jenny Ladd (owning class) called "affinity groups" was an important developmental step. While, ultimately, the insularity of Donuts lacked the opportunities to work across race, class and culture that I increasingly longed for, the gifts it gave me and others were extraordinary. I want to tell you how it changed me and why I stayed so long.

To people in my "regular life," I usually describe Donuts, the original name of the Threshold Foundation community, as "a national network of social change philanthropists." But that is just the tip of the iceberg.

Backstory

Throughout the 1970s, young inheritors like me, children of generational wealth who identified as activists, began creating a new kind of philanthropy insistently different from that of their parents. Their shared vision for this money was expressed as "change not charity." They sought to redefine the dynamics of giving; one consistent feature of these locally-based foundations (Vanguard, Haymarket, Liberty Hill, Headwaters and more) was their approach of delegating grant-making decisions to community activists to effect systemic change.

Among those inspired and engaged by this movement to change how philanthropy happened, was a young inheritor of a New York real estate fortune named Josh Mailman. But Josh felt that these funds and their people were too didactic and lacked the kind of spiritual community for which he felt a longing. In 1981, with the help of his friend Richard Perl, Josh looked for like-minded inheritors. They composed a letter that they sent to everyone they could find who they thought might have wealth and shared values. The letter began:

> My name is Joshua M. I was born into a wealthy, liberal family in New York City 27 years ago. Since my childhood, I have had a dream of peace: A world without war and a shared understanding of a common unity within and among all peoples. I have been struggling to see what can create this world and how money relates to this process. ... A quantum leap in the thinking of millions of people is necessary to

July 16, 1981

Dear _____:

My name is Joshua M. I was born into a wealthy liberal family in New York City 27 years ago. Since my childhood, I have had a dream of peace. A world without war and a shared understanding of a common unity within and among all peoples' I have been struggling to see what can create this world and how money relates to this process. This is where I have gotten to:

A quantum leap in the thinking of millions of people is necessary to transform this world. How can this be brought about? How do we attain a feeling of connectedness that opens our hearts and minds to the entire human family? I believe that profound societal change requires a critical mass of individuals who have experienced a personal awakening to great feelings of love. This type of change cannot be bought and sold. Nevertheless, money can be used to support those who are able to nurture the seeds of perennial wisdom that lie deep within us all, through what they do and who they are.

Having talked with many potential donors throughout the country, I believe there is a real constituency for a public foundation with a new focus.. The guiding principles would be simple: everything is alive, everything is interrelated, all life is sacred. As a hard-nosed visionary, I would encourage service-oriented programs (in the areas of holistic health care, local self-reliance, global spirituality, unitive politics, etc.) whose staff demonstrate the value of personal transformation as a catalyst for profound institutional change.

I am asking those of you who are interested to come to a meeting tentatively scheduled for the weekend of September 12-14 outside of Denver, Colorado. I suggest the following agenda:

1. To discuss issues related to personal growth, sincere spiritual development and inherited wealth, facilitated by an experienced group leader/participant.
2. To share proposals that might meet the guidelines and discuss them while we are together.
3. To create a Board of Directors/Donors/Advisors, regionally diverse, to oversee an initial grand making period.
4. To begin looking for an Executive Director with experience in the foundation community and a similar personal attunement.
5. To create an initial fund of $250,000.

This letter is the result of thoughts brewing over the last few years. While choosing to initiate this process, I don't own it and I don't want to do it by myself. I see myself as an active participant among others. The agenda for the conference and the resulting foundation is ours to create together.

I am sending this invitation to 75 people who have personal wealth, all of whom are friends or friends of friends. Having been a participant in conferences dealing with Inherited wealth over the past five years, I am sensitive to the need for confidentiality. If There are other people you think might be interested in attending this meeting, please let one of us know before contacting them.

Please get in touch with me by August 3rd, or with Richard P. after August 3rd, to Let me know if the dates and location are convenient and with further suggestions for the agenda, etc.

In Truth, Service and Love,

Joshua M.

transform this world. ... I believe that a profound societal change requires a critical mass of individuals who have experienced a personal awakening to great feelings of love. ...

Twenty-one people answered his call, gathering in September 1981 in Estes Park, Colorado. At the outdoor closing circle, this band of rich kids who felt common purpose and wanted to continue to meet considered what to name themselves. At that moment, a cloud formed above them in the shape of a ring: "Doughnuts!" whispered one of them as a joke, and the name stuck. Nutty people with dough. (Later, we simplified the spelling to *Donuts*.)

"Doughnuts!" whispered one of them as a joke, and the name stuck. Nutty people with dough.

Nina and Eric Utne were Donuts, and they were eager to sponsor me to join the community. The guideline at the time was that a prospective member needed to have a million dollars to qualify (later the financial criteria added "or give away $25,000 a year" so that the group wouldn't be open only to people keeping their money), be on a spiritual path and have an interest in personal growth and "social change philanthropy." Another Donut would call and interview me before I could attend a meeting.

I passed muster, and in January 1990, my then-husband, Tim; our one-year-old, Jamie; and I traveled with the Utne family to

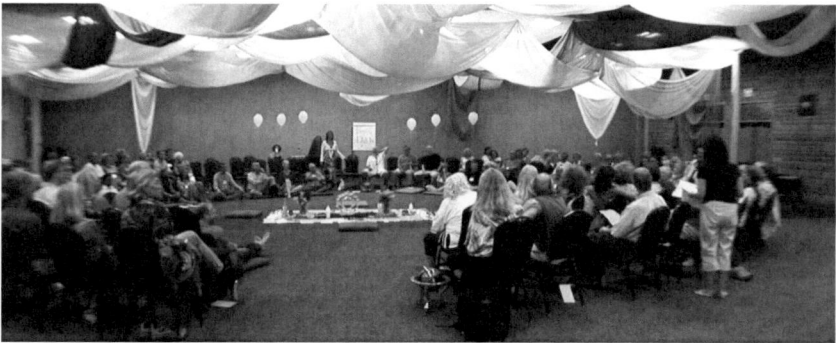

2011 photo of Donuts return to Estes Park, Colorado, thirty years after its founding there
(Courtesy of Threshold Foundation)

a Donut meeting in Sedona, Arizona. The gathering began with an orientation for the few dozen new members attending. First was the telling of money stories. A 30-something named John started by identifying as the son of the founder of the Kenner toy company (Easy-Bake Oven! Spirograph! "It's Kenner! It's fun!").

I was captivated and felt relief at the prospect of not hiding any part of myself, of having a place to speak the details of my own story: how my great-grandfather was a robber baron who accumulated wealth in the Gilded Age by leading mergers and acquisitions to create companies like Nabisco, Diamond Match and American Can. I would get to explore in community this inner conflict between the values instilled in me by my religiously grounded, civil-rights activist parents and the inherited wealth from their ancestors. I hadn't explored this with others but knew I was living with dissonance that I worked with in meditation and in my journal. The compartmentalization was so extreme, and the cultural taboo so strong, I didn't even speak of it in therapy!

The culture of Donuts was informed by the founding members whom I came to understand as mostly the black sheep of their families. They had gone to India; discovered intentional communities; explored shamanism and interspecies communication; founded learning/activist communities and Waldorf schools; were peace, environmental and social justice activists; studied all manner of offerings of the Human Potential Movement; experimented with psychedelics; studied Indigenous worldviews; and were steeped in innovative ways to gather as a group and develop community. Donut meetings offered opportunities for personal transformation, spiritual community, exploration of social issues and education about creative, cutting-edge solutions to social and environmental problems. There were opportunities to flow money to organizations advancing such solutions. We often called it a mystery school.

By the time I arrived, nine years into the experiment, the Donuts had adopted a foundation called Threshold that offered members the opportunity to learn about philanthropy by doing. We were invited to donate money into pooled giving and be part of the giving decisions by joining one of the committees, which in the early 90s were Planet, Person, Social Justice, Peace and International. For most of the 90s and early 2000s, the Threshold Foundation granted around a million dollars annually. Over time, it was clear that the community and its teachings inspired and catalyzed member giving in other venues that was exponentially greater than that.

Finding the Donut Door

At first, while intrigued, I was also judgmental. My family of origin was, I thought, a different kind of rich. My parents made a big deal of eschewing segregated country clubs and sent us to public schools. I used to say that public schools were our religion. Growing up in Washington, D.C., I felt the cultural divide between public-school kids and private-school kids and, for sure, felt more at home among my public-school people. Now, as I consider what I had intuited as the difference, I had a sense that the private-school kids were out of touch. If I look deeper, the "out-of-touch-ness" I discerned had to do with a lack of contact and relationship across race and class. My school and church were racially and economically mixed. My family had a strong racial justice ethos, and I was aware, if unconsciously, about the class spectrum among my friends.

Also important for me was to discover a community where I could be in sincere inquiry about how to be with this inherited money in a way that welcomed so much of who I was. I hadn't begun to untangle the many contradictions in how I was raised.

I know my parents lived with that, too.

These Donuts seemed to me more like the private-school kids I knew. I assumed that most had grown up vacationing at nice resorts (like this one in Sedona!) and had live-in nannies. And, I deduced, most had not experienced mixed-class and -race communities. But what was more significant for me in that moment in Sedona was how unsettling, yet also intriguing, it felt to be sitting in a circle with 175 rich kids, most in our 20s,

30s and 40s. "Rich kid" was an identity I had never intentionally inhabited.

Also important for me was to discover a community where I could be in sincere inquiry about how to be with this inherited money in a way that welcomed so much of who I was. I hadn't begun to untangle the many contradictions in how I was raised.

I know my parents lived with that, too. They straddled communities. On the one hand, their first major decision, after my dad finished seminary, was to begin a ministry in a financially impoverished parish in Jersey City, where, for eight years, they lived among the poor in this racially-mixed neighborhood. They were Episcopal, but they were inspired by Dorothy Day and the Catholic Worker Movement, which combined direct aid for the poor and homeless with nonviolent direct action. I was born at the end of their time in Jersey City, and what I know of it comes from how it informed our enduring family culture, family stories and the book my mother wrote about it when I was 13: *The People on Second Street.*

They worked tirelessly and with beautiful devotion, AND they could retreat to my father's mother's bucolic and bountiful farm, with its mansion, fresh cow's milk, homegrown vegetables, and full staff just a half hour away. They continued to spend the month of August in the Adirondacks, where my father's family had a wilderness retreat that could accommodate the whole growing family. They continued to socialize with the people they grew up with, loyal friends until the end. We kids had a sense of Mom and Pop coming from a culture that they had left. There were jokes about my parents being "traitors to their *clahss.*"

As I write today, I see that I was raised in a way that normalized such contradictions. I don't remember any guidance or teaching about how I was to be with this inherited money. I had some awareness of older siblings having given money to radical activists and to the American Friends Service Committee. Only recently, for this essay, have I begun to ask for details and amounts. For instance, in the late 60s, my big brother gave tens of thousands of dollars to the Black Panthers' breakfast program and The Pit River Tribe in California, which was fighting off a Pacific Gas &

Electric project. Somehow, I knew that my father had a private foundation from which he gave gifts, but again, it was not part of any family conversation I remember.

Occasionally I would receive requests for donations from people who seemed to understand better than I that I had the financial wherewithal to give. When I was 21, one musician friend asked for a loan of $5,000 to make a record. I said yes and, years later, forgave the loan. Fifty years later, he is still a musician and still a dear friend. One of my brother's friends had started the Big Apple Circus and asked for a donation. My sister asked for support for a feminist press. But mostly, the money and my identity connected with the money stayed in the closet. I didn't consider myself a candidate for philanthropy. Being in Donuts meant coming, at least partially, out of the closet.

Culture and Practices

Despite my initial judgments, I found Donuts to be smart, interesting, curious, brave and accomplished. I was attracted by their activist and seeking spirits. And, thankfully, they had a sense of humor about themselves! Looking back, I think what drew me was the culture of experimentation, a chance to be part of systemic social change and the collective commitment to cultivating intimacy in community through inner work.

Important, too, was tending to the unseen; in our shared work at Donuts, we placed a strong value on what I would now call "other ways of knowing." For instance, when we gathered in a circle — and we always gathered in a circle — two member-facilitators would ask for empowerment from the group. The rest of the Donuts would provide empowerment through wiggling our fingers at the facilitators. These "twinkles" were also used in lieu of clapping, out of concern for sleeping babies in the circle. The facilitators would then invite "heart keepers" and "witnesses to the process." The heart keepers would sit in meditation during the session, "holding the heart" of the group. The witnesses would pay attention to the process, track the energy and communicate when they noticed a deviation from what had been intended or if the group was going off kilter in a harmful way.

There was also a ritual, central to every meeting, that provided the group cohesion. For one or two evenings at each five-day meeting, members were invited to share what was on their heart, at the deepest level. I remember at my first gathering, several members who had cancer talked vulnerably and honestly about their experience facing death. Another member told about the death of her infant son. I was deeply moved and attracted to this practice of being real and vulnerable. My mother had lived with similar courage, as she faced her death when I was 17. I remember thinking that these are people I would want around me when I die. This and other rituals deepened trust among members, which was essential to the surrender of cultural norms about money and conventional pathways to social change. Sometimes, the ideas were too far out even for me, but for the most part, the Donut values and practices were meaningfully revolutionary and freeing.

The experiments kindled in that Donut fire were powerful and far-reaching.

In the 90s, it became apparent to me that in the broader social change philanthropic movement I encountered, Donuts were thought of as "woo" and self-referential, navel-gazing. Elsewhere in this anthology, *Donuts* is referred to as the "soft pillow" of donor communities. While that characterization is not completely wrong, it misses what has ultimately been, for me, the profound gift of Donuts: On those soft pillows, we were creating a potent community through ritual, song, prayer, profound personal work and learning

It led me to the path I am still on: to be part of undoing unjust systems by first understanding and unlearning my own allegiance to them.

about social movements and how to give money to grow them, as we sought to cocreate a different world. The experiments kindled in that Donut fire were powerful and far-reaching. For me, being part of the community from 1990 to 2020 enabled the development of skills and leadership, and gave me the relationships that led to the work that ensued. And we also moved money, funded long-lasting projects and got things done.

But first, Donuts helped free me; it supported me to integrate my whole self: artist, activist, producer, mother, owning-class inheritor. I developed self-compassion for the complexity of living all of those identities. It led me to the path I am still on: to be part of undoing unjust systems by first understanding and unlearning my own allegiance to them. I was able to develop a sense of myself and my values not because someone external to me told me how I should be, but because I was supported to do the work of self-examination, held by the love of community, the guidance of spirit and exposure to new-to-me ideas.

For a spirited 33-year-old with privileges and possibilities, this was the community and experience I needed. Yes, Donuts were woo and inwardly focused, and it was just the right medicine for me. After all, I was woo and playful *and* a serious person with gifts I wanted to offer the world. But first I had to figure out where and how I belonged.

Recently I did a little research about the origin of the Donut practices. I asked an original member, Peter Callaway (who first uttered the word *Donut* to describe the cloud!). He cited practices imported from Findhorn, the intentional eco-village community in northern Scotland, founded in the 1960s. I asked Robert Gass, who I knew had been involved at the beginning of Donuts. He became well known in movement circles in the late 90s for cofounding the Rockwood Leadership Institute, which teaches movement leaders to "lead from the inside out." Here is part of Robert's reply.

I was invited (and paid) by Josh Mailman to facilitate the 2nd Donut gathering at the Rockefeller estate in Arkansas. Josh had been to my Opening the Heart workshops and felt the group could use some help after what he described as a chaotic first meeting. In that first meeting, I did a full daylong Opening the Heart workshop — went very deep. I heard from some people later that they felt this was when the group fell in love with itself and fully bonded. I facilitated other parts as well, including bringing the group together in song in ways that had not happened so far. ... It was a pretty unruly group, carrying a fair amount of confusion if not trauma about their wealth. In addition to a strong facilitation role in the next couple of meetings, I tried to be intentional in helping the group develop rituals and processes to become functional. The essential task was to help people find collective purpose and trust sufficient to transcend people's personal agendas.[1]

Singing was a throughline at Donut meetings from the beginning
(Courtesy of Threshold Foundation)

These practices served to tend the fire of the community, enabling most of us to trust the process, fall in love with each other and reveal more of ourselves than we would in most settings. I attended Donut meetings for 30 years and sat on the board for eight of those years, often leading or coleading the agenda design. Meetings were usually five-day affairs, two to three times a year, starting in 1990. I once counted attending more than 60 in my day!

In the Threshold funding committees, we used an attunement process Robert Gass had introduced, to make decisions about

1 As Donut Andre Carothers recently told me about Rockwood Leadership Institute's founding: "I did see Robert in action at a Threshold meeting. I had been thinking about leadership development and taking classes and immersing myself in the subject since about 1990. ... When I saw Robert in action [at Donuts] I reached out to him later [to invite him to work with me], and he said no. I asked him to think about it. Then, one strange day, I was way up in Idaho, skiing with a friend, and I ran into him in this obscure ski rental walk-up in Sun Valley. He looked at me and said, "I guess I have to do this now, right?" And I said, "Yes, you do." And we started working together in 1999. We assembled a team of trainers together, ultimately numbering about 10, around 2005."

whom to fund and for how much. We spent significant time on conventional due diligence, with committee members making and reporting on site visits and how the organization did or did not align with the committee mission. Then one of us would lead a guided meditation to invite contemplation and "listen for" a power beyond our rational minds to reach discernment. While sometimes it felt like negotiating with our eyes closed, most of the time, it was miraculous how the numbers would add up to the amount of money the committee had to give. It felt like we were truly tapping into another level of knowing.

When I described the process to a fellow donor organizer who had come up in a different culture, he was horrified to hear this. "If I were a development director of an org being funded," he said, "I'd have some feelings about some rich people sitting around tapping into their third eye as the way decisions were made about whether you gave me the money you stole from my community."

On the one hand, fair enough: a moment drenched in unearned privilege wielding power. And yet, the part about the third eye? This was one of the more revolutionary dimensions of Donuts: to bring engagement with spirit into work with money. Not as a prosperity-gospel thing, but to incorporate humility about the limits of our rational minds, to recognize a greater power and to surrender to that. And to consider that this money could carry with it something sacred: our loving intention.

This was one of the more revolutionary dimensions of Donuts: to bring engagement with spirit into work with money. Not as a prosperity gospel thing, but to incorporate humility about the limits of our rational minds, to recognize a greater power and to surrender to that.

Donut Meetings and Healing Portals

And then there were the often-epic Donut meetings. At some conference center, college campus or resort — a dance floor, a hallway, a meeting room — they all blur together. The time in Saratoga, New York, my second meeting, when there was a sunrise ceremony led by Haudenosaunee elders (Leon Shenandoah and Oren Lyons among them) because the Threshold board was engaged in a project to support Indigenous elders in the lead-up to the 500-year anniversary of Columbus' arrival.

That night in a grief circle where, by the end of the night, there was a huge pile of loving and emotional bodies in the center of the room. Or in Hawaii, when the agenda facilitators decided that the agenda was to have NO AGENDA, to experiment with what would happen in the void of no plan.

2011 photos of Marian facilitating a Donut session (Courtesy of Threshold Foundation)

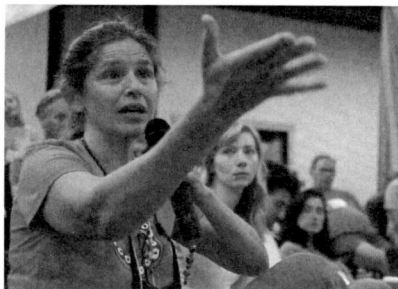

In the late 90s, in Watsonville, California, working with Jungian psychologists Arthur Colman and Pilar Montero to explore the nature of the boundary between the individual and the group, being taught through radical experimentation how individuals "carry" things for the group. The time somewhere in Oregon when I sang "Tempt Me," the R and B song I wrote, and got three of my Donut gal pals to sing backup. The time another often-inappropriate, often cross-dressing Donut stripped off his shirt on the dance floor, and I enthusiastically followed suit. Later, I was mildly chastised by the board because of what the "children might think."

We were messy with each other. We were sincere. We were passionate. Many were — especially in the early years — immature and acted out. As in all groups, there was a wide and wild variety of personalities. And Robert Gass was right: There was a "fair amount of confusion if not trauma" about the inherited money.

159

Those who stuck around, in the main, shared a passion to heal and evolve and to be of service.

Deep meaningful times for me personally also surface in memory.

The time I read to the group from my mother's Jersey City memoir. We were meeting just blocks from where our family lived when I was born, where my parents spent those eight years in ministry in a financially impoverished interracial neighborhood. Earlier in the day, Nina Utne and I had walked over to scope out where I had spent the first year of my life. It happened to be the day of Mom's 92nd birthday — though she'd died at 50. That evening, it felt so meaningful to be able to read from the epilogue of Mom's book, where she tells of a visit in her Washington, D.C., living room, 20 years after we left Jersey City, from one of the Black kids, now a man, from the old neighborhood:

> "Before you came," he said to me finally, "we had very little hope, but you started a chain of things. There was the camp and different experiences like that, and when there was nothing else to do we could go to Grace Church and hang around. You were the first white people we didn't hate. There was love and care for a long time." I must have looked startled, because he touched my arm as we sat on the sofa and went on to explain, "You're too hard on yourself. You mean you didn't know people remembered the love? Anyone could tell you. Even the guys who don't give a damn about God will admit that when you pin them down."

A few days later, I visited a friend in New York and told her the story of reading from Mom's book. I also said how sad I was to have lost the copy of the book Mom had inscribed for me many years ago. My friend, whom I hadn't seen in decades, stood up from her dining room table, pulled a copy of the book off the shelf and gave it to me. I opened the book, and there it was! Inscribed, "For Babby [my childhood nickname], who used to sit in her stroller and watch Second Street go by. With much love, Mommy." Later that day, I was with a healer recommended by a Donut friend. My mom visited me as I lay on the table. She said to me, "That death is loss is a lie."

That seemed a miraculous string of events and it feels like it characterizes the kind of profound and healing portal that opened for me because of this community: a spring from which to drink, a pathway for my becoming. It seems to me that through Donuts and Threshold, I was able to begin to integrate my money life and class privilege into a path of self-actualization.

My hope is that my commitment to continued transformation is ultimately in service of becoming who I need to be to be part of what my friend and teacher Orland Bishop calls "hosting a new future." And, for me, that "continued transformation" requires a lot of humility and willingness to look at what is hard to face; the entrenched beliefs that perpetuate the kind of privilege and disconnection that wealth and class engender. The future I want to host honors all life and our sacred interrelatedness. It's as though early colonizers, including my ancestors, cast a spell that created amnesia about our connection to earth and each other. I want to be part of reversing that spell.

> My hope is that my commitment to continued transformation is ultimately in service of becoming who I need to be to be part of what my friend and teacher Orland Bishop calls "hosting a new future."

The Money

And then there was the money. After that first Donut meeting in 1990, things shifted immediately for me. On our plane ride home, my then-husband, Tim, started a conversation with a woman sitting to his right. Our toddler, Jamie, and I were to his left. It turned out that Tim and this woman had gone to the same Catholic grade school in St. Paul. She was a Catholic nun named Pat Thalhuber, in her late 40s when we met, who told us she had been "journeying with" Native people for more than 25 years. Sister Pat had just received the blessing of an eagle feather from an Indigenous elder. We became friends, and I sponsored her project leading restorative justice circles to Threshold's Person Committee. Later, I made a $10,000 gift to her myself, my biggest gift to date.

That same winter in Minneapolis, having recently cofounded Concerts for the Environment, we decided to produce a concert in support of the 20th anniversary of Earth Day events planned on the National Mall in D.C. We needed $75,000 as a deposit for the venue. Co-founder Tom Sellars asked if I would lend $25,000. At first it seemed outlandish. I thought, "I'm not someone who can do that," a habitual reaction. Then I realized that I actually did have that much money that I could use in service to what I cared about.

As I write this 34 years later, it seems so obvious! But there is something strange and disconnecting that happens when money comes as an unbidden inheritance. The questions can be paralyzing: "Whose money is it? From whom do I need permission to do anything with it? What am I supposed to know to be able to make wise decisions? Where do I learn about this? What values should underlie my choices? What are my values?" Now, having worked for decades — as a coach and facilitator — with people who have wealth, primarily inherited, I have seen this kind of paralysis play out repeatedly. There is also often an underlying insecurity, and sometimes grief, associated with the money, since many people inherit early as a result of a parent's premature death.

For me, at that early moment in my evolution, with the Earth Day concert, with excitement about using money as an expression of something I cared about, I said yes.

Cut to a weekend in January 2025. I am visited by a beloved Donut friend who is a farmer, acupuncturist and Buddhist practitioner named Vinnie McKinney. Raised in East Texas and Little Rock, she has tended Elixir Farm in the Ozarks of Southern Missouri for 50 years, raised vegetables biodynamically and started a Chinese medicinal seed company.

Vinnie was financially eligible for Donuts — back when the financial criterion was $250,000 — because of a family investment in oil wells. She was the first president of Donuts, is now 80 years old and is very clear about the gift essence of Donuts. She says the community enabled us to be with others who had shared values outside of conventional thought and practice. It gave us the confidence and support to follow our values outside of the "supposed to" world.

Vinnie was first brought to Donuts by a woman from Little Rock named Ella Alford. Ella was afraid to venture to Donuts alone, worried that these people might try to fleece her, take her money. But, by Vinnie's telling, the eventual story for Ella was that being in the community gave her the confidence to follow her love of the Ozark land she inherited from her father and create the Ozark Regional Land Trust in partnership with a local activist. She eventually put the Alford Forest, more than 4,000 acres of Ozark County, into a land trust in the late 80s.

She also donated hundreds of acres to the land trust to enable a community of lesbians that had sprung up out of the 1970s back-to-the-land movement, to live on that land. At Hawk Hill, the women built houses on land-trust-owned land, lived there and raised their families. They are still there, now in their 70s and 80s.

Another Donut used her inheritance to develop a refuge for species on the edge of extinction in Glen Rose, Texas. Krystyna Jurzykowski devoted her life and money to its development, cocreated a nonprofit and made a gift of the 2,000 acres and all that was developed there into Fossil Rim Wildlife Center. She bought High Hope Ranch, adjacent to the preserve, which she recently gave to a biodynamic land trust, Living Lands Trust, all 1,000 acres of it. It now serves as a retreat center, a biodynamic farm (food sovereignty for the local community) and habitat conserved for native flora and fauna.

These beautiful things are real and lasting and came through a human born into the capitalist culture of hoarding money and land who followed a different path, nurtured by a community of fellow seekers to transform an inheritance into a gift.

There are questions in any process of giving or redistributing money that we who do this work to help facilitate the movement of money and power are obliged to continue to ask: Who decides? And who decides who decides? What is the role of the person who has the money? And to whom must they be accountable? It is an ongoing and important conversation.

Professionalizing the Work

It was through Donuts that I found my new work convening and coaching people with money. In the mid-90s, after supporting my family for seven or eight years with income from my invested inheritance while I had the privilege to raise my kids, tend to my creative development and work without pay, the money was running out. I needed to supplement and eventually replace that income through earning. I was able to translate my experience into a series of consulting assignments.

In the midst of that work, I received a call from Grant Abert, a Donut friend who had just become president of Threshold. He wanted me to join the Threshold board, known as "the Circle." Sitting in my cubicle on the top floor of Butler Square in downtown Minneapolis, I saw a crossroads: Grant was inviting me onto a path that felt full of promise and more an expression of what I wanted to bring and who I wanted to be in the world. Yet I couldn't financially afford to go to the meetings and provide so much time without being paid. "I would really like to work with you Grant, but I can't afford to do that right now." Grant replied, "How about if I pay all of your expenses?"

I made the decision to turn back toward the Donuts. Following that return, and at a hard time of transition in my own life, I became the lead on agenda development for Donut/Threshold meetings. In a step away from Donut culture and tradition, I was paid (modestly) for the work. I chose to host the agenda team of about seven people at my Donut friend Vinnie's place, Elixir Farm.

I was nervous but also excited to step into leadership. What I remember is that Vinnie and her farm partners devoted themselves to supporting my success. I had never had that experience before.

Peter Callaway, one of the original Donuts, lived on the farm. His boyfriend, George, was a great chef and was assigned to cook for us. Others brought the food up to where we were meeting. Vinnie visited when needed to provide long-term wisdom about the community.

I had the feeling of being re-parented. "Oh," I thought, "this is how it feels when you have people who are committed to your becoming." Wow. I still get teary-eyed when I think of that. Maybe the essence of Donuts is about healing the world through first providing for our own healing and becoming.

Class

Following that retreat in 2003, the first time I led an agenda, I chose the theme of money. Despite the fact that we were called together as a community *because* of money, we rarely went deeply into money itself. I found this frustrating and wanted to face it head on. "Let's talk about money!"

And it is not just in rich people's circles that people avoid talking about money. No matter where you are, money is a great taboo! But how to grapple with it and understand its effects if you don't discuss it?

Later in 2003, I also led an agenda about class. I invited Donut Jenny Ladd and her working-class work partner Felice Yeskel, who had cofounded Class Action, an organization dedicated to exploring issues surrounding class and identifying means of dismantling classism. They led a session that is still vivid in my memory more than 20 years later. The objective of the session was to illuminate the workings of class in our lives and consciousness.

The 100 of us - overwhelmingly white - gathered in the room and were instructed to identify our family's class status when we were 12 years old. We were to interview each other as we mingled, asking questions that would reveal markers of class. "Did you go to private school?" "Did you own your own house? "Did you have household staff?" Through these conversations, we were to place ourselves at the appropriate place on the spectrum of class status at the age of 12. Despite everyone in the room identifying as someone with wealth, or married into wealth, our 12-year-old class statuses represented a surprisingly huge spectrum.

Once we found our spot on the spectrum, we gathered with the four others closest to us and told stories of what this class status meant for our lived experience. From these stories, we were able to name our groups.

Because my group of five discovered a shared sense of duty and privileged access to vast swaths of land, we named our group Noblesse Oblige, Running Through the Trees.

We were the third from the "highest" social class in the room. I remember the top called themselves Sprezzatura (Italian for "effortless grace" or "studied carelessness"), and some in that group boasted European royalty in their extended family. The "lowest" named themselves True Grit and included a man who had grown up in North Dakota in a home with dirt floors and later became a successful Phoenix-based lawyer.

Somewhere in the middle was the upwardly mobile group Cocktails by the Pool. That exercise taught me so much. It not only made visible all the unspoken inherent class distinctions, but I discovered in myself class-based assumptions and projections I was unconsciously making, that I had been raised to make. I was quite certain that two people were fibbing about where they belonged on the spectrum. In my mind, one had chosen higher (a striver!), and another had chosen lower (ashamed!).

This for me was as revelatory as Jenny and Felice had hoped. The class structure in the U.S., while rarely discussed, is real and influences our behavior, relationships and access. Even as my financial assets decreased, my class status gave me positional power. I would do well to be aware of this power, both to use it for good and not to wield it unconsciously.

It isn't easy to undo the mindset and dismantle what hundreds of years of class-based capitalist culture has engendered. Not only is it about unlearning, but the systems to hold money and class structure in place are intense. For example, one Donut friend told me that his father had created 600 trusts over the decades of owning a family business to avoid paying taxes! One outcome of this is that the beneficiaries of these trusts have very little freedom to redistribute the money.

In my coaching of mostly women with inherited wealth, the paternalistic, condescending attitudes of trustees and financial advisors — what some call the "wealth defense industry" — are stunning. Once I accompanied a client to meet a prospective wealth advisor who advertised himself as a socially-conscious "impact investor." The presentation included a slide with the warning: "Shirtsleeves to shirtsleeves in three generations." This is to tell the inheritor not to be a fool by giving or spending it all, or you will end up like your grandfather or great-grandfather, working with your hands, in shirtsleeves.

Sometimes, in my later coaching work, I have felt my role is primarily to give permission and encourage my clients to follow their knowing. To say "YES! Your way of thinking is legitimate! You have permission to follow your instinct!" The investment advisors (by training) protect the culture of wealth accumulation that both enables their profession and their own very specific financial interests. To peel away takes confidence, courage and support.

Inclusion and Race

There were some Donuts who in their other-than-Threshold work centered poor and working-class leadership and cross-class alliance building that had not been part of Donuts. Two in particular, Barbara Meyer and Paul Haible, initiated and did the challenging culture-shifting work of establishing a process to engage "community partners" — people from the communities that the grants were to fund — in the grantmaking work.

Because Donuts did so much intimate, personal work and had a commitment to confidentiality, we were sometimes confused about what was required to protect privacy. In hindsight, I would say, while I was there, we erred on the side of protection and exclusion. While agreements are critical to any community's integrity, I now know we missed out by not having more frequent and robust integration as partners of like-minded social change agents from other class backgrounds.

An extraordinary chapter for me came through another of Barbara Meyer's offerings, work with Lillie Allen. Lille is a Black woman whose vision began with bringing together Black women and girls to talk about the realities of their lives, envision together and organize for justice in the early 80s. The work grew to include white women. One of those women was Barbara Meyer. (In the early 90s, Barbara transferred her family foundation assets to the community it sought to serve, the still active majority-Black Southern Partners Fund).

Barbara brought Lillie Allen and her Be Present Empowerment Model into Donuts, where many of us became engaged with her work to liberate us from the effects of racism — this is deep, subtle and time-intensive personal work. The promise of the process, as Lillie describes it, is to "know yourself outside the distress of oppression, to listen to others in a conscious and present state to build effective relationships and sustain true alliances through transforming conflict and building trust."

My friend Roger Milliken remembers a meeting with Lillie at Stone Mountain, Georgia:

> **She had us in a spectrum of privilege. I was at the top of the heap in all the categories except I wasn't a jock. I was standing in the middle of a long line and feeling all my privilege and the sense of separation it creates and not wanting that separation. She came up to me sticking her finger in my chest and said, "We need you in this movement. We can't have a movement unless there is room for all of us." Powerful and empowering and healing. I have carried it with me ever since. Particularly into rooms where the narrative is "Your wealth is the problem. We don't need you." This to me goes back to the Funding Exchange — given that the wealth comes out of injustice the best thing you can do is give it away and disappear.**

It's complicated, right? On our way to eliminating capitalism, how do we build that movement, that world, where there is room for "all of us" but doesn't privilege those with privilege?

It was a relief to do work about race in Donuts; the rarely spoken was spoken. While healing and greater awareness were surely underway for me and other Donuts, I would say now that

that work could only go so far in a mostly white and wealthy community. Many Donuts continued work with Lillie in Be Present's interracial spaces.

My current answer to the question about how to build a world where there is room for all of us, that doesn't privilege privilege, is this: Do work about money and class and deepen trust in multiclass, multicultural, multiracial communities.

And similarly, with racial healing, through my more recent experiences, I have come to the not-surprising conclusion that having interracial proximity, learning each other's stories and deepening trust through relationships make up the only path to true understanding so we can eliminate white supremacy separatist culture.

> My current answer to the question about how to build a world where there is room for all of us, that doesn't privilege privilege, is this: Do work about money and class and deepen trust in multiclass, multicultural, multiracial communities.

Play BIG

In 2004, when the Donuts no longer wanted to pay a member (me) to lead the agenda team, I was approached by a Donut named Carol Newell to work with her. She was my age, 48, and while we knew each other from years at Donut meetings, we hadn't yet forged a close relationship. Carol had inherited a fortune from the company her grandfather founded. (Initially the company manufactured curtain rods in upstate New York and eventually merged with Rubbermaid.)

In partnership with another Donut, Joel Solomon, Carol had been doing environmentally-oriented giving and investing to support a sustainable economy in British Columbia. Carol was the anonymous funder, Joel the co-visionary and implementer. Their partnership started in 1992; they considered the damage done in the 500 years since Columbus' arrival. What good could they do with a 500-year future vision? What was unusual then is they saw the opportunity to do what Carol would later call "whole portfolio activation to mission."

Joel had a business background through helping to manage his father's shopping mall business, so he had the chops to implement their mission to put the money to work to support an economy that was good for the planet and people. This included investing in businesses with a mission that was as important as making a financially successful enterprise. Carol's comprehensive strategy for this regional approach came to include environmental philanthropy, seed-capital investing in mission-aligned businesses, convening and political giving. Under each of those categories is a mind-bending trove of creative moves (see Joel Solomon's book, *The Clean Money Revolution: Reinventing Power, Purpose, and Capitalism*).

Their work was instrumental in supporting the expansion of a powerful environmental movement in British Columbia. The roughly $60 million that Carol was willing to put toward the building of this movement has generated a profound legacy of work that continues to make waves decades later and includes enterprises that have lasted past their "spend down" of Carol's inheritance.

Carol initially had two motivations for this next phase of work: to make it known that a woman was funding the Endswell Foundation and Renewal Partners and to influence her financial peers, thereby leverage exponentially more than her fortune could. She was in search of a partner to help her do this.

We imagined together what that could be. As I drew Carol out, to understand her vision, among the things she said was, "I just want people to play big with their money!" By which she meant, "Use imagination! Have vision! Don't hide behind the rules of money in our culture!" Carol called those unhelpful rules "money manners." We convened gatherings for people with tens of millions of dollars for the next 14 years.

This engagement with Carol to create Play BIG was the beginning of the professionalization of my work as a donor organizer, coach and convener focused on changing people's ideas of what money could be and do. It led to my involvement with Lead with Land, Jubilee Gift, Just Economy Institute and Jubilee Justice, experiences with numerous stories for another time. It

2017 photo of Donuts meeting at Hollyhock Learning Centre on Cortes Island, B.C.
(Courtesy of Marian Moore)

also led me to work with the Trust Web and Elspeth Gilmore, whose story is included in this anthology.

Liberate the People

A Donut friend, Paul Haible, who had worked at the Vanguard Foundation in the early days and led the Peace Development Fund for decades, told me recently that once in the 90s he was with our mutual friend Indigenous activist Winona LaDuke and complained about Threshold meetings. I'm guessing he felt impatience with the pace of change and release of money. Winona said to him, "Paul, you need to go to those meetings because we can't."

Paul was often grumpy at Donut meetings, and I asked him once why he kept showing up. He said, "I come to liberate the money." My rejoinder was that "I come to liberate the people to liberate the money to liberate the people..."

Orland Bishop, who studied money for more than 20 years,

has called money "our most significant unconscious agreement." In other words, we are obedient to entrenched and unconscious beliefs about what money is. My work now is to examine and transform those entrenched ideas through intentionally practicing new ways with money, in groups across race and class and culture. These "new" ways are based in relationships, in trust, in love, in shared aspirations.

For me, the work is about creating the conditions for people to see their way forward, out of conventionally held notions of what money is for, to find their own expression. I see that my work is to enable an environment that allows for a shift in consciousness about money, to reimagine what money can be and do, to remake the culture and rules.

As I wrap up this story of how I came into this work with money and class, through the long and treasured experience with Donuts, I think about my parents. I honor how they radically challenged the expectations of their class and culture. They took stand after stand for love and for justice, and they placed that value deep inside me, like a seed. I've been so fortunate to find communities that gave me what I have needed for that seed to germinate, to grow roots and leaves. And it is on me to keep learning, growing, flowering and passing the seeds along. ▪

THE COOL RICH KIDS MOVEMENT

William "Billy" Upski Wimsatt

Billy Wimsatt is a longtime leader, writer and strategist on building progressive movements and power. Billy wrote his first book, *Bomb the Suburbs*, at the age of 24, and his second, No More Prisons, three years later, in 1999. With its chapter "The Cool Rich Kids Movement" *No More Prisons* became one of the most effective tools for bringing young wealthy people into this burgeoning movement. He went on to found the League of Pissed Off Voters and, more recently, Movement Voter Project (MVP). MVP is one of the largest progressive electoral funding intermediaries in the country, with over 45,000 donors. It moved over $100 million in the 2020 and 2024 election cycles.

Here is an excerpt from *No More Prisons* (1999, pages 44-55).

In the summer of 1997, I got a mysterious package in the mail. It contained a magazine called *More Than Money Journal*. The subtitle read, "Exploring the personal, political and spiritual impact of money in our lives." It also contained a brochure telling me about a conference in Seattle for "The Next Generation of Philanthropists." Yes, it's true, there is a decent-sized network of rich people who give a shit (future rich people in my case) who go to conferences and talk about their money. How to invest in more "socially responsible" companies and how to give it away. It is all very serious. An acquaintance of mine who'd had a hunch about my financial situation put me on their mailing list.

> Yes, it's true, there is a decent-sized network of rich people who give a shit (future rich people in my case) who go to conferences and talk about their money.

The conference offered "a safe space" for "people of wealth." I didn't know what to think of it all. Well, to be honest, I thought it was ridiculous. I couldn't picture myself sitting in a room with a bunch of rich people talking about money. I couldn't relate to it and it gave me the creeps. But deep down, I was intrigued.

So, like a good self-schooler, I went. I went expecting to meet all these clueless rich people who had no connection to the grassroots and no idea what they were doing. What I found instead blew my mind.

First of all, one of the women there was an old friend of mine, an environmental activist from Chicago who I never would have guessed was rich. Then there was Trish Millines, one of the few black millionaires at Microsoft. She used her money to start the Technology Access Foundation in Seattle for young people of color to learn computers. John Moyers was there, the son of TV host Bill Moyers. John is head of the Schumann Foundation, and he spoke passionately about funding organizations that fight to get big money out of politics.

The conference was amazing. People were friendly and down to Earth.

Everyone there was either doing amazing stuff or was trying to figure out how. I learned so much so fast. I learned that I have a lot to learn. I didn't know anything about financial planning or estate planning or the art and business of philanthropy. I just knew I wanted to use my money and my time to do extraordinary things. And I knew I wanted to help other young people make their impossible dreams come true.

The conference was a turning point for me. I realized that there were all these other rich people trying to figure out how to give their money away wisely. The idea is to support groups that work for "change not charity." We're not just going to put Band-Aids on the symptoms of social problems — we're going to go change the root causes that are creating the problems in the first place.

It makes sense.

You have to be more of a detective. You don't just say, "Oh, look at those flood victims on TV. Poor them. Aren't they unlucky/ stupid for living there? Let's send money to the Red Cross so they can pile more sand bags."

Instead you are skeptical. You say, "Wait a minute, why are there so many more floods now than when I was growing up? Could it be that the auto industry, in cahoots with developers, construction unions, local zoning boards and the Federal

Government have spent the last 50 years paving over America's open lands with subdivisions, roads and parking lots so that the water has nowhere else to go? What organizations are successfully fighting this? How can I support them?"

A whole world was opening up for me. The conference was put on by a foundation called A Territory Resource.[1] ATR is part of a loose-knit network of renegade foundations around the country which were started by a small group of rich people in the 1960s and '70s. They come from a spectrum of backgrounds and use a variety of strategies. Some give specifically to grassroots efforts for social change. Some do socially responsible investing. Some fund micro-enterprise. Some put activists on their boards in order to share their decision-making power with the people on the ground.

Some, like Responsible Wealth, in Boston, fight against unfair government policies that benefit the rich, and use their stockholder status to introduce share-holder resolutions which challenge companies to stop using sweatshops or cancer-causing chemicals. (They need to add to their list the prison industry!)

One of the people I met at the ATR conference was Anne Slepian, one of the founders of the magazine *More Than Money*. She and her husband Christopher Mogil had been activists in West Philly when they unexpectedly inherited money. They went around interviewing all these other rich people who had done creative things with their money from Ben Cohen of Ben & Jerry's to George Pillsbury (of the Pillsbury Family) to Millard Fuller (founder of Habitat for Humanity) and a bunch of other incredible people most of us have never heard of. Phil Villers went to Harvard Business School and made $80 million in computers just so he could give it away. Tracy Gary helped start

---

1 A Territory Resource would become Social Justice Fund Northwest in 2005.

dozens of organizations with her inheritance, including one of the first battered women's shelters in the U.S., and the San Francisco Women's Foundation, each of which became a model for countless similar organizations across the country.

Anne and Christopher turned the interviews into a book called *We Gave Away a Fortune*. They started an organization called More Than Money, (formerly The Impact Project), which works with rich people — especially new inheritors — to think creatively about their resources, and the personal dilemma of having more than others. They publish a journal called *More than Money* for socially-conscious rich people to share their stories. And they do theater and organize groups to get rich people talking about the unique options and dilemmas that come with having more money.

One organization, United For A Fair Economy, which is the parent organization of Responsible Wealth, includes both rich and poor people. They employ a full time street artist, Andrew Boyd, who organizes hilarious stunts, like this one:[2]

Today [in September 1996] on the steps of the State House in Concord, New Hampshire, as Steve Forbes announced his candidacy for President, United for a Fair Economy launched its latest campaign, "Billionaires for Steve Forbes."

At first, UFE staffers and volunteers, smartly dressed in pinstripe suits and formal dresses, held innocuous signs and led supportive chants such as "Forbes in 2000," and "Run Steve Run!" A large hand-painted banner carried Forbes' slogan, HE WANTS YOU TO WIN.

However, each of the signs had another sign behind it. At the moment of his announcement, the large banner was pulled away to reveal another that read BILLIONAIRES FOR STEVE FORBES — BECAUSE INEQUALITY IS NOT GROWING FAST ENOUGH. Meanwhile, the hand-held signs suddenly read, TAX CUTS FOR US, NOT OUR MAIDS, TAX WORK, NOT WEALTH, and FREE THE FORBES 400. What a lift he must have felt from his billionaire boosters as they chanted "Let workers pay

---

2 The story below describes a political theatre action organized by United for a Fair Economy in 1996.

the tax, so investors can relax," and other supportive slogans they had devised in his honor!

All major press were there: CBS, NBC, ABC, CSPAN and many others.

The Most Effective Thing You Ever Do

Small renegade grassroots foundations now operate in most areas of the country. In Chicago, we have the Crossroads Fund, which I recently found out was started by the parents of someone I went to school with. One of the other people on the Crossroads board of directors is the father of one of my friends I used to do graffiti with! I also learned that Crossroads gave a grant to the Autonomous Zone, which is an anarchist punk center down the street from the Vision Village and if we had applied to Crossroads for a grant, there's a good chance we could have gotten it!

The more I learned about philanthropy, the more I realized that practically every "grassroots" organization and community leader I had ever heard of gets a lot of their money from a very small number of cool rich people. Grassroots organizations don't usually like to talk about it. They talk about how they are of the people, by the people, for the people, and to a large extent that is true. They do depend on $25 contributions and the support of a wide base. But take away that one behind-the-scenes cool rich person and most of these grassroots organizations are fucked.

> The more I learned about philanthropy, the more I realized that practically every "grassroots" organization and community leader I had ever heard of gets a lot of their money from a very small number of cool rich people.

Every hell-raising magazine from *The Nation* to *Mother Jones* to *Adbusters* to *In These Times* to *The Progressive* depend for their survival on half a dozen cool rich people. It was a hard lesson to learn. But it filled me with hope. What if we could double the number of cool rich people who are funding social change from say five hundred to a thousand? Then we could double the number of organizers on the street, lawyers in the court rooms, lobbyists in Congress. Double the number of investigative reporters. There are so many people who want to do progressive work who can't because there aren't enough activist jobs. People come out of law school to become environmental lawyers and they end up having to defend corporations because they have to pay off their student loans. Environmental groups can't afford to hire them. The same goes for radical artists and journalists, forced to get jobs in advertising and public relations.

Five hundred more cool rich people could change all that.

Five hundred cool rich people could change the political landscape of this country.

Now don't get me wrong. I'm not saying philanthropy will solve all our problems, especially not the way 99% of it is done now. I'm not saying cool rich people are any more important or worthy than any other people. Poor people are made to feel like they aren't worth anything and that's wrong. I don't want to feed into that by focusing on rich people for a while. We need billions of people from billions of backgrounds trying billions of strategies to save this planet. It's just that every serious effort to change things takes people with money who understand how to support a movement.

* * *

Consider these statistics. There are about five million millionaire households in the U.S.[3] That's approximately one out of every 50 people. So, if you are a social person (not a hermit) and you are not currently serving a life sentence in prison, then chances are you will have the opportunity at some point in your life to get to know a number of people who are, at the very least, millionaires. Most of the time you will not know they are millionaires. Half of the time, millionaires don't even realize they are millionaires. My parents didn't realize they were. People usually have their assets tied up in many different forms such as houses, trusts, mutual funds, stocks, bonds and retirement accounts.

Less than 1% of all charitable giving ends up in the hands of people who are working to change the system. As Teresa Odendahl has pointed out in her ironically-titled book *Charity Begins at*

---

3 This number is from 1999. In 2024, there were around 24 million millionaire households in the U.S.

178

Home,[4] contrary to popular belief, most charity money does not go to help poor children help themselves. The vast majority of money goes to big churches, big colleges, big hospitals, big arts and social service organizations which either directly cater to privileged people, or which treat the symptoms of social ills without ever addressing the root causes.

* * *

Over the next 50 years, the upper classes of my generation stand to inherit or earn the greatest personal fortune in history, while the lower classes both here and internationally will continue slipping deeper into poverty and debt.

That's where the Cool Rich Kids Movement comes in. Actually there isn't much of a "Cool Rich Kids Movement." That's just what I call the loose-knit network of maybe 100 of us young people with wealth who are in conversation with each other, and who support each other in taking small but significant actions. We are asking our parents to teach us about money. We are helping our families make responsible decisions about investments. Some of us are getting on the boards of family foundations or helping our families to start them. We introduce each other to amazing grassroots people to break the isolation of wealth. We are just in the process of getting organized. We had our first conference last spring, sponsored by the Third Wave Foundation in New York. More are planned.

My goal is to get more young people with wealth in on the

---

4 Teresa Odendahl, *Charity Begins at Home: Generosity and Self-interest Among the Philanthropic Elite* (Basic Books, 1991). This book shares a detailed and thoroughly researched history of the first few decades of social justice philanthropy, from Conference on National Priorities to the Funding Exchange, and the women's philanthropy movement.

conversation. With five million millionaires in the U.S., even if we only spoke to the coolest 1% of all millionaire kids, that's still 50,000 people!

One half of the money I give away every year goes directly to grassroots youth activist organizations that I have a relationship with. (No, I don't make them kiss up to me. I just give it to them, thank them for their hard work and if they feel funny about it, I remind them that the only reason I have the money in the first place is because I've been so privileged and so many people have helped me. So it wasn't really "my" money to begin with. Often times I have to *insist* that people take my money. We've all had so many bad experiences.)

The other half of my money I donate to organizing people with wealth. That may seem strange at first. Why give money to people who already have wealth?

From all my experience with grassroots organizations, I believe that organizing people with wealth is the most powerful work I do. And paradoxically, it is some of the hardest work to fundraise for because everybody including rich people thinks, "Why give rich people more money?" And that's why only a few dozen people in America have the job of helping rich people figure out how to come to terms with and do cool things with their money.

I think we need more of those people in the world.

* * *

There's very little room in our culture to talk about having money and funding renegade work. Most rich people be like, "See you later." And most grassroots people be like, "It's easy for you because you're rich." There's resentment either way. People who aren't rich can play a huge role supporting us. So many of my friends who aren't wealthy act like, "Ha ha ha, going to your rich kids conference." That's not going to make me want to talk to you.

180

If you are truly down to change the world, don't try to score points by alienating your rich friends with snide remarks. If you take the time to truly understand us and support us as people, more than likely, we will do the same for you. Rich people don't choose to be born rich any more than poor people choose to be born poor. The sickness of our society damages us each in different and complicated ways, and we sometimes forget that rich people get damaged too. Not just in a mocking way, like, "Oh, they're so spoiled." But in a real way. One of the most common ways privileged people get damaged is that we are taught not to talk about money. We put a wall around ourselves, and then it is hard for us to be honest with people who aren't rich. This makes us cold and creates a vicious cycle of not trusting and not sharing ourselves or our money.

> The sickness of our society damages us each in different and complicated ways, and we sometimes forget that rich people get damaged too.

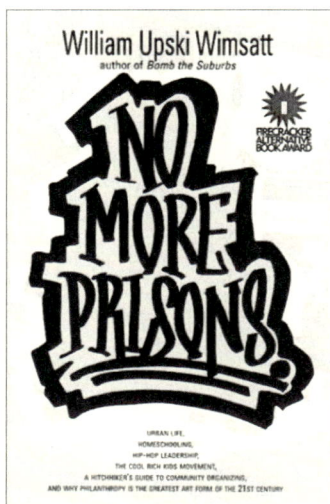

There are only a few of us out here doing this work, which is why I have been thrust into the spotlight. It's a little ridiculous actually that I am speaking for rich kids when I haven't even inherited my money yet. But there was a deafening silence and someone needed to come out here and give us a bold public voice. Do you have any cool rich friends who may be looking for people in similar situations to talk to?

Hint: You do.

Please please please pass this along to them.

It just might be the most effective thing you ever do. ∎

William Upski Wimsatt
author of *Bomb the Suburbs*

FIRECRACKER
ALTERNATIVE
BOOK AWARD

NO MORE PRISONS

URBAN LIFE,
HOMESCHOOLING,
HIP-HOP LEADERSHIP,
THE COOL RICH KIDS MOVEMENT,
A HITCHHIKER'S GUIDE TO COMMUNITY ORGANIZING,
AND WHY PHILANTHROPY IS THE GREATEST ART FORM OF THE 21ST CENTURY

WHAT I LEARNED FROM RG... AND WHAT YOU CAN TOO

Michael Gast

2014 photo from Michael's RG retirement party.
Michael is wearing the unicorn horn party hat in the middle. (Courtesy of Michael Gast)

Retirement

Greenwich Village. 2014.

I'm 34 and I'm at my own retirement party.

People mingle in the kitchen and the living room of my dear friend and former co-worker's family brownstone. Old rugs on the floor, photos and art everywhere, tall ceilings and big flower vases. I've been staying at this house and attending events in that living room for years now. I've been a part of board meetings, dance parties, deep talks, big cries and big arguments, all in that space.

I'm calling it quits. I've been working at Resource Generation (RG) for six years and was involved as a volunteer member for five years before that. I was 23 years old when I went to my first Resource Generation conference.

This is a lifetime for RG. It organizes young people with wealth, ages 18-35. The cross-class, multiracial board and staff have always been almost exclusively people in that age range. I've become the old (white) man in the organization.

There are speeches. I tear up. No surprise for anyone who

knows me.

So many people I love are there. Friends. Partners of friends. RG members. Board members. They have been my peers and comrades and colleagues. There's laughter and teasing. Part appreciation, part roast. Someone tells the story of the time I ended up naked except for a small towel, locked out of a friend's mom's apartment during an RG work trip to NYC. A former co-worker talks about how during my first week at work, I sent the staff meeting notes to the 500-plus person NYC chapter email list.

I came into RG in 2002 as an unsure, guilty, self-conscious, class-fascinated and class-conscious, scared young man.

I am leaving in 2014 a much more confident and self-assured mid-30s organizer and leader. I'm still scared, still self-conscious and class-fascinated, but I've learned how to love myself as a person with wealth and move myself and others toward greater integrity, honesty and action. Countless people have helped me learn and grow. They've helped me become a social justice donor and an organizer of rich people.

I've grown and so has the organization. By 2014, RG has a dozen staff and a million-dollar budget, almost 500 dues-paying members and more than 10 local chapters around the country. We're more than 85% funded by our base, who are moving tens of millions to movements because of our work with them. Resource Generation is starting to run campaigns and has an updated and bold mission and vision, a clear commitment to developing the racial justice leadership of all its members and growing programming for young people of color with wealth. RG is thriving: There is so much I am proud of.

After everyone goes home, I walk out into the cold, brisk New York City winter night and wonder. What do I do now? How will I keep organizing myself and other wealthy people for social justice? Where will I find another multiracial, cross-class community that helps me liberate myself and my people with love and rigor?

★ ★ ★

As I write this, it's 2025, and the questions that I left my retirement party with still animate my life. I'm 44 now. A dad and a middle-aged man and not retired at all from the work of organizing the rich. Since my time at Resource Generation, I have been a development director, fundraising consultant, donor advisor, donor organizer and facilitator to many social justice organizing projects. I have helped move tens of millions of dollars and many hearts and minds.

And, yet, even more than a decade after that "retirement" party, RG still has a permanent spot in my heart. It was my political home for much of my 20s and half of my 30s. It's where I told my money story for the first time, made my first giving and financial plan, experienced my first successful four-figure fundraising ask, led my first delegation and became staff of a lefty nonprofit for the first time.

In my conversations over the years, I have found that much of what I learned at RG is quite useful to the work of social change and social justice organizing, and yet its contributions remain little known and understood.

Writing this piece, I've found it difficult to come up with a few simple lessons to share. Instead, I've decided to focus on a handful of stories and do my best to articulate lessons from each of them. There is so much more I want you to know and learn, from me and many others. There are many RG innovations and experiments that will not be covered here.[1] But this is where I will start today, with some stories.

* * *

RG's Founding Years

RG was founded in 1998 to organize the next generation of wealthy young inheritors into the world of social justice philanthropy.

It was both a departure from what had come before and built off previous efforts like the Funding Exchange, the feminist politics and peer-to-peer consciousness-raising efforts of the women's

---

1 Some of the topics I don't cover in this piece, and would love to see written about, include giving plans, local chapter organizing, curriculum development, racial justice programming, the Redistribution pledge, local and national campaigns and campaign partners, changes in RG's mission over the years, Occupy, and reflections on RG's organizing culture. I hope to return to these topics in the future and recruit others to share their stories as well.

philanthropy movement, and the personal transformation experiments of the Threshold Foundation.

As Laura Wernick writes in her 2009 dissertation:

> Resource Generation, originally called Comfort Zone, was officially founded as an organization by young inheritors Tracy Hewat and Lynne Gerber around 1998, when they were in their late 20s and early 30s. The Comfort Zone was organized in 1995 as a collaboration of donors and activists from Boston Women's Fund, Haymarket People's Fund, Impact Project (More than Money), Peace Development Fund, United Black and Brown Fund, and Youth on Board. This group of organizations came together when they learned of a conference called Next Generation, which was to occur on the West Coast, for young progressive donors. The collaborators assumed that a lot of people, including people from the east coast, would attend and get excited and motivated about progressive philanthropy. Lynne and Tracy saw their role as plugging those returning attendees from the east coast into a progressive philanthropic network locally.
>
> Tracy and Lynne had been actively involved in progressive philanthropy. Tracy had been active with Haymarket Peoples Fund, and Lynne was working for Peace Development Fund and had also been involved with Haymarket ... When the group met for the second meeting, they learned that the original purpose of their meeting, the Next Generation conference, was cancelled due to a number of reasons, including lack of attendees.
>
> This east coast collective continued to meet, however, to talk about why it was exceedingly difficult to find young progressives with wealth.
>
> They had a number of theories, explained Tracy:
>
> *[T]he left on the whole was, you know, we're very bad advertisers. So there was probably a huge group of people who had no idea that such a thing was happening, number*

one. Number two, the stereotypes of young wealthy people were awful. There had just been an article in Newsweek [Forbes] called "Affluenza," that was ... famously about the ... Paris Hiltons of the world ... [T]he stereotype was so bad that nobody in their right mind would want to go spend a weekend with a bunch of people who acted like that, so we needed to do a little education around that, and, that typically, American kids growing up [as] "owning class" were told, rather consistently as kids, that they were middle class. They simply didn't identify as being in the top 5% or 1% of American wealth holders. They had no idea, and so they didn't see it as being a conference for them.

The collective decided to put together what was referred to as "the little packet" of information that they would use to do outreach to young progressives with wealth, particularly to college campuses in and around the Boston area, where they were located. They wanted the packet to provide specific information about how people could start if they wanted to learn more about the impact of money on their lives and what they could do about it, in a non-judgmental way. "It also had to have a hard cover," said Tracy, because the nature of that material could be scary and overwhelm the recipient at first glance, and they "wanted it to be able to go under somebody's dorm room bed, and stay there for three years, and come out looking the way it did when it went under. That was kind of the litmus test for design for this thing." The packet was divided into the categories Haymarket used in their conferences as guiding areas, which many found helpful: personal, political, technical and giving.

We named it "Money Talks, So Can We," in response, in many ways, to my experience of being at that first [Haymarket] conference and talking about how much money I had for the first time ... the talking part seemed like a really important piece of this, so the name was rooted in that. (Tracy)

In 1996, prior to becoming an official organization, the collective named their collaboration The Comfort Zone. By May of 1997, with the financial support of the founding organizations, they printed 500 copies of *Money Talks, So Can We*. One hundred went out the first day.

They initially sent the packets to all of the liberal and progressive young people they knew were wealthy, or who they thought could have wealth, in addition to those who had helped them in some way ... They had set up a telephone answering machine at Peace Development Fund, and almost immediately we started getting calls from people saying, "Hey, this is my story. Where are you? Who are you, and are there more people? ... [H]ow do I find people like me?" And that felt really exciting; it felt like ... we had produced the right material, for the right moment. (Tracy)

Tracy responded to every caller personally. She often spent a great deal of time on the phone, or meeting people in cafés throughout the northeast. Very often, it was the first time the callers had spoken about their wealth with anyone outside of their families.[2]

What lessons do I take from this early history?

1. RG was set up to answer a question important to leaders in the world of social justice philanthropy: "How do we find more young wealthy people to fund this work?!" Unlike almost every other group before them, RG was not a foundation or grantmaker. It did not have a formal way for its constituents to give together as part of its work. This difference took some of the focus off fundraising from the young wealthy people they engaged and put more of the focus on building a base of young people with wealth, developing dynamic political education and introducing constituents to a whole ecosystem of groups. I think RG became a laboratory for developing the practice of organizing the rich, in part, because it wasn't a foundation or grantmaker.

2. From the beginning, RG put an emphasis on cross-class,

2 Laura Wernick, "How Young Progressives With Wealth Are Leveraging Their Power and Privilege to Support Social Justice: A Case Study of Social Justice Philanthropy and Young Donor Organizing" (Ph.D. diss., University of Michigan, 2009).

multiracial leadership. Unlike Threshold Foundation, and similar to the Funding Exchange, RG believed in the importance of representative leadership for the perspective it brought and the accountability, however limited, it enabled. At the same time, RG relied, at least at first, on staff who were young people with wealth. Tracy and Lynne's class background helped them connect with peers and build relationships, which was crucial for growing the community.

3. RG built off many decades of experiments in organizing the rich. Some of the lessons and practices they borrowed from previous generations include the use of caucus spaces;[3] the importance of peer support and role modeling; an understanding of the basic tenets of "donor organizing," as mostly clearly articulated by Anne and Christopher Ellinger;[4] and a commitment to addressing people's feelings about money and class, not just focusing on the technical blocks of giving.

From Comfort Zone to the RG House

By 2002, founding Executive Director Tracy Hewat passed the baton to Hez Norton, RG's first executive director who was not wealthy. Hez came out of LGBT youth organizing in North Carolina, where they started a statewide network for LGBTQ youth focused on leadership and organizing called North Carolina Lambda Youth Network.

As Hez shared with me in an interview in 2023:

> When I was at RG, I wasn't thinking "Oh, this is the next iteration of that [Lambda Youth Network]," but looking back,

---

3 *Caucus spaces* are separate meetings or gatherings organized for people who share a specific identity or experience. The purpose is to create spaces where participants can freely discuss common experiences and challenges that might be harder to talk about in mixed groups. Caucus spaces can be organized by class background, racial group, gender or sexual orientation, to name a few, and they are often considered essential to meaningful coalition and community-building efforts.

4 For more on Anne and Christopher' approach to donor organizing, read "A Brief History of Organizing the Rich Toward Justice," in this anthology.

it was similar in many ways. It [RG] was a great support network for young people with wealth across different sites in the country. But there was this whole set of young people with wealth, particularly our Jewish constituents, who were ready to organize, not just talk or quietly donate — similar to how in North Carolina, there were LGBTQ young people who were ready to organize. Yes, they needed the support network too, but they were ready to get into action.

This is just my analysis, but RG's queer constituents [young people with wealth] were ready to organize as well because, most often, they'd already had some kind of break with their family around their queerness. So another break around money and politics wasn't as scary. We had some constituents who just wanted the support group, but then we had this whole other set who were like, "Yeah, and what else can we do?" For some, they might not have had access to their money yet, or maybe it wasn't that much, but they wanted to do more.

Pretty soon after that, we hired Karen [Pittelman]. Allison [Goldberg] had started her own project about family philanthropy and merged with us. So all of a sudden I had two wealthy people on staff who were ready to talk about money and organize. I thought, "Let's get some organizers in here to support them" — like Naomi Swinton, who'd been at Grassroots Leadership for 20-plus years; plus Jethro Heiko; Kenny Bailey; Kalpana Krishnamurthy — to start talking about what organizing looks like and how to build a Donor Organizing Institute and weave organizing through all the programs.

We started thinking about RG like a house, you walk in, and if you want the support room, it's over here. Family philanthropy? Over here. Want to organize? Over here. We wanted everyone to organize eventually, but we knew folks might not be ready immediately, and that was okay.

Do what you need to do, and hopefully we'll get you to organize because we want everyone there.

But I wouldn't say I knew what I was doing.

I love reading Hez's words. This RG house was in the process of being built when I got involved in 2003. I walked into a house under construction. The foundation had been laid; many of the walls and rooms were formed. I was astonished at what was taking shape.

2004 RG Staff Photo. *Left to Right:* John Harrison, Allison Goldberg, Hez Norton, Sally Bubier and Karen Pittelman. (Courtesy of Karen Pittelman)

What do I learn from this part of the RG story?

RG developed its organizing model by being responsive to the interests of the young people with wealth involved, particularly its Jewish and queer-identified constituents, who were itching to take bolder action. This constituent-led energy was matched with and guided by a team of experienced organizers willing to offer training and support.

* * *

Finding RG and Taking My First Steps

I was 22 when I first read Billy Wimsatt's book, *No More Prisons.*

It was the early fall of 2003, my favorite and the hottest time of year in San Francisco, the city where I was born and raised — and that parts of my family have called home for five generations. I was living in the Mission District with my college roommate and bestie. Six months before, the U.S. had invaded Iraq. Outkast's new double album *Speakerboxxx/The Love Below* was playing regularly on our living room boombox.

I was a young wannabe radical, a recent Vassar College graduate. Like many well-meaning young do-gooders, I had spent the last year working for an AmeriCorps program, making $12,000 a year, plus the bus pass and $4,000 educational stipend.

I was politicized in college through friends; a fieldwork program at a local prison; exposure to the burgeoning youth movement in the Bay, particularly the "No on Prop 21" campaign;[5] and a semester abroad in South Africa. Teachers of color I respected and admired told me, "Work from your own experience, in your own communities," but I had no idea what that looked like as a young white boy from the wealthy, private school world of San Francisco.

No More Prisons was just the right book at just the right time. Reading Wimsatt's chapter about "the Cool Rich Kid's Movement," I found someone I felt was speaking directly to me and could help answer these questions about my role in multiracial, cross-class movements. It was an exciting day.

The author, Billy Wimsatt, was a 25-year-old artist, organizer, hip-hop head and author of an underground classic *Bomb the Suburbs* — a former graffiti artist and breakdancer, a political thinker, a white Jewish guy and a sorta wealthy, sorta middle-class kid (a little bit like me!). He spoke directly to the part of me who wanted to be cool and down, and needed a lot of support to understand how to claim all the parts of myself in service of the movements I cared about.

In the "Cool Rich Kids" section of the book, his subchapter titles are "How Break Dancing Got Me Into Philanthropy," "In Defense of Rich Kids," "The Cool Rich People's Conference" and "Money Talks So Can She: An Interview With Tracy Hewat." Each section opened up a challenging and intriguing perspective

---

5 Proposition 21 was a racist ballot measure that would increase sentences for a whole bunch of juvenile offenses. It was on the ballot in California in 2000. There was a vibrant, youth-led "No on Prop 21" campaign organized around the state.

on how to relate to the class privilege and wealth in my life and communities.

The last page of that section had a resource list. I jumped on my aqua green clamshell Apple laptop and dove in, looking through the websites listed: Third Wave Foundation, Resource Generation, Responsible Wealth, United for a Fair Economy, *More Than Money Journal*, *Grassroots Fundraising Journal* — all organizations and projects I had never heard of.

In the internet wormhole that followed, I found gems of information. On the Resource Generation website, I read that my sister's best friend from high school, Mahea, was on the board. I also discovered that the Making Money Make Change conference (MMMC), RG's four-day retreat for young people with wealth who cared about social change, was going to be held in Marin County, California, in just a few months.

I reached for the wireless phone on our kitchen table, walked to my room and called Mahea.

"Are these good folks? Will you be there? Should I sign up?"

"Yes! I'll be there! You should totally come. They're good people. I'll hold your hand. It will be great... and a lot. And I'll be there with you."

I was scared and committed — horrified by the idea of identifying as a young person with wealth and compelled by the chance to finally talk openly about money, wealth and class in the context of the social justice values I aspired to and the movements I wanted to be a part of. I would use some of the $5,000 my Nanna gave me when I graduated college to sign up for MMMC.

For the first time, I was being organized to move toward the wealth and privilege in my life.

* * *

It's Saturday night. I'm sitting in a big conference room. I've made it. I'm at my first Making Money Make Change conference in Marin County, California. As it was for its first decade, the conference was put on by Resource Generation, the Funding Exchange, the Tides Foundation and the Third Wave Fund.

Seventy young people with wealth and class privilege sit in chairs in a circle. We each have one minute to tell our money story to the group. We have been asked to tell it honestly. Try to cut through the myths and share the real deal.

We have known this was coming for two days. I've prepped in my pod (a small group that met three times throughout the conference). We've been encouraged to say numbers.

Thirty-five people speak before me.

Oh, the stories I hear.

Money made from railroads, oil, property development, a cheerleading business, art, Publishers Clearing House, tech start-ups, divorce, the lottery, Hallmark greeting cards, stolen land, slavery, button factories, grocery store chains, razor wire and much more.

People give numbers. "I've inherited $300,000 and will inherit much more." "I make more in a year than my parents made in a lifetime." "I've inherited $25 million and my family's net worth is between $1 and $2 billion." "I inherited $150,000, I make $300,000 a year, part of my family is poor and in debt and the other part goes on vacations to Europe." "I married into a wealthy family and now have access to millions."

People look tense, relieved, nervous, proud. There are tears. Some hold hands. It is part group therapy, part smart-ass organizing strategy. It's my turn.

My mom's dad, Waring, was a WASPy stockbroker from a multigenerational wealthy New York family. His grandfather owned a national grocery business in the 1800s and used the proceeds to buy up lots of land in Rye, New York. A hundred years before that, one of my ancestors on that side of the family enslaved Africans on their farm in New York. My grandfather struggled with alcoholism, had a stroke and lost the money he'd inherited by the time my mom was five.

My grandma on my dad's side, the Jewish side of the family, was married three times and widowed twice. Her second husband, my grandpa Leslie, ran a family business on the Lower East Side of NYC: Blum Knitwear. He was on his way to becoming a millionaire when he died of a heart attack at the age of 43. My grandma's next husband, Harold, became wealthy working as chief counsel [head lawyer] for Hess Oil. The money from Hess Oil was made primarily from refineries in Saint Croix. Money from my grandma paid for me to go to private school, and I've inherited something like $65,000. I'm not sure how much money my grandma has but I would guess it's over a million dollars.[6]

Both my parents are homeowners in San Francisco. My dad runs his own architecture business. My mom works as tech support for nonprofits. My Nanna's wealth subsidized many parts of my family's life, including the house we lived in, the launch of my dad's business, private school education for me and my siblings and debt-free college.

The timer goes off. It's been a minute. I exhale and sit back. I'd spent most of my college years hiding the fact that I was there thanks to a trust fund. Now I'd just told 70-plus people all about it. This is quite a change.

A wave of exhaustion hits. A tingly sensation. I look around. We're already on to the next person.

It is a lot. The stories back-to-back are a lot. An extensive history of hard work, innovation and creativity, as well as capitalism, colonialism, immigration, land theft, sexism and slavery. I'm riveted.

In the liberal world of San Francisco private schools that I grew up in, everyone pretended they were middle class, even when they

---

6 When I asked my Nanna her net worth that Winter, she did a double take ... and then told me she had around $3 million dollars. At the time it felt like so much money. These days, less so. I was taught early on in RG that so many of us with $$$ are taught to compare ourselves to those above us on the class ladder, minimizing our wealth and never noticing how much more we have than others. I've always found it useful to counter these tendencies by claiming my familial and personal connection to the owning class and my place in the global 1.5%

owned big homes in expensive neighborhoods. No one talked honestly about how the wealth we controlled might be related to the poverty of others. As a young person, I was incredibly curious about exactly how much money the adults around me actually had — and never got to ask.

Hearing people's money stories, with numbers, was a revelation. I felt like I could listen to that sort of honest truth-telling all day.

* * *

My first MMMC in 2003 already had many of the components of what made RG such a powerful space for transformative organizing.

The workshops covered personal, political and financial topics, with titles such as "Navigating Cross-Class Relationships," "Who Wants the Estate Tax?" and "Creating Your Social Justice Giving Plan." There were full group activities, like the money stories exercise I previously described, as well as plenary sessions. From what I can remember, the plenary speakers for some of my first MMMCs included Eli Pariser from MoveOn.org and Van Jones, who, at that time, was leading the Ella Baker Center for Human Rights.

We took the money survey, where everyone is asked to answer a long list of questions about you and your family's money, how it's made, how it grows, the taxes you pay (or don't), what it's invested in and how much you're giving. The survey even had questions such as "How open are you about the wealth in your life with your friends and community?" On Saturday night, all the surveys are compiled, and Sunday morning, there is a PowerPoint presentation of the data.

Especially in those first years, I found the sharing of the survey results a horrifying and sobering experience. What would inevitably be reported is that the young people with wealth in the room had control over many hundreds of millions of dollars and, through family, access to billions more. The survey would show that we were collectively paying a quite low amount in taxes and giving much, much less.

It laid out exactly why the cosponsoring organizations (RG, the Third Wave Fund, the Tides Foundation and the Funding

Exchange) wanted to mobilize these young people with wealth to give more and take responsibility for the money and power in their lives and in their families. I remember wanting to bar the doors and lock us all in the auditorium for a week until we figured out how to move that money NOW!

⋆ ⋆ ⋆

A few months later, I walk up the three flights of stairs to the top-floor apartment I share with two friends. I walk down the carpeted railroad flat hallway and emerge into the living space.

A flashing red light appears on the answering machine on the table. I press the Play button and hear the voice of Karen Pittelman, RG staff organizer. My heart skips a beat. I'm so excited to get her message.

I had come away from MMMC lit up. Energized to take responsibility for the wealth and connections to wealth in my life, and use it in support of the movements for justice that I believed in.

She invites me to attend a Resource Generation leadership training called the Donor Organizing Institute. I pump my arms in delight.

Reading back through the stories from this time in RG, from *No More Prisons* to MMMC to the Donor Organizing Institute...

What Lessons Can I Pull out for Future Generations?

1. **The importance of published stories in the expansion of this burgeoning movement. Books and short publications, newsletters and blogs, because they can be read in private, have helped bring many rich people into this work. From** *Robin Hood Was Right* **in the 70s and 80s, to** *Money Talks and So Can We* **in the 90s, to** *No More Prisons* **and** *Classified: How to Stop Hiding Your Privilege and Use It for Social Change* **in the 2000s, publishing and promoting books has been a successful strategy for growing the base.**[7]

2. **Relationships matter. I don't know if I would have made it to**

---

7 See the Bibliography in the endnotes for more information on these books.

my first MMMC without the reassurance of a trusted friend. Peer-to-peer outreach and relational organizing matters and is vital to bringing wealthy people into political and organizing homes.

3. Money stories are a foundational place to start helping wealthy people find our self-interest in breaking from the class training we've received.

RG Trains Me To Be a Leader and Peer Organizer

On a snowy Boston weekend in early 2004, I walk into a living room at Walker Retreat Center. I'm there to learn how to become a peer organizer with 15 other young people with wealth involved in RG.

Experienced organizers Kenny Bailey and Naomi Swinton lead us through role-plays where we practice how to lead a one-on-one meeting. We try out telling our money stories in new ways, as organizing tools to inspire others to action. We learn about the intertwined history of race, racism and philanthropy in an interactive timeline activity.

At the end, we stand in a circle and make commitments to each other for the bold actions and organizing experiments we're going to try out when we go home. I commit to giving half of my trust fund[8] and to helping grow the RG Bay Area chapter. The staff give us hats, RG business cards and a gold chain with a money sign on it (maybe a cancelable move today, but still funny to me). I am officially deputized to be a young rich kid organizer. I'm thrilled.

One of my favorite things about RG during that time is that it had a sense of humor about itself and us as young people with wealth. A series of animal cartoons that personified class-privilege

---

8 A significant part of my first years in RG involved creating and developing a financial plan and a giving plan. Through RG workshops and publications such as the Social Change Financial Planning Notebook, I was supported to develop a financial plan, where I both saved more, gave more and moved my investments in alignment with my values. When I developed my first giving plan, I shared it with my family and friends, inspiring others to escalate their giving as well. Early on in RG, I learned that getting my financial house in order, and learning to give more generously and systematically, was fundamental to being able to organize other wealthy people to do the same.

patterns. Funny limericks for each of the money myths. The monthly newsletters, written by former staff member Courtney Young, regularly made me laugh. The lightness and levity helped me look at hard topics like money, class, racism and family that I otherwise might have shied away from.

What Do I Take Away From this RG Memory?

1. **The importance of developing a leadership ladder. RG offered multiple opportunities for its constituents (i.e., unpaid participants) to move into more and more leadership. Once I read a book, I could go to a conference. Once I went to a conference, I could be invited to a leadership training. Once I attended an organizing training, I could develop and grow my local chapter. There were always new ways for me to develop my skills and contribute to building this community and movement.**

2. **It was life changing to have spaces to learn the hard skills involved in organizing wealthy people. It wasn't just assumed I would know how to do one-on-one outreach or lead a meeting. I was given chances to practice and develop my confidence and craft. I was given the responsibility to put these skills into action by going to find other wealthy people like me. I was being coached and mentored into leadership step-by-step.**

Praxis Groups and Giving Circles

It's 2010. Instagram has just been released on the iPhone, *Hunger Games* and the first *Harry Potter* movies are making millions at the box office, and I'm spending my late 20s living in Seattle, Washington.

I'm in the living room of a friend and fellow RG member in the Capitol Hill neighborhood. I look around at six other young people with wealth and class privilege sitting on the floor and in cushy chairs, in a simple, IKEA-decorated living room. There's a computer engineer who works at Google, a few teachers, a therapist, a foundation staff person and several nonprofit workers with inherited wealth.

We're talking about what to do next. We've been meeting for the last year on a semi-regular basis. We pick a new topic every time we meet. We often discuss our giving, investment or financial plans. We talk about how to navigate cross-class relationships, how to structure loans to friends, and how to talk to our families about money and giving on our next fancy family vacation.

It's winter in the Northwest. It's cold outside and quite dark at 6 p.m. The curtains are drawn. I like the group, and it's hard that who shows up always changes, and we can't always go deep or continue conversations from previous meetings.

Someone in the circle suggests that we close the group to new members for a while. They suggest that we commit to meeting for the next six to eight months, just us. Each meeting, one or two people will get to workshop a challenge they're taking on, for which they'd like support.

Heads nod. We look around. That seems like a good idea. It's an increased commitment to each other, and that is what I want. I'm already working at RG at the time, and this is certainly a group I am all-in on.

Without being aware of it at the time, we had just decided to start RG's first praxis group.

At the first meeting of our now closed group, we set up the structure. Start with check-ins, where we report back on the commitments we made at the last meeting and share what we've accomplished. One person has 15 minutes to talk about a question, challenge or idea. The group then gets 10 minutes to ask clarifying questions. Finally, the group shares feedback, advice, input and reflections. We always close with each person's new commitment. It could be anything — "make a multiyear donation," "talk to my financial advisor," "look at my investments."

Early on, like the lefty nerds that we are, we call it a Praxis Group.[9] *Praxis* is the Greek word that means theory plus action — and is a favorite of many Marxists and wannabe Marxists, like many of us.

---

9 For years my wife thought it was called a "Practice Group."

By the end of the eight months, we're thrilled with what we've done. We are closer and more committed to each other. Each person has moved forward their money- and class-related goals in significant ways. We are a bonded and tight leadership team ready to take on more! Several of us suggest we continue praxis and expand the experiment by running two praxis groups next round. Hands are raised; leads are assigned.

Another idea comes from our close relationship with Social Justice Fund Northwest (SJFNW). It has been funding progressive organizing efforts in the Northwest since the 1980s. More recently, it has been working to reinvigorate its community and donor base, engaging younger donors like us. Staff people at the organization have mentioned wanting to try cross-class giving circles.[10] Heads nod and more hands are raised. We decide to help develop SJFNW's first round of cross-class giving circles in 2010.

Not even two years later, praxis groups and social justice giving circles have seen significant success for both RG and SJFNW. RG starts sharing the praxis group model with its chapter leaders around the country as an excellent base-building and leadership development strategy. It is a success everywhere people try it, and it is soon being used to build the leadership of subgroups within RG, like people of color, Jews and men.

Today, praxis groups remain a core organizing tool within RG. The curriculum has grown (the current RG praxis guide is 48 pages long), but the basic idea of a closed group of young wealthy people supporting each other to turn theory into action has made a huge difference to many. (Note: This is not a new tool. The women's movement used consciousness-raising groups extensively to build a fighting force of feminist female leaders.)

At the same time, the first Social Justice Fund Northwest giving circle is a huge success. It combines political education with opportunities to share money stories, participate in class-caucusing, learn fundraising and give money to local organizations. The first group exceeds their fundraising goal and

---

10 A giving circle is a form of collective giving where a group of people pool their financial resources and decide together which organizations, individuals or causes to support.

raises over $150,000.

Within a few years, almost all of SJFNW's grantmaking is done through giving circles. There is a vibrant multiracial, multigenerational community lit up by the work of SJFNW. New energy and resources are brought into SJFNW. Other social justice foundations, many of which were part of the Funding Exchange, hear about how SJFNW has been transformed and the money it's moving and decide to develop their own versions of cross-class giving projects.

At this point, in 2025, nine foundations run giving circles using some version of this model, and there is even an organization to coordinate and support this work called the Giving Project Network. There are so many that can claim their place in the lineage of giving projects; humans coming together to collectivize resources and share them with their communities is an ancient tradition — and I'm proud to share Resource Generation's piece of the story.

What Do I Take Away From this Story?

RG's work was able to grow and develop in important ways when it employed tools and lessons in community organizing and political education from other movements, like the women's movement.

Having small consciousness-raising groups for peer education and accountability was extremely helpful in:

1. Increasing access to peer-support caucus spaces.

2. Creating exponentially more leadership opportunities for members.

3. Providing collective accountability for members to move forward their individual goals around leveraging their wealth and privilege.

When paired with "action projects," RG members got into cross-class communities, talked openly about money and class and learned how to fundraise. That was a magic combo.

The RG community would experiment with different types of "action projects": giving circles, like the ones at SJFNW; versions from the Movement Generation Support Committee, coming out of the Bay Area chapter; and the Gulf South Allied Funders, a national group of RG members that partnered with the Twenty-First Century Foundation, Threshold Foundation and Women Donors Network. Together, they moved $1 million per year for three years to the equitable rebuilding of the Gulf South after Hurricane Katrina.

Every time, we saw young people with wealth learning how to speak up, work together, partner with and financially support poor-, working- and middle-class-led efforts for justice.

Over and over in Resource Generation, we saw that caucus spaces + cross-class action projects = more leaders, more money, more power.

Over and over in Resource Generation, we saw that caucus spaces + cross-class action projects = more leaders, more money, more power.

RG Almost Closes Its Doors

Any honest introduction to Resource Generation, and really any part of this world of organizing the rich, should be clear that this work has always been messy, full of contradictions and conflict, heartbreak and hurt feelings.

What examples can I share? Here are a few that come to mind:

I remember sitting in a room with Elspeth Gilmore, when we were co-directors of RG, preparing to lead the opening plenary at a Making Money Make Change conference. I was shaking with fear, tears rolling down my face. I was so scared! I was scared to be visible, to share my thinking, to "get it wrong," to disappoint the many people I respected in that room. Yet, this was my wildest dream come true. I was leading this organization that I cared so much about, and it was absolutely terrifying.

Another memory is standing in the Oakland RG office, getting angry at a staff member who made a mistake on a fundraising letter. It wasn't cute. We ended up in a mediated conversation with a board member. Our relationship had been hard for some time. I felt upset and victimized, vented to my wife and stayed up nights thinking about it. But I was the associate director, I had more positional power; I had treated this staff person with disrespect. I needed to own up and apologize, and I did. My apology didn't fix everything, but I was glad for the support to own my mistake and attempt to repair it.

The challenges aren't just interpersonal; they're organizational too. RG almost folded multiple times in its first decade.

The challenges aren't just interpersonal; they're organizational too. RG almost folded multiple times in its first decade.

Around 2005, Hez left as Executive Director (ED), and Taij Mootelall was hired for the position. Taij was an accomplished fundraiser and racial justice activist, both in her Indo-Caribbean community and through her leadership in Blackout Arts Collective.[11] She was also brand new to Resource Generation, had no relationships in the community or direct experience with the work, and was entering as the first person of color to serve as the Executive Director (ED). What was already going to be a challenge, quickly turned much harder.

Within weeks of starting, Taij learned that RG was struggling financially. As well, there was conflict and burnout amongst the staff. In a classic setup for a woman of color ED in a largely white organization, Taij was handed a difficult situation, not of her own making, and the responsibility to clean it up.

By the spring of 2006, with the financial situation still tenuous, RG's fiscal sponsor laid off the staff. With the help of several board members, and some emergency fundraising, Taij raised the money to keep herself and one other staff member, Jamie Schweser, on board.

Taij moved the organization's office to NYC, where she lived, and worked long hours to rebuild. RG never closed and did regain

11 The Blackout Arts Collective, started in New York City in 1997, was a group of artists, organizers, students, and more working to empower communities of color through the arts, activism and education. The organization still exists, but has since evolved into a national network who collaborate on select projects, still utilizing art to push for progressive social change.

its footing. Part of what got the organization through was a grant from the Kellogg Foundation for work with young people of color with wealth. This money was used, at least partially, to keep the organization afloat.

At future board meetings, this time became known as 'the special period,' invoking the term used in Cuba for the time of economic hardship in the early 90s. Taij, alongside many other leaders from that period, deserve a ton of credit for ensuring the organization survived.

The second time RG faced a financial crisis was during a subsequent Executive Director transition in the early 2010s. Again, an executive director of color was hired with extensive organizing experience but few, if any, relationships with the membership.[12] Within a few years, fundraising slowed and the organization, once again, faced a budget shortfall. Issues of money, race, class, power, communication and culture were threatening the long-term viability of the project.

RG emerged from these difficult periods with important clarity on key structural issues – the board needed to up its game around financial management, and the organization needed to be more systematic about asking all its constituents for financial support. These were important lessons the organization needed to learn in order to grow. That said, RG has operated with a significant financial safety net because of the wealth of its base. This has allowed it to weather hard times in ways other organizations might not.

If building functional cross-class, multi-racial teams was easy, everyone would be doing it!

As I like to say, if organizing the rich towards justice was easy it would have already been done! If building functional cross-class, multi-racial teams was easy, everyone would be doing it! Let's not pretend that it's ever been comfortable, even as it has always been so worthwhile.

---

12 Since 2017, RG has been led by executive directors of color in Iimay Ho and Yahya Alazrak. Both were on staff for several years before moving into the executive director position. This slower move into leadership seems to have worked quite well.

What Lessons Do I Want You to Take From These Stories?

1. **Expect this work to be hard and messy.**

2. **Expect classism, racism, sexism, anti-semitism, and other oppressions to show themselves over and over in the work. It is not a failing of any organization that these oppressions show up. It is just where we're at as a society.**

    We need to attend to all the ways these oppressions poison our work and the lives of our leaders and members. Let us get skilled at addressing them, without resorting to either harshness or liberalism.[13]

3. **Learn and practice the art of navigating conflict, repairing relationships, owning mistakes, and handling attacks.**

4. **Bringing people into leadership without significant experience or relationships with the wealthy community they will be leading can be a real setup.**

Launching a Membership Program

In 2010, after the second financial crisis, the board adopted and the staff launched a membership model for the organization. In a membership model, a classic structure for community organizing groups, every young person with wealth who came in contact with RG would be asked to become a member by donating $250 or more per year. This was a big change.

In RG's first decade, the organization had been hesitant to ask its own constituents for financial support. It relied on a small number of major donors and foundations for the majority of its budget. This was a problem when losing a few major donors could (and did) send the organization into financial trouble.

The membership program was meant to shift all that and enable RG to be financially supported by the young rich kids it organized, helping RG's constituents take responsibility for the financial health of the organization for the first time.

13 In this context, I am using "liberal" to mean avoiding disagreement for the sake of a false sense of unity.

It might seem like a no-brainer today, but at the time, many were hesitant to consistently ask RG's base for support. There was significant resistance among constituents to fund RG at all, this program for rich people (like them). In the first years of the program, we supported numerous RG member leaders to talk openly about why they were becoming an RG member and why their giving to RG was a worthwhile investment. The community at large needed help understanding that a dollar to RG meant exponentially more money out the door to movements. Many

> **There was significant resistance among constituents to fund RG at all, this program for rich people (like them).**

young people with wealth in the community needed help seeing that it was OK to invest in a political home for rich people like themselves. It took time to move away from a service orientation, where young people with wealth could drop into individual RG programs and get what they wanted without being asked to support RG's long-term success.

After several years of one-on-one meetings, membership asks at retreats, fundraising emails explaining the program, and "We are RG" stickers sent to every dues-paying member, the culture had changed. RG became 80%-plus funded by individual member contributions. This base of support included a team of major donors, who named themselves The Tracies, after RG's first executive director, Tracy Hewat. Each member of The Tracies gave $10,000 or more per year, for three years or more. This crew of multiyear major donors, alongside the broader membership base, gave RG the financial foundation to be confident and bold as it planned for the future.

Where Are We Today?

Everything happens sitting or standing around in circles.

I'll always remember Taij Moteelall leading us in a closing activity at Making Money Make Change during her years as executive director, from 2005 to 2008. Everyone from the retreat stood in a circle — young people with wealth, there as participants, alongside a mixed-class group of staff, the board and presenters.

It was always a multiracial, multigender, cross-class group.

"My liberation depends on your liberation."

She would ask us to, one at a time, look to the person to the left, make eye contact and say, "My liberation depends on your liberation." Then that person would look to their left and tell the next person. And the next. Until the message went all the way around the circle. It might sound hokey and forced but it felt real. We had just spent four days breaking all sorts of class rules, talking openly about money and wealth, committing to redistribution and greater courage and integrity. In my mind, I could see the relational bonds being wound around each of us as we closed out the retreat.

It's no coincidence that young people have always been in the lead of many of the world's most revolutionary and hopeful efforts. Young people are more able to remember what we are all born knowing: that we are all connected and meant to play and enjoy each other, oppose what is unfair and do big things. It is not surprising that an organization like RG, as a community of young adults, has been at the forefront of efforts to organize the rich toward justice.

As Iimay Ho, RG's executive director from 2017 to 2021, wrote in their June 2021 farewell blog post to the RG community:

> If you've been involved in RG, you've probably heard someone talk about funding the "movement ecosystem" and "anchor organizations" within those ecosystems. This is referring to the web of relationships that organizations build with each other, and the best practice of supporting many different kinds of organizations to support the health of the overall ecosystem. "Anchor organizations" are ones that are deeply intertwined with many different organizations and increase the overall strength and capacity of the network.
>
> I'm going to stake a claim that RG is an anchor organization, especially in the ecosystem of donor organizing and social justice philanthropy. RGers have gone on to become founders of, or core organizers within, Regenerative Finance, Solidaire, Donors of Color Network, and Movement Voter Project. We supported the launch of Resource Movement (Canada) and

Resource Justice (UK). Our members take on leadership in their family foundations, start their own social justice foundations and giving circles, or are leaders and active participants in giving projects at social justice foundations around the country.

As I write this, in 2025, Resource Generation has the largest membership base of people with wealth and class privilege, attempting to work for redistribution, of any group I've heard of, now and in the past. Several more international sister organizations have launched: Resource Transformation in German-speaking countries in Europe and Resource Generation Australia. Research by Laura Wernick, associate professor at Fordham University, has shown that RG involvement increased overall giving for all young people with wealth in their programming, with dues-paying members giving 16 times more than before they got involved.[14]

2009 photo from RG Board and Staff Retreat (Courtesy of Michael Gast)

RG Staff photo from 2023 MMMC (Courtesy of Resource Generation)

14 L.J. Wernick, "Critical Consciousness Development Impact on Social Justice Movement Giving Among Wealthy Activists," *Social Work Research* 40, no. 3 (2016): 159-69.

While RG has many imperfections and challenges, it remains a foundational part of the broader ecosystem and a vital learning lab for this work.

Lessons and Questions

Reading through these stories, reflecting on a handful of the cherished memories from this time of my life, I am left with a few reflections:

Structure matters. So much of what RG has accomplished is based on borrowing and adapting organizing models and structures from previous efforts in poor, working- and middle-class communities. These structures, from local chapters to praxis groups and a membership model, have helped RG scale its work. Let's keep on learning from cutting-edge organizing models and modify them for this unique constituency.

Cross-class, multiracial leadership is important and helpful. Don't leave rich people alone. FUBU (for us by us) rich people organizing has significant limitations. Rich people organizing without caucus spaces has significant limitations. We need both.

Shame and guilt don't work — community and kindness, coupled with high expectations, do. If wealthy people are supported and lifted up, we can look at the hard stuff (like the ways we've profited off of slavery, genocide, war and exploitation) and work to repair what we have done. A mix of fun and humor, alongside real talk, is a winning combination. We can hear the hardest things if our tone conveys kindness, belief and respect. And, always, always, keep expectations high. Don't agree or collude with our bad behavior. Give us real work to do in care of our own liberation.

Racial justice is for everyone. Create racial justice programming for white wealthy people. Create racial justice programming for people of color with wealth. Give everyone the chance to learn how to fight against racism, separately and together. Taking action against racism won't make things easier, but it will make so much more possible. There is no just society, healthy economy or liberated future without an end to racism.

Be rigorous about money. We (the rich) will lie unless you force us to be honest. And then we will still try to lie. Giving plans and money surveys, praxis groups and one-on-one coaching all matter. Communal accountability matters. Make us say it out loud, with others, and then check in on us, again and again. Once we get wealthy, we are fighting against a system that is meant to keep us wealthy and uphold the power structure. Doing anything different takes a ton of work.

Help the wealthy give up the search for being rich and righteous. Make a long-term plan to give back the money individually and structurally. Help wealthy people make a plan to break their dependence on inherited wealth and extractive finance. Prepare for a world where we have won!

Figure out what it means to be well nested in working-class-led movements. Figure out what it means to build working-class power. Let's not be satisfied with the individual divestment plans of the wealthy. Let's not be satisfied with supporting a bunch of middle-class nonprofits or individual mutual aid efforts. Let's win structural change for working people.

Make space for the feelings, and don't believe the feelings. Doing this work brings up hard stuff for everyone. About our early money memories and money messages. About our internalized superiority and inferiority. About our isolation and loneliness. Make space for people to process those feelings. And remind people that those feelings are old and don't need to be acted upon. This work will often be uncomfortable and that's OK.

There are so many questions that still need to be answered. What are a few of the questions I'm thinking about today?

1. How do we create entryways for wealthy people who are more mainstream, new money, straight, and corporate to get involved in this work? This more 'normie' part of the owning class holds the majority of the wealth

and institutional power, and is one that RG and other redistribution oriented groups have mostly failed to engage.

2. What is our north star? Over the years, RG's mission has shifted from "leveraging privilege for social change" to "redistribution of land, wealth and power." What is the world we are working toward, and how do we create effective strategies to get there? How can we be even clearer about where we're going while making room for everyone to get on board?

3. How do we have goals and a strategy that aren't just about being the most righteous individual rich people but about building the power of the multiracial working class? For too long, we have been satisfied being the rebellious rich without being connected to the labor movement or part of a real plan for winning power for working people.

The fire that was lit when I was 23 is stronger than ever. So much of the way I lead now is due to my time with Resource Generation and its transformative organizing model.

RG has expanded my imagination of what is possible. I have passed the metaphorical baton to the next generation in RG, but I'm still here, as part of a growing intergenerational movement. All of us together, this ragtag, brave and holy crew, have seeded so much.

It's been a decade since I left my RG retirement party wondering, "What do I do now?" It turns out that I get to keep on learning and growing, with courage and humor. I can look back, learn about my lineage and bring all my ancestors and mentors with me. I get to move forward with everyone I met from my first MMMC until now. I can keep on holding hands as we step together off a new cliff, walking into the unknown, watching as the ground reappears underneath our feet.

There is so much more to do and to say. So many more stories to tell. But I will always be thankful for where it all began. ∎

CHILDHOOD LESSONS

Nigel Charles

Nigel Charles has been a professional donor organizer since 2017. He started as the director of donor organizing at Bread & Roses Community Fund in Philadelphia. There, he led a cross-class, multiracial crew in learning how to become skilled, bold, class-conscious donors and fundraisers to local social justice organizations and movements. These days, he works at Solidaire, organizing its primarily white and wealthy individual member base to understand their own stake and strategic role in collective liberation movements and embrace their power and protagonism as donors, fundraisers and peer organizers.

This piece was originally published in December 2024 on the Organize the Rich Substack.

I've been reflecting a lot on childhood lessons, ways of being I naturally absorbed while growing up in a working-poor, single-parent Black family.

Unknown to me then, the wisdom of the poor, the immigrant and the Black family was being embedded in me and would become guideposts that lead me in my work as a donor organizer.

The wisdom of the poor, the immigrant and the Black family was being embedded in me and would become guideposts that lead me in my work as a donor organizer.

There was no perceptible way that "little Nig-ee" (my grandma's nickname for me) could know that, many years in the future, he would be organizing towards a world of racial, economic, social justice — but in hindsight it makes sense.

By the sixth grade I had a keen understanding of the ways that access to resources impacted the quality of my education, food, healthcare and life. I understood that poverty is expensive — families who had better access to a grocery store were paying less for the same food I got at the corner store. I understood that government-run programs had preferential treatment based on social location — free lunch at my all-Black elementary school paled in comparison to the lunch at the downtown magnet school I attended for middle school. I understood that we did not all have the same access to information — I could only carry home a limited number of books from the library while other students could do research on their household computers. I also saw how my people resisted these systems, creating hope and pathways to a better future.

In this essay I reflect on some of the childhood lessons that I've found most useful in my work. I want them to be known and seen. I want to celebrate and honor the power of my family and my

Nigel's third birthday party at his maternal grandmother's house in Philadelphia (Courtesy of Nigel Charles)

community, and the way they have enabled me to move others.

Woven into my story are glimpses of a different world. In this world collectivism, connection and community are embraced, shaping the ways we move and interact with each other.

For much of my life I did not know that these early life lessons were different from the ones many wealth-holders were receiving in their formative years. It wasn't until my time at Bread & Roses Community Fund in Philadelphia that I learned their full power.

At Bread & Roses, I worked with cross-class, multiracial and intergenerational groups who believed in the power of community organizing to challenge existing systems of oppression. Through the Giving Project model, we brought together cohorts of community members across race and class to engage in political education, organize resources — people and money — and make grants to local community organizing efforts in Philly. As the director of donor organizing, I would share my stories with these groups to deepen our sense of connection, only to find that the values I believed to be universal — such as belonging and responsibility to one's community — felt foreign to many of the wealthier people in our community.

It was while leading those groups, sitting in on those meetings, that I realized that these lessons could be especially supportive to owning-class people looking for different ways of being, different ways of moving money and different ways of relating to their families and loved ones.

Now, in my role as a donor organizing strategist at Solidaire Network, I have come to see these lessons as one of my movement superpowers. I experience over and over that my mom, my pastor, my family and my community are always with me, helping move the hearts and minds of the wealthy people I organize.

> **I experience over and over that my mom, my pastor, my family and my community are always with me, helping move the hearts and minds of the wealthy people I organize.**

Political Education Weekend at 2018 Gender Justice Giving Project at Bread & Roses Community Fund (Courtesy of Nigel Charles)

The Meaning of Family

My mom emigrated from Trinidad and Tobago to the U.S. at the age of 18, with very little means. She raised my brother and me on her own, figuring things out in ways I still find hard to fully grasp. As the sole provider for our small family unit, she ensured that we understood the value of each dollar. We knew how to take advantage of discounts while grocery shopping, how to stick to a budget and how to make things in the house last. As she was solely responsible for two boys, no one would critique her for keeping her focus narrowed on the two of us, but family had a much more expansive definition to her.

We learned that family is about who's invested in you and who wants the best for you — not just bloodlines. Your mom's best friend's kids are your cousins, the family friend who checks in on you is your uncle and the congregation members you see every week are your siblings. We contributed to the betterment of all of our families' lives, and they did the same for us. And none of that got in the way of us improving our lives.

One day, out of the blue, my mom told us we were moving from our one-bedroom apartment into a house — no warning. But that's how she was: always finding ways to improve our lives, for all of our family. Our home became the place for family gatherings, where tired mothers dropped their babies off for a night of rest, and for folks in between living situations to stay for a while.

In this work I've learned that my expansive understanding of family is a shift from how many wealth-holders are socialized. Oftentimes, the emphasis in wealthy families is on preserving a rigid idea of "legacy" tied only to your blood relations. In practice this can mean that land, money and institutional power must stay within the family, with any larger sense of social responsibility limited to a token commitment to charity.

My upbringing proved that two things can be true — the family unit can be taken

> In this work I've learned that my expansive understanding of family is a shift from how many wealth-holders are socialized.

care of while investing in the lives of others. Even more than that, we could take on more people as family, making their challenges our own, and build a stronger system of support along the way.

Do the Right Thing

Walking home from school with an honor roll certificate in hand, I began to plan what I would do with the $1 for each "A" I would receive. I had received $4 for my grades at the end of the last marking period, so my current seven As felt lush. Although my teacher had written on the bottom of my report how I had the tendency to distract other classmates when I had completed my work, I was confident my mother would have grace on me.

I strutted down the street, dreaming of all the snacks I would buy at the corner store. This was not a time for budgeting! I had grand plans to splurge on all the snacks the corner store could offer. When I got home, I considered calling her on the phone to share the news, but thought better of it. She was still at work and I wanted her full attention. Once she was home I would break the news and receive my reward.

Imagine my shock when my reward was given in the form of a life lesson, not physical currency: "You do what you're supposed to because it's the right thing to do." It felt like my mom was moving in slow motion as she lovingly reminded me that my education was the real reward.

It would take me years to understand that she was also saying that we did not have extra money at the moment, and even longer to fully understand what she meant about the "real reward."

The expectation for a reward in the world of philanthropy is a real phenomenon. For the right amount, your name can be added to an acknowledgment, a program or even a building. I remember hearing the frustrations of wealthy donors, from a lack of acknowledgment, spilling over during the 2020 Uprisings [triggered by George Floyd's murder] and the Standing Rock protests [to stop the Dakota Access Pipeline in 2016-2017]. While movement leaders were focused on the immediate safety of activists and the urgency of defeating a disastrous pipeline, many donors struggled with the same thing my third-grade self did.

They did not understand that the movement groups, much like my mother, had nothing left to give to them.

In practice, I try to prepare donors early on: when you give, the organizations you support might not be able to acknowledge you right away. The chronic underfunding of movement work, maxed-out staff, and a general lack of fundraising capacity and training often result in traditional development-related tasks being neglected. As frontline organizers put their bodies on the line to create a just and equitable world for us all, we should approach them with patience and grace. Whether a donor receives a thank-you or not, the "real reward" will likely take years (maybe decades or generations) of consistent effort before it can really be enjoyed and appreciated. Like my mother taught me, I encourage the donors I work with to do the right thing because it is the right thing. Giving isn't about the pat on the back; it's about doing what needs to be done.

What if we saw our giving to movements in ways beyond acknowledgment/reward? What if we saw our contributions as a way of becoming a part of movements, adding our resources, skills and experience to the cache of tools we use to craft our collective future? What if we focused on the "real reward": a just and equitable world for all of us?

What if we saw our contributions as a way of becoming a part of movements, adding our resources, skills, and experience to the cache of tools we use to craft our collective future? What if we focused on the "real reward," a just and equitable world for all of us?

NIGEL CHARLES

Illustration by former Solidaire digital organizer, Bronwyn Walls (Courtesy of Solidaire)

All of Us or None of Us

My brother and I loved playing video games. We saved money from birthday cards and found odd jobs just to buy used games at the local Electronics Boutique, blocks away from our house. We would carefully trade in old games to get new ones whenever we could.

One fine day, my mom decided to help us buy a used Super Nintendo to add to our gaming collection. So much had to go right to make this moment possible. My mother didn't often have extra money to contribute to larger recreational purchases, but the used console being on sale and a small bonus from work opened up a window for us. My brother and I had to contribute as well, trading in some of our video games for store credit and using up our savings. We were so excited to have multiple game systems! It was to be a glorious time.

Plot twist! Our mother had other ideas than letting us stockpile multiple video game systems. Our good fortune meant we would be passing along our old Nintendo system to someone else, namely our cousins, who had recently moved from Trinidad & Tobago to Washington, D.C.

We tried to resist as she had us pack up our old Nintendo. We shared our grand plans of collecting multiple systems and games to fit any mood. We discussed the economic benefit of holding onto it, knowing that video game consoles accumulated value over time. She was resolute; she refused our plan to "move up" without bringing others with us. Our moment of blessing meant we could be a blessing to someone else.

Our moment of blessing meant we could be a blessing to someone else.

We couldn't hold onto something for an expanded benefit when others didn't have. We couldn't hold onto something for future benefit when others could benefit from it right now.

This story is about video games, but as children, the games were our wealth. Although we were raised to share without having to be asked, this moment pushed our growing edges, asking us to put theory into practice. We had clear systems for how to take turns playing the game, brought our system to the houses of friends who didn't have one so they could enjoy it and let friends borrow games at times. But this moment required more of us. This moment asked for us to let go.

Letting go can be hard even when it is aligned with our values. My brother and I knew that an upgraded system would meet our entertainment needs, but having excess was our aim at that moment. To have more games to choose from than we could ever actually play felt like a luxury we had worked hard for. It took my mother to remind us that our luxury was directly related to our cousin's lack.

Grounded in her experiences as a Trinidadian child in a working-poor family, my mother was able to provide clarity on how our motives were misaligned with our family's values. She understood the relationship between lack and excess better than we did, and provided guidance in a challenging moment.

Similarly, working-class professionals in the philanthropic sector often tap into their experiences to provide greater perspective to owning-class donors. In my personal story this type

Nigel leading a Community Organizing & Change session with community members who are part of Philadelphia's Millennial Advisory Committee (Courtesy of Nigel Charles)

of guidance meant making a difference in my cousins' lives. In the philanthropic sector this guidance can mean making a difference in policies that impact millions of lives.

As I work with wealthy donors I often lovingly push their growing edges, asking them to move more money to movements for justice. In many cases their self-imposed limitations are cemented in lessons of individualistic upward mobility, creating legacy foundations that last in perpetuity, and fear of losing the social benefits connected to their wealth. Ironically, these same people share with me that they crave community, want to meaningfully engage with their family outside of foundation giving and feel limited by the unwritten rules of how they must behave in certain social settings. To them I offer my stories of a different way of being and different ways of thinking about what is enough: a world where we embrace collective responsibility and contribute where we have abundance.

The truth is that we never actually missed that old Nintendo.

Filling the Barrel

My childhood church remains integral to my understanding of collective giving. Most of the members of that church emigrated to this country from the Caribbean, leaving family members behind. In fact, many of them came to this country with the primary goal of sending resources back to others. Many quickly realized that climbing the class ladder was way harder than they expected, making it challenging for them to fulfill these commitments to their loved ones. Still, they leaned on the practices of collective giving that they had previously learned and benefited from.

Every now and then a church mother would show up to the church with an empty 55-gallon barrel and a list of people in mind who needed help. The case never had to be made — just an announcement to our congregation and people moved to action. For the next few weeks, we all gave from our excess and invited our friends and family to do the same. None of our wardrobes or pantries were the largest, but it never took long to fill the barrel, or several, with clothing and food.

I love to reflect on this story because it reveals a simple

Nigel *(right)* outside of his childhood church with his older brother *(left)* (Courtesy of Nigel Charles)

truth about collective giving. None of us could fill the barrel alone, but together it never took long. I am encouraged that in the philanthropic world, collective giving programs, like the Philadelphia Black Giving Circle and Network, are being developed throughout the field, providing opportunities for connection and increased giving.

Still, I have a deeper desire for donors resourcing movement work. I long for a day when all donors, especially wealthy donors, commit to and find a place of political home, much like the members of my childhood church found a spiritual home. Our sense of home created the opportunities for our church mothers to clearly communicate the needs of others. It provided a centralized place for people to give their donations. It helped us to coordinate quickly and invite our extended community to participate as well. It also meant that when people were in need, they knew where to find us. Through the safety and trust of this congregation, our contributions were valued, and we could take pride in our shared achievements. I think these components can directly translate to the more formal world of philanthropy. I hope that as owning-class donors continue to engage in collective giving projects, they also seek places where they can build community and be politically grounded.

Lessons that Shape Us

One of the most enjoyable parts of this work for me is telling my stories and creating space for donors to share theirs. As we share with each other it becomes apparent that the lessons that ground me show up in their lives as well, regardless of their background. Moments of collectivism, community and connection are a part of the human experience, regardless of the socio-economic status we were born into.

Whatever your background, I encourage you to identify your own personal stories where these themes make an appearance. As you reflect, explore the feelings that come up for you. No matter how these values show up in your life or the lives of your ancestors, you carry these stories and experiences with you and deserve to spend time reflecting on the parts that are fulfilling. You can do this even while challenging any messages of individualism, isolation and competition that you find, and that are in opposition to the vision of the world you want to bring into being.

Everyone has something positive from their heritage they can identify with, and it is important for us to look for those spots to ground us as we give and organize. Just as I have my mom and my community at my back, supporting me wherever I go, I want each of the wealthy people I work with to feel and claim the humanity and courage of the people who poured into them.

So what's your story?

What lessons did you learn about wealth and giving as a child? How do your childhood lessons on collectivism, community and connection inform the ways you give now?

I'd love to hear your story! ▪

WHAT IF WE EACH TOOK RESPONSIBILITY FOR ORGANIZING PEOPLE WHO SHARE OUR CLASS BACKGROUND?

"ORGANIZE MONEY BEHIND ORGANIZED PEOPLE"

Interview With Leah Hunt-Hendrix

Leah Hunt-Hendrix is the co-founder of Solidaire and Way to Win, two of the leading groups organizing the rich toward justice in the United States. She received her Ph.D. in religion, ethics and politics from Princeton University and recently co-authored a book, *Solidarity: The Past, Present and Future of a World-Changing Idea*. She was born and raised in New York City.

This piece is taken from a two-part interview published on the Organize the Rich Substack in June 2023 and November 2024.

Mike: How did you come to participate in engaging wealthy people around social justice?

Leah: My mom's father started an oil company, Hunt Oil. My mom inherited a portion of that company and started receiving dividends from it in her 30's and 40's. With her sister Swanee, she started a foundation called, at first, The Hunt Alternatives Fund and then called The Sister Fund, which focused on women and girls.

Ever since I was little, I watched my mom work as a donor organizer.[1] I wasn't interested in philanthropy, but in my 20s, I did start thinking about my class background. I was always interested in inequality, especially from having moved around and living in Manhattan and then also living in rural New Mexico. From a young age, I was really struck by inequality in America.

I found Resource Generation, where you were leading at that time, and that was very helpful in learning about class privilege. During those same years, I was in grad school studying political

---

1 Leah's mom, Helen LaKelly Hunt, is a powerhouse wealthy donor organizer, one of the early supporters of the women's funding movement, cofounding the Dallas Women's Foundation, The New York Women's Foundation, the Women's Funding Network and Women Moving Millions.

philosophy and I found Mark Randazzo, who was running the Funders Network on Trade and Globalization (FNTG).[2] I was really interested in international affairs and political science, and I ended up going as part of an FNTG delegation to the World Social Forum.[3] It was very inspiring and I learned a lot there about global grassroots struggles.

I decided to spend a few years living abroad, in the Middle East. I came back to work on my Ph.D., and pretty soon Occupy Wall Street started. I was interested in getting money out of politics at the time — the Supreme Court had recently ruled on *Citizens United,*[4] and I'd joined the board of an organization working to reverse that decision. So that interest, and the graduate work I was doing, which involved a study of democracy and social movements, made me want to go down to Occupy every day to listen and learn about the perspectives and strategies people had there but I couldn't really figure out my role. As a wealthy person, it just felt wrong to be leading direct actions or doing something like that. I worked for a while in the Orientations Working Group where I set up a welcome table. I thought that could be a good role for me. But then a friend was like, "You know, your role should be organizing rich people." It wasn't necessarily what I wanted to hear; it certainly didn't sound like the most fun job, but it made sense.

> But then a friend was like, "You know, your role should be organizing rich people." It wasn't necessarily what I wanted to hear; it certainly didn't sound like the most fun job, but it made sense.

2 FNTG was a philanthropic intermediary that worked alongside the global justice movement for many years, moving wealthy individuals and foundations to support people's movements primarily in the Global South. FNTG turned into EDGE Funders (Engaged Donors for Global Equity).

3 The World Social Forum is an annual gathering of civil society organizations from across the world. From the beginning, it was meant as a left, grassroots alternative to the Davos summit in Switzerland, where the political and economic elite meet and attempt to set the vision for the future. The World Social Forum's first meeting was in 2001 in Brazil.

4 In *Citizens United*, the 2010 case, the United States Supreme Court ruled to allow corporations and wealthy donors to spend unlimited money on elections.

In 2012, as the Occupy movement began to wane, I was part of a small group of friends thinking about what we would do next. I was able to hash out some ideas with them about what it would look like for me to do more funder and wealthy people organizing. I had joined the Democracy Alliance, which was started in the early 2000's as a political donor community, to understand how political and funder organizing worked. And a group of us basically decided we're going to build something similar, but with a progressive orientation. We started calling this project Solidaire, and I began working on it with Farhad Ebrahimi.[5] Billy [Wimsatt] was a huge support;[6] it would not have happened without him. Billy taught me how to facilitate conference calls, how to make spreadsheets, how to follow-up with people and be an organizer. We started building this new group. About eight of us started having monthly dinners and hashing out what it would look like, how it would work. We created some initial bylaws of what would become Solidaire.

So that's how it all started.

Mike: What do you see as the lineage of your work organizing wealthy people? And who have been your mentors?

Leah: Definitely my mom. She showed me that this was actually a thing to do, and that it took a lot of work but could be really impactful and transformative for the people involved. I loved that her community was a lot of the people she organized with. That seemed very meaningful. Also, my Aunt Swanee and Tracy Gary.[7] I always think of Tracy as the high mother of donor organizing. I learned a lot watching them all organize a movement of wealthy women donors that accompanied the women's movement. They created foundations with cross-class boards, and an attention to

---

5 Farhad Ebrahimi is a wealthy inheritor, organizer and strategist who most recently was the founder and president of the spend-down Chorus Foundation and, now, in 2025, works at Solidaire.

6 Billy is Billy Wimsatt, founder of Movement Voter Project, co-founder of Solidaire and author; an excerpt from his book *No More Prisons* is featured in this anthology.

7 Tracy Gary is a long-time leader in the women's philanthropy movement and in the world of social justice philanthropy. She is the co-founder of many organizations including the Women's Foundation of California, Women Donors Network, the Women's Funding Network, Resourceful Women, Changemakers and Inspired Legacies.

the role of race. They were second-wave feminists, in many ways, but my mom welcomed the "third wave" — in fact, the Third Wave Foundation (now Third Wave Fund), led by Amy Richards, Cat Gund, Rebecca Walker, Vivien Labaton and others, rented space in the Sister Fund's office, so some of those women also became great mentors to me.

2018 photo from a planning meeting with movement leaders, figuring out Way to Win's priorities (Courtesy of Leah Hunt-Hendrix)

Mike: Are there any stories from this work that you want future generations to particularly know and understand?

Leah: Perhaps I'll tell the story of the founding of Way to Win, because it's also a story about how building a new institution can help shift an ecosystem.

As I mentioned, I was a member of the Democracy Alliance (DA), which was a very important organization in many ways. The DA has done a lot to organize high-powered, major dollars, and move political resources. I'm very excited about their new executive director, Pamela Shifman. And I think that the DA has shifted away from the critique I'm about to offer, but historically, it had a pretty elitist, white, male dynamic. For example, we heard a lot of complaints from organizations funded by the DA that they were treated as "vendors" to do the donors' bidding, rather than as partners who had visions of their own, that were informed by their expertise from the ground.

One time there was this exercise at a DA conference where we were sitting at circular tables and they had a couple of questions for each table to discuss. One of the questions was, "Which do you think is more important to focus on going into 2016, racial justice or electoral politics?"

That's when Tory [Gavito] and Jen [Ancona, co-founders of Way to Win] and I were like, "Oh my gosh, this whole thing is just built on the wrong paradigm." There seemed to be a lack of understanding among the political establishment that a massive number of Americans are disenfranchised and disempowered by racism, and that questions about race have a huge impact on electoral politics and vice versa. You just can't separate racial justice and electoral politics. Think about the Southern Strategy[8] — one of the main tactics used by the Right since the 1960s (but also throughout American history). The Right uses racially divisive language to assemble its base. It's a fundamental component of American politics.

You just can't separate racial justice and electoral politics.

So it was 2016. The establishment was all in for Hillary. They would never entertain Bernie as a viable candidate. And that was frustrating. There was just this confidence that Hillary was the God-ordained next president. Then Trump won. But was there a deep rethinking about our previous assumptions and strategies? Not at all. The same people who led the charge into 2016 pulled together after the election to dictate the way forward, simply blaming their loss on Comey and the FBI and the fiasco around Hillary's emails. I was so mad, I rage-wrote an article about this that got published in *Politico*.[9]

At the next DA conference, the strategy they were laying out for the next period was exactly the same as the strategy going into 2016 — basically, TV ads and a focus on the Midwest, no real attention to the South, to young people, to people of color, to questions of ideology. That's when I started texting some people I saw as allies. We had a text thread with Farhad Ebrahimi, Billy Wimsatt, Tory Gavito, Jen Ancona, Ashindi Maxton, Jason Franklin, and a couple other people who were at the conference.

---

8 The Southern Strategy was a Republican Party electoral strategy to increase political support among white voters in the U.S. South by appealing to racism against African Americans.

9 "The Wrong Way to Rebuild the Democratic Party," *Politico*, February 24, 2017.

I called an emergency meeting. We left the lecture hall and went into a side room to talk.

It was basically a broom closet. We all squeezed in.

Through that time, between 2012 and 2017, Farhad and I had both been participating in the DA and building Solidaire. The idea was, let's build something on the outside and let's work to also help move this organization from the inside. But after 2017, I felt like we needed a venue to discuss new political strategies and really deal with what was happening in the electoral landscape.

So in that little broom closet, we decided to write up a concept paper for a new political funding vehicle, a new political community.

I wrote the first draft of the concept paper, and Jen and Tory added lots of edits and comments to the Google doc. They were just so engaged and brilliant. Tory had the idea of calling for a "New Southern Strategy" — a strategy used by the Democratic Party that recognized the role of race in politics, and could take back the South. Jen had ideas about messaging and building a narrative shop. We knew we wanted to focus on funding long-term organizing, not just astroturf strategies every two years and bad TV commercials.

Pretty quickly the three of us were building this new thing together. All three of us had other full-time jobs. I was still running Solidaire. Tory was running the Texas Donor Table [called the Texas Future Project]. Jen was vice president of the Women Donors Network. So we just kept hot potato-ing the building of this new institution to each other, each as we could hold it. Then finally, Jen and I both agreed that Tory should be the president. We sat her down and helped her to realize that she could leave her job and take this on, we would raise the money and it would be okay. That was a big leap!

We pretty quickly built a table of supporters like Quinn Delaney, Steve Phillips, Liz Simons, Molly Gochman. It was Quinn Delaney who actually named it Way to Win. We consulted with tons of state-based groups and partners in the field to understand how the old model was broken, and how to fix it. We would have these small meetings around the country where we would just take a lot of input from these initial donors and partner organizations on how to build it. It was a very collective process.

And then it was off to the races. Alabama Senate elections in 2017: black women, like DeJuana Thompson,[10] were responsible for beating the horrible Republican candidate. National and congressional elections in 2018: Justice Democrats started building "the Squad," with our support.[11] And then a full-on strategy to flip Georgia and Arizona in 2020, which we did!

Mike: If you could identify a few priorities for progressive wealthy people organizing in the next five years, what would they be?

Leah: For me, the drama of politics is about organized people in opposition to organized money. Part of our work in the progressive donor world is to organize money behind organized people or, to say it differently, divert financial resources from the ruling class towards the multiracial working class so that they can build a better society for all.

I would argue that progressive wealthy people should focus on two key priorities, the two pillars that uphold our social and economic system: one priority should be rebuilding the labor movement, which is the institutional representation of the working class. If that pillar is strong, benefits will flow to all of society more broadly. And the flip side of that coin is restraining corporate power, which is the vehicle that endows the few, the elite.

It was labor unions that won the weekend, the 8-hour work

---

10 DeJuana Thompson is founder of Woke Vote, an organization designed to engage, mobilize and turnout African American voters in the South.

11 Justice Democrats is a progressive political action committee and caucus founded by leaders in Bernie Sanders' 2016 presidential campaign. It works to elect progressives, often those running against more mainstream Democrats. "The Squad" is an informal progressive and left-wing coalition in the U.S. House of Representatives forming part of the Democratic Caucus.

day, and child labor protections in the wake of the Industrial Revolution. Labor unions benefit all of society because they expand the safety net, they fight for standards and conditions that impact everyone, and they give a political voice to the working class, which is the majority of society. When the labor movement was at its height in the mid-20th century America had the strongest middle class, and the lowest level of economic inequality, we've ever had.

But exactly because of its power, the labor movement has been under attack. Companies have waged fierce anti-union campaigns, and our labor laws don't provide sufficient support for workers trying to unionize. The right has passed so-called "right to work" laws in many states making it harder for unions to get funding to organize. Labor density (the percentage of workers in unions) has decreased from almost 35% in the 1950s to about 10% today.[12] Nevertheless, we are in a movement moment, and people around the country have been taking steps to build new unions in recent years, such as at Starbucks, Amazon and Trader Joe's.

One reason I think unions are so important, as opposed to just funding traditional non-profits, is that philanthropy is riven by a fundamental contradiction: while it often says its aim is to help those with less, it's the product of amassed wealth, made on the backs of underpaid workers.

Wealthy philanthropists might genuinely want a better world, but most waver in their belief that the working class should actually have powerful institutions that can challenge the status quo [or their profit margins]. For this reason, philanthropy can't build the world we need. The interests of wealthy donors are almost always in opposition to pro-redistribution anti-inequality movements and policies, and the fickleness and ability for these donors to control or withdraw their support creates too great of an obstacle to really tackle questions of economic inequality head on.

Rebuilding the labor movement is crucial because it's an institution that is self-funding [funded by its members' dues] and can wield power independently of donors and the owning class.

12 Union density remains around 10%, as of 2025.

There is a role for people in philanthropy to help grow the labor movement, help unorganized workers get organized, support strike funds, provide legal defense, or advocate for pro-worker and pro-union policies. But once unions are established they no longer need significant grant-funding, and that's a really good thing.[13] Through labor unions, working-class people can fight for what they need, without being dependent on the benevolence of wealthy donors. Self-funded and member-funded poor and working-class organizations are the way out of the paradox of philanthropy.

I should acknowledge that the labor movement has had a lot of problems: racism, sexism, corruption. But it doesn't have to be that way. There have been a lot of changes in the field over the past several decades, and a recognition that women of color are in many ways at the center of what we mean by "the working class." They are the majority of domestic workers, service workers, restaurant workers, all of whom have been getting organized. There are also reform movements within major unions like the Teamsters and United Auto Workers. Philanthropy can play a meaningful role in these efforts. For example, I've been working for the past several years

Rebuilding the labor movement is crucial because it's an institution that is self-funding [funded by its members' dues] and can wield power independently of donors and the owning class.

with Teamsters for a Democratic Union, which is a grassroots group of Teamsters who have fought to make the union more democratic and representative.

To my second priority, we have to find ways not only to build up workers' power but also restrain corporate power. Efforts like reviving anti-trust laws, or fighting for progressive taxation, may seem wonky but are crucial to the fundamental balance of economic and political power in this country.

---

13 In case it's not clear, Leah absolutely believes that there is a role for foundations and wealthy people to financially support labor. That is the fundamental premise of her current project, Democracy Takes Work. And, at the same time, it's so helpful that labor, because of membership dues, is not dependent on philanthropy.

The Chamber of Commerce is one of the biggest obstacles to progressive organizing in the U.S. For example, the Chamber of Commerce sued the Consumer Financial Protection Bureau — the agency created by Elizabeth Warren to protect consumers — in an attempt to declare it unconstitutional. The Chamber also ran ads against the El Paso Climate Charter ballot initiative. Over and over, you'll find them opposing the public interest. One organization I support is Revolving Door Project, which has a tiny budget, but punches far above its weight to ensure that people appointed to federal agencies aren't just representatives of big corporations who will bend the rules for private gain, but instead, are truly public servants who will fight for the public good. ...

We have to find ways not only to build up workers' power but also restrain corporate power.

Mike: Thank you. I'm excited about every piece of that. What is going well in moving wealthy people and wealthy institutions toward those goals, and what are the blocks that you run into?

Leah: There are not a lot of donors in this space. I think that's probably a legacy of the age-old battle between the working class and the owning class, and the ongoing reality that philanthropy is the legacy of the owning class. People who've made millions or billions often did that in opposition to the demands of labor, by driving down labor costs [i.e., decreasing wages and benefits while increasing automation]. For younger people in wealthy families, who may not have made the money themselves, I think the obstacle is often that they don't have a positive personal relationship or experience with unions.

There's a gulf between the worlds of philanthropy and unions. And since unions can't take philanthropic dollars directly since they are not 501(c)(3)s, that gulf has been slow to be bridged. However, as I mentioned, there are ways for philanthropy to support the project of rebuilding and strengthening the labor movement through 501(c)(3)s and those resources could actually be crucial.

I do think the anti-monopoly movement has gotten more popular, and more foundations like Omidyar and the Sandler

Foundation have become involved, which is fantastic. But we need a lot more education in philanthropy about how corporate power is often part of what's eroding the public goods that would benefit us all.

Mike: Just to underline the point you made, I grew up disconnected from unions. My introduction to activism came through nonprofits and social justice philanthropy — worlds quite separate from the labor movement. From what I've seen, many progressives from wealthy backgrounds share this experience. We either superficially support organized labor but have little real relationship, or we've absorbed the anti-union attitudes that are so common in professional and wealthy circles. Or both! What are your thoughts on how to get more wealthy folks involved and supporting these efforts?

Leah: I think we need to proactively organize a cohort of funders to go through a process together that would involve going to union rallies, having one-on-ones with workers and with labor leaders, and studying the history of the labor movement. It was labor that won so much of the New Deal and so many of the big social programs we got in the mid-1900s. We need to start a process of deep education on this topic.

Mike: What moved you onto this track?

Leah: Much of it was my concern that there's no ideal place to end up in terms of the relationship between philanthropy and nonprofits. There's just no way out of the power paradox. Either nonprofits don't have sufficient power OR they have power, but then they're tied to the interests of the donor class.

Working-class-led organizations that are funded directly by their members have such a better form of accountability. And while the labor model isn't perfect, at least there is a form of internal democracy. They are directly accountable to their members, because that's who they're funded by. I'm interested in the Working Families Party model of having grassroots community organizations and labor on a governing committee together.

There could be other ways to structure organizations so they are accountable to the members they're trying to serve, even while they take money from wealthy supporters at the same time. There's

Left to Right:
Leah, Astra Taylor
and Maurice
Mitchell of the
Working Families
Party (Courtesy
of Leah Hunt-
Hendrix)

no perfect situation. There will always be internal conflicts. But it's better when those can be hashed out democratically instead of decided by the donors.

Mike: What are the relevant pieces of political education that you think are needed within progressive donor networks to strengthen solidarity and support for worker organizing efforts?

Leah: People need to have an analysis of the bases of power in society and the fulcrums that can move those. As I said, unions can be a source of real power. So can the Chamber of Commerce. So can any major industry or interest group lobby. On any given issue, you need to start with a power analysis.[14]

I also think about the movement ecosystem work that has been developed by Paul and Mark Engler and Carlos Saavedra, and taught through the Momentum Community and its workshops. I

14 In this context, power is the ability or capacity to achieve a goal. A power analysis maps how and by whom power is exercised to cause and maintain the social problems we seek to change — it considers unequal power relationships within society and how power is used toward political, economic and social agendas that cause problems. An analysis defines the problem, the agenda of those who are causing the problem, the conditions you want to change, the decision makers, who is unorganized, who is organized in support, and opposition and strategies for change.

would run wealthy progressives through those trainings a million times.[15]

Then we need history — history of the labor movement, of right-wing philanthropy, of how any major social policy was passed. People need a real understanding of how large-scale change takes place. And we can't be afraid of looking at the role of politics and policy, and getting political.

Mike: I imagine it's not so easy to talk about, but are there challenges being a wealthy person who's so visible and is leading this work in big ways? I don't think most people really understand the challenges of the type of visible leadership you've taken on.

Leah: I've taken some risks in being visible in hopes that it would inspire other people who have this class background to do something similar.

But journalists love to flatten it, make it about the "rich liberal girl," make it gossipy. During Occupy I spent a lot of time with a journalist to try to tell the story of why a wealthy person should stand with Occupy Wall Street. Then the editor slapped on "Occupy's Heiress" as the title, which was embarrassing. I was profiled in a book more recently, hoping the author would focus on my work, but a lot of what was written tried to make me seem like a hypocrite, talking about the working class while drinking a matcha latte.

This makes me tear up a bit! It feels vulnerable. But I want people to know that if you have inherited wealth, you can do more than just buy fancy things. And I do hear about positive ripple effects from the articles I've done, so I think telling our stories is still worth the risks.

Mike: I have so much respect for you, Leah, and for the stands you've taken. And I've seen over and over again how our [wealthy] people who take stands get patronized. Especially if you're young or a woman, you get patronized and portrayed to be naive or vapid.

---

15 Paul Engler and Carlos Saavedra detail a specific model of organizing that combines "structure" and "momentum," organizing traditions to unify and energize mass movements to create change. As of this publication, courses are taught through Ayni Institute, and a series of articles were published about the model in *Ecologist* in 2024.

That's bullshit. I hate it. The tears are welcome. What you have to say here is important.

Leah: Thank you. There are not a lot of people you can talk to about this stuff. I never want these challenges to be construed as a "woe is me" story, where I'm looking for pity.

A frustration I sometimes have is that if you go public as a rich person about the work you've done helping fund movements, you can get smeared by both the right and the left. But if you don't talk about it, then a lot of work is behind the scenes without people really understanding what went into it.

And you can get kind of pigeonholed. When people call, it's usually about money. When my older sister dabbled in philanthropy, she told me "Leah, don't get involved in philanthropy. You're not that level of wealthy." And I wouldn't have, except at Occupy I felt requested to use my class privilege to support the movement. But it really locked me into this "wealthy person movement fundraiser" identity. I have a Ph.D. from Princeton but people are more interested in my access to wealth than my ideas.

That's a smattering of the challenges. If I'm totally honest, it's often been quite hard to be in this role. I'm curious what might feel more rewarding in my next phase. I love the political education stuff we've talked about. Our conversation is reminding me that I love that and am good at it. Maybe there's something there.

Mike: Thank you for sharing all that. We have to get better as a movement at supporting wealthy people to take the risks that you've taken. The big economic transition that we need, the working-class power we need to win, is going to take more of us being as bold as you've been. And we don't yet know how to hold and support wealthy people consistently when they do that.

What would you say to younger wealthy folks who are inspired by what you've done? How do we hold them with more care?

Leah: I would say in the Solidaire early days, having a small crew that really knew each other felt really good. We could talk about the hard things together. So having your own little cohort to go through this all with is what I would advise anybody. Join a community, find people who can support and challenge you, and if the ones that exist don't work for you, start one.[16] Start by reading a few books together, try funding a few projects together. Just be in community, and don't worry about being perfect. There will be contradictions, but we can all just do the best we can.

Mike: That tracks with my experience too. Having a small crew you can share everything with is so important.

Thank you, Leah, for taking the time to talk. ▪

---

16 A message I learned early on, from Resource Generation and many others, was "Discourage wealthy people from starting new organizations!" It remains a necessary counter to the common thought that, armed with our many degrees, resources and connections, we [the rich] are uniquely and best-suited to lead on any given issue or topic. Instead, I was taught to encourage wealthy people to join established projects and learn how to be reliable participants and contributors. I still think this is good advice! And there are many examples of projects started primarily by wealthy people (including Solidaire and this one, Organize the Rich) that I absolutely am glad exist. All to say, I think of this message and hold this tension as I read Leah's suggestion.

"WHO'S GOING TO REACH MY PEOPLE BUT ME?"

Interview with Sharon Chen

Sharon is an important leader in US based efforts to organize the rich towards equity and justice. She is the board chair of Donors of Color Action, board member of Women Donors Network, and emeritus president of the Progress Alliance of Washington [the C4 state donor table for WA]. She became wealthy, along with her husband, working for Microsoft in the 90's and 2000's.

This interview is from November 2024 and was published on Organize the Rich in May 2025.

Mike: I've been using this question recently as one way into the conversation: What's your earliest memory of money?

Sharon: It's Fall, Halloween time, in central New Jersey. Metuchen: a small town, two miles in diameter. What flashes in my head is my mom holding my hand while I carry one of those little UNICEF boxes that you take to collect quarters and dimes when you go trick-or-treating. Those boxes were a great excuse for me to learn about the different coin shapes and counting. I loved that.

Mike: Was it your neighborhood or did you drive to a wealthier neighborhood for trick-or-treating?

Sharon: Back then we didn't drive to other neighborhoods. I didn't even know there were wealthy neighborhoods. The UNICEF boxes came from school. We took them home and returned them afterward.

Mike: Wow. I have that memory too. I remember walking around with those UNICEF boxes, and being very excited about it.

Sharon: Who doesn't love knocking on doors and getting something from people? It was more fun than selling Girl Scout cookies. Looking back now, where I lived was a straight-up middle-class neighborhood. I didn't think of it as middle-class

239

then - I had no concept of class.

Mike: Similar question – what's your earliest memory of taking political action?

Sharon: It's later than you'd think! Probably when I started board service for the Washington Toxics Coalition, now called Toxic Free Future. This was about 20 years ago. At the time, I didn't realize how difficult it was to make change in the public sphere.

Working at the Washington Toxics Coalition on chemical-policy reform, I initially believed education was the key – if people just understood the facts, they'd make the right decisions in the legislature. I quickly learned this was wrong. Science rarely determined how people actually voted on bills.

For a while I thought, "Oh, it's just that one bad politician. Once he's gone, things will be okay." What seemed to me like common-sense decisions about inappropriate use of toxic chemicals would be resolved. But no, you take out one legislator and there is still this never-ending stream of much bigger issues blocking your way.

That was my earliest activist work. I was in my early 30s – coming to these realizations later than I'm proud of.

Mike: What's your class and race background, and how did you come to this work of organizing the rich toward justice?

Sharon: I'm the child of immigrants from Taiwan who met in the US in the late '60's. There wasn't substantial wealth in my family growing up, though I consider my upbringing very privileged. I didn't go hungry, didn't worry about housing. I was warm, safe, and dry. My parents made it clear my priority was to do well in school.

I was fortunate to go to school in the '90s. I had a knack for math, science, and computers when computers were brand new. It's funny – I started college at Princeton University as an Engineering major and didn't switch to Computer Science right away. It took two years of hemming and hawing about it because computer science was deemed risky – who knew what this flash-in-the-pan computer science might be?!

[laughter]

Engineering was considered reliable. This was in the early '90s, and I was one of three women graduating in a class of 25 people in computer science. Now it's a massive department, but back then it was little. I was the only engineer of the three women in our department - the other two got Bachelor's of Arts degrees. And yes, I was the only woman of color.

Mike: That's a big deal!

Sharon: My degree led to a full-time job at Microsoft. That's basically the story of my good fortune.

I also married another "Microsoftee," so for a while, we were a 'double income and stock options' family. I eventually had three children, but after the second one was born, I semi-retired. It wasn't really retirement – it was more like, "I don't need to work for pay anymore."

I love computer science and the puzzles I got to solve, but working in technology in the 90s as a woman of color... I'll just say... it wasn't great. I always thought: I need to figure out what to do when I "grow up."

During that period we moved to Taiwan for two years. Why not? I'd always wanted to live in another country. Growing up as a kid of Taiwanese immigrants, I had some basic Mandarin language skills. I'd always dreamed of living in a Mandarin-speaking place because it would be easier for my kids to pick up the language at that age.

My husband continued working with Microsoft in Taipei. I focused on developing my language skills. The kids went to school – I went to school too.

Mike: This was after your early retirement?

Sharon: Yes, after early retirement.

Mike: So basically you're parenting full-time but also learning Mandarin and living in a new country?

Sharon: Right, because my personality won't let me just do one thing. *[laughs]*

Mike: Hah, I'm starting to learn that.

Sharon: These were the Obama years, 2008 to 2010. I had a great time *[laughs]*. But realistically, my language skills were never going to be sufficient to work in Taiwan. Learning Chinese and becoming literate as an adult is a huge investment. So that and other family factors brought us back. We'd considered staying - we loved it there! But Seattle was home, so we returned.

Shortly after, I rejoined the Washington Toxics Coalition board around 2010, getting involved in issues I cared about. I had the financial flexibility to not need another tech job. I could do whatever I wanted. I'm a seeker type of personality - I felt in my gut how I wanted the world to be, while still learning how it actually works. During that period, I kept asking myself: what is my highest, best use?

I am a wealthy person. I live in Capitol Hill in Seattle. That's a part of my identity that cannot be denied. There's no hiding that I don't worry about money. When I go to the grocery store, I don't look at prices. When my kids come with me, it's only a matter of "Is it going to be healthy for you?" not "How much does it cost?"

As an immigrant kid I fought and worked so hard for my Ivy League education. It's part of my background. Now there's some aspects about my privilege that I don't love, but I have it. *The most wasteful thing would be to not use it.*

My background and willingness to use it makes me fearless. I'm never going to be in a room and feel a certain type of fear. I'm subject to imposter syndrome like any other woman, particularly as a woman of color. But this idea that I'll talk to somebody and feel like they're somehow above me – it's just not going to happen.

This Ivy League degree gave me that. So many super talented, amazing people I work with don't necessarily have that same confidence. If I can be their tour guide or representative or ambassador into wealthy spaces, then I will do that.

Also, I know what it's like to be a wealthy person thinking about where to place resources. I want to help fundraisers, organizers and other wealthy people by explaining what my barriers were to giving away more money faster and what ultimately helped me escalate my giving.[1]

---

1 Reading this now, I want to know what Sharon's barriers were to giving more and what ultimately helped her escalate her giving! A subject for another conversation.

NOW THERE'S SOME ASPECTS ABOUT MY PRIVILEGE THAT I DON'T LOVE, BUT I HAVE IT. THE MOST WASTEFUL THING WOULD BE TO NOT USE IT.

Sharon Chen

Mike: One of the reasons I wanted to interview you is because I heard you talk about how important it is for the rich to go towards the wealthy people in their lives, rather than away from them. YYou were talking about this dynamic where wealthy people become politicized around inequality, see how unfair our economic system is, and then turn away from those "bad rich people" in their lives.[2] You talked about how that's the opposite move we need to make – we need to go towards our people and organize them. Can you tell me more about that lesson?

Sharon: First, I understand the inclination. Sometimes I may not want to share where my [Ivy League] degree came from depending on the group I'm in.

Mike: You don't wear your Princeton sweatshirt everywhere you go.

Sharon: I don't. *[laughs]* Although I have one – I have several!

Mike: I love your honesty.

Sharon: As I had my eyes opened to the ways wealthy people can act badly, there was a bit of shame – "Oh gosh, my people did this!"[3] It's embarrassment, not wanting to be associated with that group.

But where my mind goes is: if not me, then who? If not me, then who, literally – who's going to reach my people but me?

As someone who came to understand how the world works

---

2 There are certainly times when it makes sense for rich people to distance ourselves or break off relationships with individual wealthy people in our lives because of their negative impact on us. Healthy boundaries are different from this organizing orientation Sharon and I speak to here.

3 I asked Sharon what she meant by "this." She wrote "I'm referring to behaviors that are a result of wealthy people's economic/social standing that are not helpful to anyone, including ourselves. The biggest one that comes to mind in the context of philanthropy is the notion that we know better than the professionals we are partnering with, such as nonprofit staff or movement leaders. This notion is based on an incorrect assumption that people with money are smarter and that our role as funders is to evaluate the work of organizations we support. Once we've decided WHAT kind of change we want and assessed WHO we want to work with, we need to trust the HOW to make change to someone who has literally developed PROFESSIONAL skill in the area. A little humility and willingness to learn goes a long way. Too often we get in the way of the change we want because we are confused about the role of our money. We approach our philanthropy as some kind of consumer behavior and it holds us back from the positive impact we could achieve with the dollars."

relatively late in life, I believe in people's redemption. If I believe in my own redemption, then why wouldn't I believe in other people's redemption?

I mean, I got a degree in computer science. If you had told me at 20 years old that I would be interested in politics 20 years later, I would have thought it was a joke. In some sense, back then, I didn't care about people. I didn't care about how big societal decisions were made. I thought, "What a mess! No way I want to get involved in that!" *[laughs, raises hands with palms out to signal "stop"]*

I was subject to the same cultural messages that many people face: that politics is messy, it's unfeminine. As a woman, you're uglier than you would be otherwise if you think about politics. It's crude and uncouth.

I think those messages are part of patriarchy and there to make sure women don't get involved.

When I started thinking about politics not as this ugly thing but realized that "politics" just means "how people make decisions"... then why wouldn't I want to have some influence or connection to that?

Mike: Amen. Some people who identify as progressive or left have an allergy to power. They think if you have power, you're bad, and because of that, try to avoid it, even to the point of being anti-leadership and wanting flat structures. The fact is, we need to be able to learn how to build, hold and wield power.

What helped you turn the corner from the techie engineer who didn't really care about people to somebody who did? Were there certain mentors or experiences that politicized you, that got you on this track of seeing the world differently than what you thought it was?

Sharon: There are many things, but what comes to mind is that in 2014, Tamir Rice died.

I just couldn't wrap my head around how a 12-year-old child could be left to bleed out over hours while police officers stood around. He wasn't killed instantly. He was shot and left there. His sister was literally feet away, restrained in the back of a police car and not allowed to comfort him in his last hours. The inhumanity was just so striking in a way that I didn't understand.

However, it's not like he dies and the next day I awaken knowing how the world works. But that part of me that's a seeker – asking *why, why, why* – was lit at that moment. I started to read, to listen, to pay more attention to the ways that race informs everything. It put a richness, unfortunately, to understanding our history that I didn't have.

Mike: We don't get that history.

Sharon: It's shameful, actually. I got the best education this country can provide - public school in a relatively rich suburban New Jersey, then an Ivy League university.

But looking back, the holes in my education are profound. I didn't know much about the Black Panthers, but if someone had asked me, I would have said, "Oh, I don't know anything about them, but I think they're like a radical, dangerous group." Which turns out to be exactly what the FBI intended. The reality is they came up with school breakfast and lunches, and community health care.

Mike: Yes!

Sharon: My initial attraction to advocacy and activist spaces was through the environmental route, understanding that the root of climate change isn't merely too much carbon in the atmosphere. You have to ask: Why is there too much carbon? It really comes down to how our culture and how our economy works, based on exploitation and extraction.

I work a lot now in environmental justice spaces, and I'm interested in solutions that address that root cause. There will always be people working on technological solutions, like better batteries. But it's been proven that with more efficient light bulbs, we don't use less energy – we just leave lights on more often.

Technology is not the answer.

Mike: Amen.

I want to switch gears a little bit. You're in the leadership of two different types of donor groups - Women Donors Network and Donors of Color Action. What's the importance of those two spaces for you?

Sharon: I'll start with Women Donors Network (WDN). We talk about the difference in girls' learning in school settings when boys are around. Those gender dynamics play out even in wealthy donor spaces. I'm a relatively new member, just 6 or 7 years, but it's been around for 20 years. What we've learned over that time is that without the male gaze, women will be more radical. They won't feel a need to defend their sense of justice.

> Without the male gaze, women will be more radical. They won't feel a need to defend their sense of justice.

Looking at the history of decisions at WDN, the willingness to take risks on potential grantees is amazing. One of my favorite stories is about a member who met LaTosha Brown. LaTosha wanted to rent big buses to drive around the South getting people registered and out to vote.

Mike: I've heard of her. She co-founded Black Voters Matter.

Sharon: Yes, this was before anyone would give her the time of day - WDN said, "Ok, we'll give you the $70k you asked for your vision of buses."

Left to Right: Kaniqua Welch, The Kresge Foundation; Monica Atkins, Climate Justice Alliance; Sharon Chen, Donors of Color Network; Denise Collazo, Faith in Action; and Ning Mosberger-Tang of the Innovo Foundation. (Courtesy of Sharon Chen)

The payoff was incredible. They started bus tours in 2018. Their 2020 election cycle bus tours went to 15 states and are credited with helping increase Black voter turnout in Georgia elections, including the crucial 2021 Senate runoff election won by Reverend Raphael Warnock.

I'm hopeful there will be a world someday where we don't need women-only spaces like this. But the reality is, having women make decisions without the pressure of the male gaze is important.

Mike: Last time we talked, you mentioned the power of spaces for women to strategize about how to take on sexism and patriarchy in their families and relationships, especially around taking ownership of money. You mentioned some leadership development practices you learned in WDN. Can you talk about that?

Sharon: Women and gender-expansive people tend to police ourselves and how we use our power. WDN is a space where we reflect on our tendencies, push ourselves to speak up, to take action, to trust ourselves. We once had a trainer come in to lead us through power poses and vocal exercises. Literally, we practiced taking up space and using our voices.

Those of us who are not men tend to feel like we need more preparation, study and education before taking action. I'm reminded of studies about women applying for jobs – we tend to shy away from job postings that are a stretch; we want to have all the qualifications. That's not as true for men.

Mike: No, us guys will just jump in even if we have no idea what we're doing.

Sharon: The same goes for making donations, what we often call "investments." To not leave power on the table, we need to shorten the gap between willingness and action. When we understand the psychology of our members, we can address it. We can speak intentionally about it: "Hey, self-doubt is something that's going to hit all of us. If you are planning to invest and suddenly feel a wave of 'Oh, I don't know enough,' that may be true, AND ALSO we're going to feel that way because of sexism." These are conversations we can have in a gender caucus that would be tough elsewhere.

Mike: Thank you. That makes sense. Can you talk about Donors

of Color Network and what you've found is the importance of that space?

Sharon: There are many analogous situations between the women's space and the donors of color space. At DOCN, we get to see what kinds of decisions a bunch of people of color make without needing to manage the emotions of white people. And we get to practice solidarity across race. These are muscles that need to be exercised.

Just because we're all targeted by racism doesn't mean we don't hold prejudices about each other or understand what each other face. As a person of Asian descent, I've had the opportunity to learn about the Movement for Black Lives. And my Black colleagues at DOCN have learned from me about what it's like to be Asian, and about anti-Asian racism.

Yet when we talk about many parts of our social justice movements, people of color with wealth can feel a real visceral connection. It feels less like charity.

Many of us who have become wealthy have experienced separation between us and the poor, working or middle class communities we come from because of our striving. Yet when we talk about many parts of our social justice movements, people of color with wealth can feel a real visceral connection. It feels less like charity. There's many ways we're different from white philanthropists.

Mike: Thanks for explaining those pieces. I gotta say, you have a unique organizing superpower, which is that you are a former techie in Seattle that speaks that language and knows that world. Your experience and roots in that community give you a real chance to move people and inspire other techies. I'm so glad you've gone towards this mostly wealthy community you've been a part of, rather than away from it.

Sharon: A lot of the donor organizing I do is code switching between social justice movements and this wealthy donor class. As a child of immigrants, I've been doing that all my life. I code switch between all sorts of communities, and this is just another one.

The wealthy donor class is used to being behind the microscope, but it deserves to be and needs to be under the microscope as well.

I also want to say – we're really good as a progressive left at saying "hey, it's important that we have cultural competency about this or that community." As much as we study Asians and civic engagement (or any other community of color) – guess what?! The wealthy donor class is used to being behind the microscope, but it deserves to be and needs to be under the microscope as well.

Mike: Ooh. Yes! Please tell us about the research you'd like to do on wealthy people.

Sharon: Ok. I need to give context for why I believe research matters.

Washington state is currently 49th in the nation in terms of regressive tax policy, which is terrible and quite surprising for a state perceived to be as blue as it is. We have no income tax. All our taxes are based on sales tax, very regressive things. We've climbed from 50th to 49th because we're starting to make progress with capital gains taxes.

We started making progress after being in the wilderness on this issue for decades. About 17 years ago, the progressive donor community in Washington decided we'd had enough. We knew about the libertarian roots in this region but we didn't let that stop us. We put money together for sociologists to study people's worldviews about taxes.

From that research, we figured out messages that would break through the knee-jerk "government is bad, taxation is bad" reaction. We started talking about an "upside down tax code" because the word "regressive" wasn't breaking through. We learned to focus on tax revenue as *investment* – what do you get with your money? People are willing to invest in their communities, but if you're just talking about taxation, you're on the wrong side of the conversation.

Having this experience of being in the wilderness politically for 15+ years and having the discipline to be patient – not trying to win tomorrow's election, but doing the deep cultural understanding and shifting work over the long term – that's what started to break it open for us in Washington state.

Right now we're in a similar situation, needing more wealthy progressives across the country to invest in grassroots electoral organizing. Donor organizers like me have a lot of stories about what feelings are in the way. But I'm trying to be open and not presuppose where the problem is.

I'm committed to researching this topic in a similar way to how we researched the issue of taxes in Washington state. We need to look through the microscope to get a clear picture of core attitudes and beliefs, then discern how to help wealthy progressives understand the importance of – and invest in – grassroots movements to win governing power.

> Donor organizers like me have a lot of stories about what feelings are in the way. But I'm trying to be open and not presuppose where the problem is.

Mike: Amen. I can't wait to see what you find out. Thank you for taking the time to talk with me today. I've loved our conversation. ■

FINDING A NEW WAY

We're living through an unprecedented convergence of crises, and the stakes for organizing wealthy people have never been higher. As we look forward, what lessons and experiments can we learn from as we navigate these challenging times? In this section, current leaders and practitioners grapple with where we are and where we go from here. Through intimate and honest reflections, these pieces illuminate pathways forward. This is no roadmap, but it does lead us to essential questions as we consider how to build upon what's come before.

"WE CAN'T AFFORD TO LEAVE ANY POWER ON THE TABLE"

Interview With Braeden Lentz

This is an excerpt from an interview with Braeden Lentz by Michael Gast. It was originally published on the Organize the Rich Substack in April 2023.

Mike: What do you want Working Families Party, and your WFP people, to better understand about left organizing of rich people?

Braeden: I want more of our people to see organizing the owning class as possible. To be curious about how to do it as part of a sound, uncomplicated strategy and to hold its contradictions within a coherent ideology and toward WFP's goals. Because we can't afford to leave any power on the table.

Mike: What are the stories or lessons from your time organizing wealthy people that you want others to know and understand?

Braeden: You cannot heal your own trauma about class by getting angry at rich individuals.

Most of my early years as a board member with Resource Generation were shaped by a mix of discomfort, shock, frustration, anger, sadness and grief — just to be around rich people. And I think that's the number one barrier that most working-class people will experience: the emotional contradiction of being so adjacent to the systems that hoard and harm us, and the people that system benefits. And I think the way to maybe not heal — but to make sense of the tension — is seeing and believing in the humanity of rich people. Actually believing in their liberation as humans, their capacity to transform and their ability to have a meaningful role in our movements. If you don't believe in those ideas, none of the tension inherent to this organizing project will ever make sense.

As helpful a rallying cry as "eat the rich" is to call out the urgency of wealth inequality, it doesn't work to have that mentality sink into your approach working with individual rich people. It makes a difference to see them as people who deserve liberation from our unjust class system, not just as targets to campaign against or people to extract money from. And they can tell when you bring an extractive approach, like any human can. The first lesson, I think, is the skill of being emotionally developed enough to personally hold the contradiction.

A second lesson is more tactical; it's important to remember that wealthy people, no matter where they are in their development, live within cultures and institutions. You'll need to navigate within wealthy class spaces in order to properly organize them. If you don't come from those spaces, navigating them will be a necessary skill that requires genuine curiosity and patience.

Pretending that you can organize them in the same way as anyone else is probably not going to work. For example, a lot of wealthy people with radical values will look for the easy way out: "What's the easiest way for me to absolve myself of guilt so I feel in right relationship with working-class people?" Some wealthy people will have that approach. Some wealthy people will be stuck in their owning-class culture in other ways, like they might want to have a lot of control over outcomes and only want to work on projects that they feel a sense of power over. Others may be scared of making wrong decisions in the eyes of their family and advisors and be too discouraged to act at all.

It also helps to just be upfront. It's better to be direct about when you want to have a call where you're going to ask for money. If you actually want to build a relationship with the person, tell them, "I want to have a meeting to get to know you better" and mean it. And when you're going to do an ask, let them know you want to do it and ask for their consent. Ask them if it's okay as part of setting up a meeting. Or if it comes up in real time, be like, "Hey, it seems like it might make sense to talk about funding or money now. Is that okay with you?" These are probably just basic organizing practices that I've found work.

Mike: What do you see as the strengths of how the left engages wealthy people right now? And what do you see as the weaknesses?

Braeden: What are we doing well? We are really good at making compelling, urgent pitches about crises that get rich people to take risks that they otherwise wouldn't have taken in terms of the amounts that they're giving.

For example, the surge in fundraising to defeat Donald Trump. WFP benefited from this surge moment — and as a movement, we're really great at creating stories about urgency and that "this is the most important thing ever!"

I don't think we're good at getting wealthy people to make longer-term commitments to build institutions. This is in part because of how philanthropy is structured. It's also in part because the left can be ambivalent about building institutions, and we often lack long-term plans. There is also a fundamental avoidance — to not really *want* to manage relationships with wealthy people or believe that's possible. So yeah, I see how working-class left leaders and fundraisers have exacerbated the surge and fall of money, too. I mean, we always talk shit to philanthropy, like, "Give us long-term general operating support!" But we don't actually have long-term plans that invite people into meaningful relationships with us toward big, long, multi-year general support giving. So it can be a self-fulfilling prophecy.

> **I don't think we're good at getting wealthy people to make longer-term commitments to build institutions.**

I think we're really good at explaining the moral imperative of the moment to wealthy people. I think we're good at basic political education, like getting people to understand racism and capitalism. I don't think we're good at political education about what power needs to be built to change those things. We know how to get people to turn up on the system, but we're not disciplined about explaining the theory of change needed to build and win power over the long term and the institutions we need to build to get there.

Mike: If you can identify two priorities for lefty rich people organizing over the next five years, what would they be? What experiments would you want to see the left try?

Braeden: First of all, I would love to have our organizations encourage donors to sign up for progressive donor networks, such as Solidaire, Way to Win, Resource Generation, Democracy

Alliance and Movement Voter Project. No donor network is perfect — just like no working-class organization is perfect — but it's better to lean into a community of learning and commitment than to stay isolated. I believe in collective action. It might be that some wealthy people can find political home within working-class organizations — I do think this is the case for many of our folks at WFP — but if an organization doesn't have the capacity to support them, we can't leave our people hanging.

Second, this requires the left to hold wealthy donors with less scarcity — which has many other benefits. Get them into formation and encourage them to join a donor network. It's going to be helpful to you as the fundraiser to have them be part of a network where they can fundraise for you. It's also going to be a place for them to get some of their emotional needs met about their unique experience as wealthy people — which is likely not possible at your organization. And if you actually believe that you need strong coalition partners, and that your organization cannot be all things to all people, why wouldn't you encourage your funders to support other good work?

But there's not enough of those groups for people to sign up to, and they all need more capacity!

The left should have proper infrastructure that's going to meet the needs of rich people stepping into movement in alignment with working-class vision. And then we need to hold our donors less closely and encourage them to sign up for it. Yeah. I feel like that's the top. Those are the top two things.

Finally, one even more fundamental thing that is needed: The left actually needs to consolidate its ideology and strategy.

Funding an ocean of grassroots activism, or the first people of color activists you stumble across, is not going to move us toward ending wealth inequality. We need to invest in wealthy people's understanding of how change works, to understand power building and to be committed to building the governing power of the multiracial working class to ultimately force wealth redistribution through taxes and to deliver a safety net that works for everyone and invests in healthy and vibrant communities. If we encourage rapid, chaotic giving, we are mitigating emotions of guilt and urgency, but we are leaving power on the table. Obviously, this requires the left to consolidate around ideology and strategy — when we lack strategy, this has ripple effects into the behavior of left wealthy people, too. As we consolidate around ideology and strategy, there need to be enough organizations to receive these wealthy people, and there

If we encourage rapid, chaotic giving, we are mitigating emotions of guilt and urgency, but we are leaving power on the table.

needs to be more of a generous spirit to get people into the right house in the neighborhood of organizations. Let's get wealthy people into a political home that is part of a broader multiracial working-class movement, and which is going to help them unlock the most amount of money as part of a larger strategy *and* meet their political and emotional development needs, just like people of all class backgrounds deserve.

So just all that. ▪

YOU CANNOT HEAL YOUR
OWN TRAUMA ABOUT
CLASS BY GETTING ANGRY
AT RICH INDIVIDUALS.

Braeden Lentz

IT IS NOT THE JOB OF
WORKING CLASS PEOPLE
TO MAKE RICH PEOPLE
FEEL BETTER ABOUT
THEMSELVES.

Mijo Lee

"WE HAVE THIS BIG RED SHINY BUTTON IN FRONT OF US"

Interview with Mijo Lee

Mijo Lee is the former executive director of Social Justice Fund Northwest (SJFNW) and a longtime leader in social justice philanthropy in the U.S. Since 2020, she has been consulting with individuals, families, foundations, and nonprofits as a donor and funder educator and philanthropic advisor. She is the executive director of Willow Fund, and with Rye Young,[1] Mijo developed and leads DIGG (Donor Intro to Grounded Giving), a donor education program for high-net-wealth individuals. She is on the advisory committee for the Emergent Fund, a former board member of Grassroots International, a current board member of Firelands Workers United and ReFrame, and a member of Solidaire Network.

Editor's Note (MG): I first met Mijo when she was hired as a staff member at Social Justice Fund Northwest in 2011. I was working for Resource Generation at the time and was renting office space from SJFNW in Downtown Seattle. We have been close colleagues and friends ever since. I interviewed Mijo and am sharing this piece here because of her honesty, integrity and hard-earned wisdom on the topic of engaging, advising and fundraising the radical rich, and the class dynamics and contradictions that invariably show up in the process.

Mike: Okay. Well, why don't we jump in — how did you come to participate in engaging, fundraising, and organizing wealthy people for social justice?

Mijo: You were there. You know, I got hired at Social Justice Fund Northwest (SJFNW) in 2011. I had never done any kind of professional fundraising, much less organizing of wealthy people before. I was hired because of my willingness to do a really unique and challenging job.

---

1 Rye Young is a longtime leader in social justice philanthropy. He was the executive director at Third Wave Fund and now is a donor advisor and philanthropic consultant.

Photo by Naomi Ishisaka (Courtesy of Mijo Lee)

I was later told that one of the reasons I was hired was that I had a good answer to the question, "What is your experience with wealthy people?"

I answered something about having attended New York University, realizing how rich most of my classmates were and wishing I had known how to organize them.

What I didn't realize then was that with my professional middle-class background, I'd had class privilege and had been adjacent to rich people. Like a lot of others in this work, I had learned to navigate those worlds before getting into organizing and fundraising the wealthy professionally.

When I was hired at SJF, we had just started doing Giving Projects.[2] As you well know, the very first Giving Project in 2010 was a partnership with the local Resource Generation (RG) chapter in Seattle. From the beginning of the job, I was doing cross-class organizing and community building in the Giving Projects, as well as fundraising for SJF. I was learning how to do both at the same time.

Mike: Anything else you want to say about your class background or how it's shaped your relationship to this work?

Mijo: This morning, in a workshop I was leading with staff at Grassroots International,[3] I asked a question: "What messages did you learn growing up about money, about rich people, and about giving?" This is a slight variation on a prompt that we used in every Giving Project curriculum during my years at SJF.

What I have seen in asking this question, in dozens and dozens of Giving Project cohorts, is that the answers are consistent depending on someone's class background.

---

2 Giving Projects are a model of collective grantmaking and political education started by Social Justice Fund Northwest in 2010. Giving Projects bring together a cross-class, multiracial crew to build community, learn about race and class oppression, fundraise from their peers and make grants to social justice organizations. Giving Projects draw on a long legacy of collective giving efforts in many communities going back thousands of years. For more on Giving Projects, read Michael's essay on Resource Generation in this anthology.

3 Grassroots International was founded in 1983 and provides funding and support to social movements around the world that focus on land, water, food and environmental justice. The organization works primarily with grassroots movements in the Global South.

You can pretty much script it. What it boils down to is this: Poor and working-class people are better at giving. They know how to do it. They do it all the time. They're super-practiced in it. It's not even a question. And the more privileged you are, the weirder you are about it. It's more individualistic; it's more isolated.

The dividing line that matters is whether giving is optional. Is giving something that you can choose to do? Or is it how you, your family, your community and your people survive?

Because I hadn't done that discussion in years, hearing people's answers this morning was like a splash of cold water in my face. In that moment I was reminded that *the dividing line that matters is whether giving is optional.* Is giving something that you can choose to do? Or is it how you, your family, your community and your people survive?

And by that metric, my class privilege is so clear. For us, giving was optional. We did it. My parents definitely set that example for me, but not because that's what we needed to do to survive and how we kept our family alive. It's something they did out of the goodness of their hearts.

That's something I'm noodling on today.

Mike: What do you see as the lineage of your work engaging wealthy people as part of left movements?

Mijo: I've spent a lot of time thinking about how my work is built on the legacy of the lessons learned at ATR [A Territory Resource, the original name of SJF] and the Funding Exchange.[4] And in some cases, built on the rubble of organizations that have died, relationships that have died, a lot of really rough stuff. I've heard a lot of horror stories from working- and middle-class people, who were on social justice foundation staffs, boards, or committees back in the day, about the ways they were treated by rich people.

---

4 ATR and SJF were never formally part of the Funding Exchange, but were inspired by and have been in relationship with FEX since its founding. For more about the Funding Exchange, read the report *Change, Not Charity: The Story of the Funding Exchange — A Pioneer in Social Justice Philanthropy*, by Theodora Lurie, 2017, available at www.fex.org.

I've heard stories from wealthy people who were treated badly too.

I've heard so many painful stories from all sides.

When I hear these stories, I always think, "Everybody was really doing their best. Everybody." I really do believe that the rich people, whether they were doing beautiful, liberatory things or really harmful things, were doing their best. And sometimes their best was awful. *But they were making up something that nobody had done before.* They were figuring it out. And the extent that we're able to do better now is because of the mistakes that they made. So I'm grateful for them for taking the risk and making a mistake even when they fucked up. And I'm especially grateful for all the working-class people of color who really led and actually made it work, at immense cost. You know, when they usually don't get the credit.[5] ...

Mike: Are there any mistakes that you made that you want others to learn from?

Mijo: I've never made a mistake, Michael.

Mike: We can move on then. *[Laughing]*

Mijo: Oh, my God. Well, this is an interesting one that Rye and I've been talking about.

The kind of progressive rich people that gravitate to us social justice movement fundraisers are often motivated by feelings of

---

5 In the interview, Mijo goes on to shout out a whole set of working-class people of color who were involved with ATR in the 80s through early 00s, including Alice Ito, Andrea Alexander, David Rogers, Eric Ward, Gail Small, Gary Delgado, Garry Owens, Guadalupe Guajardo, Kenneth Jones, Scot Nakagawa, Soya Jung, Susan Balbas, and Tyree Scott. She also mentions the importance of PCUN [Piñeros y Campesinos Unidos del Noroeste, a farmworkers' union in Oregon] as an organization that grew up alongside ATR/SJF and indelibly shaped its politics.

guilt and shame.[6] Ergo, as fundraisers, we have this big red shiny button sitting in front of us when we meet with people who have that tendency. Sometimes you can just see it glowing. And, you know, if you push that button, in the short term, you might get the bigger gift. I think that's even more true in the last several years, with Donald Trump and George Floyd and everything else.

The decision about whether or not to push that button is not actually a simple one. Obviously, if we're thinking long term, big picture — don't push the button. Right? We're in it for the long haul. I want to invest in this person's personal growth — but sometimes you do have real urgency. You fucking need the money and you don't know if the long haul is really going to be a thing for this person. Maybe this is your one shot. You know, it's just not simple. There have been times when I pushed that button and it was not the principled choice.

It's not the choice that's most in line with my values. I can't really defend it from a long-term organizing standpoint, but I can defend it from a short-term resource mobilization standpoint.

I've also made a mistake the other way, where I decided, "Actually, I'm not going to push because I think that I can work with this person for the long haul" and then they ghosted me and I was like, "Fucking hell!" You can gamble wrong in either direction.

So that's the debate that Rye and I have had. You know, at SJF we would ask everybody to make a personally meaningful gift. We had this whole long list of ways to define a meaningful gift, one of which was "It makes you feel a little scared." Rye is always saying how our goal should never be to destabilize somebody's nervous system. People do not make good decisions in that state. I think that makes so much sense.

At the same time, I also know fear and excitement are the same thing — not mentally, not emotionally, but physiologically.

6 Mijo emailed recently to elaborate. She wrote, "A little tangent in defense of guilt. I actually think guilt in the right amount can be useful. Like a smoke detector, it tells you when something is wrong. If you disable your smoke detector because you don't like how the noise makes you feel, you're not going to be able to fix the problem. But of course you can't have your smoke detector blaring all the time either, it'll drive you crazy (which is what guilt can do too). I do think shame is useless."

I do want people to feel excited. For myself, I know that I'm growing when I feel a little bit destabilized and uncomfortable. So I think it's a very individual determination. I think you have to get to know the person well enough to know "Is this person going to meet their potential when they're feeling kind of nervous and uncomfortable or when they're feeling very, very held and secure?" Different people need different things. And that's fine.

One thing that I've realized from talking and reflecting with Rye is that I've definitely encouraged people to make big decisions from a destabilized place. And that is something that I think a lot of organizers, not just fundraisers, but organizers in general, do. It's probably the way that I was trained as an organizer, and I don't think it's a grounded way. It will work for some people but it should not be the default. ... That was my default and that is something I regret.

Mike: I love those examples. Thank you. I could relate to all of it. I think every fundraiser can. These are important tensions you're naming.

What perspectives or tools do you use that you have found most useful?

Mijo: Hmm. The book *Classified: How to Stop Hiding Your Privilege and Use It for Social Change* [by Karen Pittelman] was very important to my education and curriculum development, training of staff, and approach to organizing. The piece of *Classified* that I use the most is "Lucy's Redacted Story." Rye and I have used it in DIGG. It's a really effective way of getting the point across about how people with class privilege edit our stories to avoid reckoning with the reality of our privilege.

Another book I've been referencing a lot with my clients is Chuck Collins' book, *Wealth Hoarders: How Billionaires Pay Millions to Hide Trillions*. That's a recent one for me. It's great because it helps make clear to my clients: "It's not that you're stupid, it's not that you're incompetent, it's not that you're not trying hard enough to redistribute your wealth — there's actually an entire industry that is devoted to preserving and growing your wealth, whether you want to or not." Talking with clients about

TO FREE THE MONEY

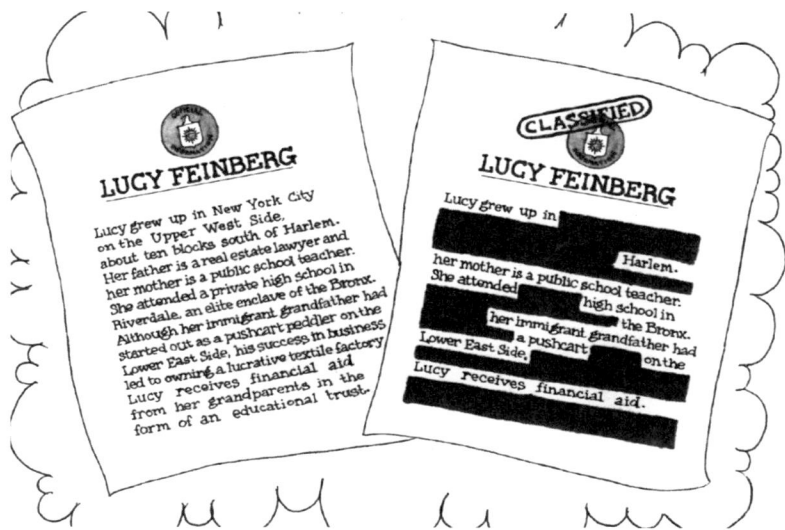

Illustration by Molly Hein (Courtesy of Resource Generation)

that has been really helpful.

Another one that was very formative for me is the book *Class Matters: Cross-Class Alliance Building for Middle Class Activists* by Betsy Leondar-Wright. She includes a chart of working-class, middle-class, and owning-class patterns. It is too reductive to use on its own in workshops. But it has been a helpful sort of cheat sheet for understanding class patterns and dynamics in this work. And her piece "It's Not Them, It's Us" about non-essential weirdness[7] — very important! ...

Mike: What do you think we're doing well right now?

Mijo: Something we're definitely doing better is asking for more. I see a shift in that. The Movement for Black Lives is asking for and receiving 10-year pledges. That's a sea change. And we are expecting more. I think that's one of the impacts of MacKenzie

---

7 Since Mijo introduced me to this article in this interview, "It's Not Them, It's Us" has become one of my favorite pieces of writing about class cultures and cross-class dynamics in activism and organizing. It was written by longtime economic justice researcher, author and educator Betsy Leondar-Wright. I write about Betsy in "A Brief History of Organizing the Rich Toward Justice" in this anthology. You can find this piece at https://classmatters.org/its-not-them-its-us/.

Scott's philanthropy.[8] Her donations have raised expectations for groups about the type and size of support they can ask for.

I am encountering more wealthy people saying, "I shouldn't be making all the decisions. This is not my money. I don't have this money because I'm smarter or more capable." That's great. And it makes it easier for social justice movement-led and movement-accountable funding intermediaries to raise money, which is always one of my top goals.[9]

Mike: What are some of the challenges we're facing now? What are some of the weaknesses of our current approach for engaging the wealthy?

Mijo: I was talking with somebody recently who works in philanthropy who said, "I spent so many years saying, 'Rich people, just get out of the way!' And now that they are doing it, I'm like, 'Oh, wait, not *all the way* out of the way!'" This is actually not healthy. There's a whole generation now of wealthy people who've been socialized and trained that if you're down, you will just write a check and not engage in any way.

And good fundraisers don't want that. They want to be in a relationship with their donors. Good donor organizers, even more so. So that's tricky.

When clients start with me, my first step is to have them fill out a worksheet on their priorities. I have some clients who say, "It doesn't matter." They think their priorities don't matter. But they do. They just do.

---

8 MacKenzie Scott is an author and the ex-wife of Jeff Bezos. She signed a Giving Pledge in May 2019 to give the majority of her wealth back to society. She has made many large donations to important progressive organizing groups, such as Southerners on New Ground, One Fair Wage, National Domestic Workers Alliance and Movement for Black Lives, as well as social justice philanthropic intermediaries like Groundswell Fund, Astraea Lesbian Foundation for Justice, Solidaire and Grassroots International. As of this publishing, in 2025, her foundation has moved over $19.2 billion to more than 2,450 nonprofits. The gifts are unrestricted ("no strings") and have a median amount of $5 million. She has yet to tell the story publicly about how she was organized towards this giving strategy.

9 Intermediaries in this context are grassroots organizations or public foundations with the capacity to receive dollars and redistribute them to key leaders and organizations using their own grantmaking process. You can find a list of social justice philanthropic intermediaries here: https://tr.ee/sjintermediaries

Because, like it or not, you are the riverbank that this water is flowing through. It is shaping you and you are shaping it. And you can't pretend otherwise. So let's just put it out on the table. If you are passionate about climate justice and not immigrant rights, that's okay. And guess what? They're the same thing anyways! But being clear about your priorities gives us direction, and that's helpful to look at and be honest about.

The whole suppression of self by progressive wealthy people, the suppression of their individual wants and needs and desires, is not a healthy impulse. It's going to lead to resentment and backlash. Nobody is going to be happy with that in the long term.

There's also this idea floating around some progressive donor spaces that you have to be in deep and authentic relationship with every organization you fund. But you can't do that. It's not sustainable.

I talk to clients about picking two or three organizations that they will be in close relationship with. I think it's helpful to encourage people to focus on a few organizations they will really show up for. The rest? Hand them off to a donor advisor to manage or give money to intermediaries — they'll steward those relationships for you.

There's a greater recognition these days that wealthy people can be organizing each other. I go to donor briefings and hear the speaker say, "Funders, go get your people; donors go get your people." But the problem is that there's little support for them to actually do that. Organizing is not something that most people instinctively know how to do. Organizing wealthy people is a really specialized skill set and it's hard.

A lot of traditional organizing has this sort of "target" or "us vs. them" type of orientation that does not translate to donor organizing, and that leads some wealthy people to think, "My dad is the enemy."

Organizing your parents carries a different kind of risk from organizing your co-workers. Your parents are the people that you love most in the world, who often know you best — and maybe they are the cause of your greatest trauma. It's just a whole thing.

Another weakness is that there are limitations to how well we can take a standard community organizing framework and apply it to donor organizing. A lot of traditional organizing has this sort of "target" or "us vs. them" type of orientation that does not translate to , and that leads some wealthy people to think, "My dad is the enemy."

To be clear, your dad might be the enemy. I'm not saying that dads are never the enemy, but sometimes that's not the right power analysis or that's not what's going to actually get you the goods.

Mike: What parts of the work or the ecosystem are the most mature and what parts are most in need of development?

Mijo: Good question. You know, it's so hard because the parts of the ecosystem that should be mature have had to start over so many times that they haven't really been allowed to fully develop.

I think of all the activist-led social justice public foundations — so that's the FEX Funds; that's Grassroots International. It's everybody that came out of that moment of the late 70s, early 80s where so many of these funds were started.

If they had actually been able to build steadily for these last 50 years — where would they be now? They would be mind blowing, right? But most of them had to do a whole "phoenix rise from the ashes" thing. Multiple times! Every one of them has been through some kind of hellacious financial crisis or leadership transition or something like that. Some of them didn't make it. So it's a painful question because I feel like they are the oldest parts of the ecosystem, and the most mature, but they've had to start over multiple times. There are a few who have been able to maintain some continuity, and that's been a really good thing.

Resource Generation (RG) has one of the most developed frameworks and skill sets around wealthy people organizing but deals with some of the same problems I just talked about. It's an inherent tension of a young people's organization to always be starting over in some ways, with a new crop of leaders, which is fucking infuriating and also necessary.

Mike: Why do you keep on using the term donor organizing to

describe wealthy people organizing?[10]

Mijo: That's a good question. *Wealthy people organizing* just sounds really clunky.

Mike: Yeah, I hear that.

Mijo: So it's partly because I don't have a better term, but I mean, I'm organizing them because they're donors, right? I'm not only organizing them as donors, but that's the point of entry. Also, any wealthy person that I'm organizing damn well better be a donor. If not, what are they doing!?

But it's a good question, because we want them to be more than that, obviously. It's also this inherent tension of whether people over- or under-identify with their wealth. If we are organizing them around that wealthy identity and at the same time trying to get people to rightsize that attachment, and let go of their wealth, that seems like a real contradiction.

I think maybe the short answer to your question is that the term *donor* is less triggering for some people than *wealthy*. Some people don't like the term *donor*, but it's a lot less triggering, controversial and divisive than *wealthy people* or *owning class* or naming any kind of class, for that matter. A donor is something that you do. Whereas a wealthy person or owning class is something that you are. And that's a lot more baggage. I want wealthy people to own their class position but it might not be possible at first.

Mike: What would you identify as priorities for lefty, rich people organizing for the next five years?

Mijo: We need to really build more infrastructure for training, coaching, peer support, to develop wealthy people into organizers.

Second, I would prioritize working on the question of how to translate our most aligned wealthy people's economic power and social capital into left political power. For many of my clients, they have family relationships with the leadership of major companies, or they are one or two steps away from really personal relationships

---

10 As I mentioned earlier in "A Brief History...", it is one of my pet peeves when people use the term *donor organizing* as code and shorthand for *rich people organizing*. For more on why, read footnote number 14 on page 76.

with top business and financial leaders and boardrooms where key decisions are made. Or they own parts of businesses that have influence and power, but they don't know what to do with that or how to organize around it strategically, and frankly neither do I. There's got to be a way that we can translate these relationships and financial power into some kind of political power for our movements.

> **There's got to be a way that we can translate these relationships and financial power into some kind of political power for our movements.**

I think the third is to create more entry points into this world and work for wealthy people. I'm biased because this is the reason that we created DIGG. We need more spaces to welcome wealthy people in.

Mike: Why aren't the progressive donor networks we already have effective entry points?

Mijo: They're not effective enough entry points because, number one, I don't think people really find them unless they're already politicized or organized to some degree. And number two, I think it's super-hard to understand what's going on, to take advantage of the programming, to vibe with the culture or any of those things if you're not already in the lefty club. I think we need more entry points and more different kinds of entry points.

This is such a small pond we swim in, of people who educate and advise and organize wealthy people towards justice and equity, alongside progressive movements. There's just so few of us. We would all be better and smarter at this if there were more of us.

Mike: Agreed. That is so much of what this project is about. There needs to be more of us. And one thing we don't do well is talk openly, publicly and boldly about what we've done, so that many more people can learn from our work and get involved.

This is our opportunity to say: "For better or for worse, we're the most experienced people you've got at this historic moment doing this historic thing." And we're shit at actually telling you about it. So let's try to change that. Let's tell you about what we've done and figured out.

Mijo: Part of the reason we don't speak publicly or plainly about these things is because we're all holding so many confidential stories. We're trying to think strategically about what we can share and what we can't. There's so much to learn from these stories, but they're hard to tell. Maybe we can anonymize them. It's a real challenge.

Mike: Last question, you were telling me a story the other day that I wanted to come back to. Can you share your thoughts on the importance of wealthy people knowing our own goodness?

Mijo: We talked about that this morning during the workshop I led. I've seen that wealthy people often come to the groups they fund seeking validation of their own goodness and worthiness. That really resonated with some of the people in this workshop, where they were like, "I totally see donors coming to us seeking validation. And I didn't really realize that's what that was. And we shouldn't try to give them that." And I responded, "You not only shouldn't, you actually can't." You can tell people, "I like you. I think you're a good person." That's a really nice thing to say to anybody. And then you should probably tell them, "And I hope you know that for yourself." I hope you're telling yourself that you're a good person because that's really the only place that can come from.

> Part of the reason we don't speak publicly or plainly about these things is because we're all holding so many confidential stories.

I remember the quote you had on your office wall all those years ago. Something about wealthy people knowing their own goodness enough to look at the oppressive things they had done and work to fix them.[11]

It didn't click for me at the time. I didn't really get it.

And now I do. I see it everywhere. Wealthy people wanting to feel liked and happy with themselves through their giving, and upset when the affirmation of their goodness that they thought

---

11 The quote is from a mentor of mine, Jo Saunders, profiled later in this anthology. The quote reads, "Imagine a world where the owning class are so sure of their own goodness that they can face unflinchingly the genocide, slavery and oppression that they have engineered and profited from for centuries and commit to backing those that can end it."

they had ordered isn't delivered to them.

But the fact is, no one can do that for them. It has to come from inside. There are some people who can deliver that feeling in a short-term way, but I am not one of those people. That's not my vibe.

There's this idea and struggle I've heard from some wealthy people. This belief that there's a big enough check to write to become a good person. Ooh. It hurts to hear that. It's been really affecting me to see wealthy people struggle with that.

I've seen over and over again what happens when wealthy people have this unmet need for validation. They've been raised with this idea, this entitlement, that if they have a need, somebody out there can meet it. This idea that they should be able to pay somebody, purchase something, leverage some power to get that need met.

If that's not happening, it's like, "What the fuck is wrong with me? Why can't I feel better?" It is not the job of grassroots organizers. It is not the job of working-class people to make rich people feel better about themselves. I do not have a problem with people saying, "Eat the rich." I do not have a problem with guillotine jokes. I don't have a problem with any of that.

But there is something I want to see left movements understand. Moe Mitchell [Maurice Mitchell, executive director of the Working Families Party] wrote about it this last year — can we be more nuanced and understanding that everybody is a whole, complex person that is more than their identity markers? Can we be more relational in our organizing? Can we trust ourselves and each other to handle hard things? Can we see ourselves and each other, in all our weird complexity, in the context of collective strategy? Can we do that for all of us, including for the wealthy people that are putting in the work, that are trying to be in real solidarity? I believe we all have so much to gain if we do. ▪

THE TRUST WEB: MONEY LIKE WATER

Marian Moore

The Trust Web is a wealth-redistribution experiment grounded in cross-class relationships and no-strings-attached gifts that has redistributed a $7 million inheritance through the trusting relational web of a dozen movement organizers, activists and artists. In this moment of massive generational wealth transfer, as dissatisfaction and frustration grow with the inflexibility and power dynamics embedded in conventional philanthropy, the Trust Web models a different relationship to money, each other and the future.

Marian Moore's role began as coach to Elspeth Gilmore and then as lead facilitator of the first phases of the process, from 2014 to 2018. The Trust Web has now moved into a new stage of storytelling and practice, with shared leadership that grew from what they all learned together as the Trust Web.

Make Something New

Imagine this: You turn 21 and you inherit the first of what will be many millions of dollars. You were raised Quaker, with a strong social-justice ethos. When the money comes to you, you are compelled to give it away. This money is not something you have chosen. You find you don't like giving it away alone, as the sole decision maker. You have felt loneliness and isolation as a result of the inherited wealth that you feel is not rightfully yours. You want to figure out how to "give it back" in community with others, to share power and lessen your lonely burden of responsibility to do it well. You wonder what it would be like to actually do this work of giving back in deep partnership.

What if you stopped wondering and stepped into sharing power and releasing millions? While money is often equated with security, is it possible that in giving away the majority of your money, you feel more secure than you

Is it possible that in giving away the majority of your money, you feel more secure than you did before? More connected, less isolated and separate?

273

Elspeth *(back row, third from right)* recently reflected, "Our relationships are the foundation for everything that we can imagine and build together." (Courtesy of Trust Web)

did before? More connected, less isolated and separate?

And now, I invite you to imagine yourself as someone from generational poverty who has never had "extra"; imagine that you work with money for your organization but have never had agency over any personal funds beyond a paycheck, nor has anyone in your family or community. What would it feel like to be entrusted with a financial gift that changes the conditions of your life, with no strings attached? Also, what would it be like to have full discretion to give away money to others? What would it feel like to be entrusted in a group with 11 others from a wide variety of backgrounds who have also been given this gift, with support and companionship that allows for transformation of your relationship to money?

And finally, imagine yourself as someone who inherited some wealth yourself and has been working for a couple of decades with other primarily white inheritors to reckon with the dissonance of holding values of justice and a lineage of privilege and money. One of those coaching relationships leads you to support the development of a small cross-class, cross-race group to work with money. To your delight and surprise, you are able to bring much of what you learned with white inheritors to the transformational work with this group, only one of whom, your original client, had inherited money herself.

In the experiment that became the Trust Web, we have stories of such experiences, and I was invited into the role of holding space for its creation and helped to guide the experiment as it formed. We didn't know where we were going; we were truly guided into an experience that felt and continues to feel miraculous. Everyone broke out of the conventional norms of giving and receiving, and moved into such a deeply trusting web of relationships that all were transformed.

> **Everyone broke out of the conventional norms of giving and receiving, and moved into such a deeply trusting web of relationships that all were transformed.**

How did this happen? Are there lessons we have learned that can serve in this moment, which is characterized by mistrust and division? That is our hope. I am honored to share my perspective of what I helped create and witnessed among the beautiful souls who participated. And there are 12 other stories that could and may be told. It has shown me how money can serve liberation across class and race, helping us do transformational work together by creating a web of trusting relationships with an intention to challenge and change "how money works." And through it, I was also changed.

Yearning

Elspeth Gilmore, a white woman raised Quaker in New York City, inherited $1 million when she turned 21. Five years later, in 2004, Elspeth began to educate herself about giving it back to social-justice projects and community, while organizing and sharing with other inheritors about class privilege and wealth redistribution with Resource Generation. She inherited another $16 million when she turned 33 and moved a few million of it back into justice work in the first few years.

In her words:

> **From the time I got involved with Resource Generation, my north star was really to give back all of it. That has served as**

275

a really powerful guide. I've given back most of the money I inherited, and it's been an incredible journey with incredible people at my side. There's this whole other piece of personal healing and transformation that is necessary to accompany this work of redistribution, that allows the money to move, but also goes a lot deeper. I am one of the wealthy people in the current world, socialized to uphold the system as it is, which obviously has devastating effects on the world and has devastating effects on me: I feel that I have to be self-sufficient, that my survival depends on me being in control, that I can't make any mistakes. The list goes on and on, the effects of internalizing white supremacy as a white-bodied person. I don't have to believe in it. I don't have to want it, but I have it.

Despite the meaningful community Elspeth had built for herself, she was still the sole decision maker when it came to writing checks. Not only did she believe in sharing power, she no longer wanted the isolation of stewarding these resources alone and yearned to do it in partnership. In 2014, Elspeth hired me as a coach to support her to create a process that would satisfy this yearning. That yearlong inquiry led to the next step, which was to invite a small group of people she cared about, with shared values, to be *equal decision makers* with her about what to do with $7 million of her inheritance. The invitations went to women whom she thought would be interested in being part of a collective project diving deep into class and money together. Two of them, who had not grown up with wealth, said yes.

In her invitations, she put relationships first and also thought about where power and wealth are not typically held in this country. The two people who said yes were women of color: Black and Latinx women. One worked in professional philanthropy and one had been Elspeth counselor in college. According to Elspeth, "It's only become more clear as the journey has progressed how important their lived experience, values, particular intelligence and wisdom have been to what was created."

Wrestling with Money

As the three initial women (Trayce Peterson, Elspeth and one anonymous person whom we will call "Sonia" in this story) began working together, they prioritized building relationships through four in-person retreats. After the first retreat, they invited me into the role of support and facilitation for what was, at first, simply a "giving project" to redistribute $7 million of Elspeth's inheritance. I was to lead a process that included the kinds of experiential deep dives I had participated in and helped lead for decades in the Donut (Threshold Foundation) community and in other work I'd done as a coach and convener. It took a while for Sonia and Trayce to trust me, an owning-class white woman they'd just met, but over time they did and, together, went deeply into their own personal money stories and experiments with giving. Through the process, they empowered each other to imagine and create together something surprising and new.

We are now, in 2025, eight years on from that first meeting. Recently, Trayce, a Black activist and teacher in her 60s, was invited to reflect on the invitation and what unfolded:

> I have been chewing on the fact that in the earlier stage of this work, Sonia and I really had to grapple with ownership. We thought we were advising Elspeth on this journey. She kept saying to us, "No, this is *our* money." The reality that the three of us, with Marian, were going to steward this set of resources was a powerful thing to accept, and it was also a responsibility.

Elspeth added that this process "feels different than past giving. My only decisions were to hand the money over and to invite people into a relationship; the rest we would figure out together." This freed Elspeth and gave her hope for a different way with money.

I recall how, at the first retreat I led in 2016, Trayce and Sonia sat in their discomfort with money itself, with the possibilities that it offered, with their distrust *and* their trust. Given that the project was to redistribute $7 million, I put 70 dollar bills on the shared altar, each to represent $10,000. Trayce and Sonia exhibited

Trust Web member/
co-creator Trayce Peterson:
"Part of my liberation is tied
to the 1%."
(Courtesy of Trust Web)

visceral resistance, even horror!

As Trayce later put it, "Until the moment with the dollar bills, we really didn't have to think about the tangible money because it was somewhere else. That day, it became very real for us, and we started wrestling with what it means to engage with money and to do it in a way that has ethical standards."

Questions and reflections emerged out of this discomfort:

"Can money liberate others? Is there enough to quiet the suffering that poverty creates?"

"There is a seduction with money, that money is everything. But it's really only a tool. As with any tool — there are other things you need."

I asked, "What do you see as possibilities for your own liberation in this process?" understanding how much was stored in their own experience and inner knowing, if only it could be revealed.

Sonia responded, "Transformation, transition, creation, living in full dignity, reconciliation, growth in my evolving role around identity."

Trayce said, "So often people who don't have money don't get to make decisions about where money goes. I am mindful of many judgments — some very valid — related to people who have lots and lots of money. But we're all interconnected! This process for me humanizes wealthy people because sometimes they seem like

Cover Page

User: Admin

Document: FTP_Guts_-O

Server: CO-C6085

Time: 11/13/2025

Selected Page Range: 1-276

Status: OK

Notes 1:

Notes 2:

Instructions:

demon spawn in my mind *and* they are human beings also. Part of my liberation is tied to the one percent."

The three practiced by each giving away $20,000 on their own and then gave $300,000 together to a national organization whose work they thought critical and where one of them had a trusting relationship with people in leadership.

As they reflected on these first experiments, they realized something was missing for them. They came to realize that they wanted to center relationships of trust in the redistribution of the remainder of the money. Just like Elspeth, they did not want to do it alone! Through our conversations during this inquiry, three core values emerged that would guide the next phase: trust, relationship and liberation. At a gathering in the first series of meetings in 2016-2017, Elspeth said:

> Being part of the Trust Web, I've gained another layer of understanding about how deeply I have internalized upholding the class system, despite my values. I can see the little pieces of humanity I've lost. I can feel disconnected in the midst of deep community. I often feel a need to be in control to feel that I'm okay. I think that I can only rely on myself, despite evidence to the contrary. All these ways that I'm conditioned help to uphold the system that was set up so the owning class could amass wealth for ourselves. It takes deep practice and community to unlearn it all, and the Trust Web has been a pivotal space of practice for me.

At the same meeting, Sonia mused:

> What if one of the buckets of money is to give to individuals rather than organizations? Individual people take a lot of risks doing what they do. What if we trust that personal needs are connected to "movement" needs? For me, this is totally new behavior, a new line of thinking. This idea is difficult for me! I'm having a range of feelings. What I'm naming is definitely what I've wanted. It feels that we are experiencing shifts in relationships, the very thing we're trying to create.

Rereading this quote now, many years after transcribing the conversation, I see this as a moment of opening that led to one of the most unusual and radical dimensions of what was to come. I remember seeing it as a crack of an opening that made me wonder if it might open further. Would they dare suggest giving to themselves? For Trayce and Sonia to consider including individuals as worthy of a personal gift is very much outside of the conventional paradigm of philanthropy. And this gesture of personal gift became a key part of the conditions that were created for the transformational nature of the Trust Web.

The Trust Web: Imagination and Creation

In April 2017, at an Airbnb by a golf course in Trayce's hometown of Tucson, Arizona, Sonia, Elspeth, Trayce and I had our final of three meetings as the initiating "giving project" pod. We invited a SoulCollage™ facilitator, MariaBruna Sirabella, to help unlock a new level for this undertaking. SoulCollage™ is a creative and intuitive process that makes it easy to tap into other levels of consciousness by creating and giving voice to small collages that are called "Neters."

I believe that working with the Neters helped free Elspeth, Trayce and Sonia from vestigial grips of conventional philanthropy that might have lingered. Such as: "Give to established organizations not individuals." "Perform due diligence on the organizations and require them to make reports to show what they did with the money." "Do not develop relationships with grantees because you will lose objectivity."

By the end of the weekend, they had decided they would each invite three more people to the group — for a total of 12. Each of the 12 (including Elspeth) would receive $100,000 for personal use (a leap forward given that Sonia had initially said that funding individuals and not just organizations was uncomfortable for her) and $200,000 to give to "social justice," in whatever way each person defined it. They invited their people into the process, including a gathering the following summer at Elspeth's family's farm, land her father had purchased in the 1960s, in the Hudson Valley of New York.

Four months later, the 12 people — now named the "Trust Web" — plus me, gathered for the first of two facilitated retreats

WHAT IS GAINED
BY GIVING
MONEY WITHOUT
IMPEDIMENT,
WHERE NOTHING
HAS TO BE PROVEN?

as they received, spent, saved and redistributed their "personal" money ($100K each) and their "social justice" money ($200K each). The group also met virtually as a full group and in pods throughout the next year and a half to build relationships, offer peer support and do personal and relational work about giving and receiving money. They were also provided both financial planning guidance and administrative help to move the money, from Elspeth's financial advisor and her staff.

The 12 hold a variety of identities: Several are artists, one a musician and farmer, four are Quaker, four are Latinas who immigrated to the U.S. Five are Black; three are white; one is Asian American. Some of the people in the group are longtime, deeply effective, social justice movement leaders. Over half identify as queer or lesbian. The youngest was in her 30s, the eldest in her 70s. A few were raised "solidly middle class," a few precariously middle class. Several were raised in poverty, not knowing where the next meal would come from. Only Elspeth (and me as facilitator) had been raised in the owning class.

Given this range, and the subject at hand, I remain amazed at the relative ease in which they operated. Each was so open during the retreats and conversations that followed. My guess is that this stemmed from the trust inherent in the original relationships; Elspeth, Trayce and Sonia had chosen people with whom they had long-term trust. Maybe it was also because there was an abundance of money and no sense of scarcity, which can be divisive. I'll also add that the original three embodied the three values they had named as essential and that stayed strong: trust, relationship and liberation.

At that first full-group retreat in August 2017, my notes say that our purpose was to "nourish, imagine, fall in love, ground, widen the lens of what is possible." We created an altar with sacred objects people brought from home. Many ancestors were pictured on the altar. One other ancestor who was part of the weekend was Bayard Rustin, close advisor to Martin Luther King and one of the most influential and effective organizers of the civil rights movement. Bayard had been very close with Elspeth's father and is, in fact, buried at the farm. On the second day, we walked together across

The Trust Web meets in 2024 (Courtesy of Trust Web)

the lawn to the edge of the woods to visit his grave. As I reflect on the power of our time there together, it's easy to consider Bayard's spirit helping to hold us.

Among our activities that first weekend was to work with dollar bills. Each person held three bills; each bill represented $100,000. My guidance was, "Money is an instrument of exchange. Each of these bills represents $100,000. You will have fifteen minutes to contemplate this money. Play with it. Take it on a walk. Talk to it. What does it mean to you to hold it? As a receiver? As a future giver?

"What is your deepest wish for this money? What in your vision can be enabled by money? What part of your vision has nothing to do with money?"

The next day, one of the exercises was for the 12 to place themselves on a spectrum from "I don't know" to "I am very clear" about what they would do with the $100,000 "personal money" they had been given in this process. They created another spectrum for the $200,000 "social justice money" each would distribute. Putting themselves on the spectrum required each to reflect and share, in all of their vulnerability and "I don't know." I remember that process as one of the times that the relationships of trust deepened in the group.

As Trayce later said, "This is a cross-class, cross-race, cross-gender experiment. It affirms this notion that difference is good. Leaning into those differences, recognizing that sometimes it'll be bumpy, will make us better people and give us a more expansive view of the world."

Money Flows

Our second full-group gathering at the farm was 20 months later, in April 2019. Most of the 12 had spent and given the majority of their money. Our intention was to weave the community more; allow each to reflect on what they had learned, how they had changed; and learn from each other. Everyone *had* kind of fallen in love, and all were eager to reconvene.

People in the group used and moved the money at all different speeds and toward many different outcomes. A number of people bought houses; a sabbatical was funded; members of the Trust Web supported innumerable people in their communities and funded organizations and political organizing. One made gifts to a handful of people to give forward, a kind of mini-Trust Web.

Recently, on the banks of the Saint Croix River — which divides parts of Wisconsin and Minnesota, an hour from my home — I attended a workshop called "Growing Water Knowledge." As one of the workshop leaders talked about water, she described its dendritic nature. *Dendritic* means "having a branched form, resembling a tree." When I reflect on the design of the Trust Web, it is also, like water, dendritic in nature. These 12 people — positioned in different communities, with vastly different kinds of relationships across class, race and purpose — were able to carry the money, and its loving intention, from the original source of trust, relationship and liberation into a wondrous variety of places in ways that money rarely flows. It was without impediment; no one had

> As Trayce later said, "This is a cross-class, cross-race, cross-gender experiment. It affirms this notion that difference is good. Leaning into those differences, recognizing that sometimes it'll be bumpy, will make us better people and give us a more expansive view of the world.

> It was without impediment; no one had to prove anything to receive it.

to prove anything to receive it. If Elspeth had remained the sole decision maker over this $7 million, it would not have had this nourishing, far-reaching and life-giving characteristic.

Now in 2025, the group is examining patterns to the giving. Everyone made gifts to individuals. Everyone made gifts to organizations. Most gave gifts toward housing, migration and mutual aid. Over half of the people gave gifts they characterized as "spiritual," and at least half gave gifts supporting community service. There were many land projects (Indigenous land return, farming, identity justice) that received money. The organizations funded included youth, education and economic justice, Indigenous sovereignty, get out the vote, housing and workers' rights.

The Money Game

One of the most memorable, lively and meaningful sessions at our second retreat was when I led them in the Money Game, something I'd learned from my time with Donuts (Threshold Foundation). To play the game, each person brings as many dollar bills as they want to "risk" to learn more about their relationship with money. In the first round, people are instructed to give their money in whatever way they are moved to, in silence. A dollar here, a dollar there, maybe all of it at once to one person. In the next session, also in silence, they are instructed to take money from others.

Lots of feelings come up about giving and taking. Some people are pleased as their pile of bills grows, while others can't give it away fast enough. Some are energized by the mischievous fun of taking; others are more quiet and passive.

For the third round, talking is allowed, and the instruction is for the participants to ask for money and allow themselves to be asked. Negotiations ensue!

Because the Trust Web included several organizers — those who professionally organize people and money and power toward social justice — this third round of the Money Game was especially electric; it came naturally for them to begin to organize the money. One person was quite persuasive, and partway into the third round, a large amount was in that person's hands. Out of that energy, people got excited to grow that amount of money and pool funds to give meaningfully to one cause together.

The spontaneous organizing out of the Money Game was "just a game" and played with not much more than $100 total. But, months later, the energy and flow of it led several participants who hadn't yet directed all of their "social-justice money" to seed funding of Seed the Vote, a new effort to win federal elections while building the political power of local groups in battleground states.

Alex Tom had been discouraged by a number of donors who felt they would not be able to pull off this new effort, Seed the Vote. He was determined to prove them wrong, and he did. Alex shares that his relationship to money and power changed through his experience of the Trust Web. He developed a different level of power and agency having received the Trust Web money and didn't feel as beholden to individual donors and foundations. Trust Web gave him and other members the opportunity to invest in new ideas. He knew there was a need and that once Seed the Vote was off the ground, others would eventually come along. Other Trust Web members who lead organizations heartily agreed. They no longer felt the same need to prove themselves, to play at being deferential instead of recognizing and practicing the equalization of power through partnership. The power differential between them and their funders shifted. And/or the experience of having a financial cushion in their personal lives *and* money to give others changed how they relate to money.

Those who did not lead organizations also experienced transformation, the causes and effects of which we are still unearthing. Trayce told me how her whole attitude toward work and money had changed.

I responded, "Oh you still have money from the Trust Web?"

"No," she said, "I don't have any more money, but what I learned from the consciousness shift about money is still with me. I have developed more confidence to follow my instincts to flow money where it is needed. I have become more confident that my needs will be met if I trust."

And from Elspeth, who initiated the whole thing because she no longer wanted to "do it alone": "The Trust Web has helped me feel in my body, in a way I'd never experienced, that I am not alone. That I just might be caught by community if I fall. I've come to understand that the fear of not being caught is what keeps me holding onto wealth."

Another thing happened with the Money Game. As I facilitated the process, sitting on the sidelines, while the often rambunctious process unfolded, one of the participants, who had been collecting money for the possible group project, wanted to put the money somewhere. I saw her look at our shared altar with the money in her hand, about to place it there. But then I saw her reconsider and look around for something. She found a little piece of Styrofoam on the kitchen counter, placed it on the altar and then the money on top of the Styrofoam. "Oh my God," I thought, "she doesn't want the money to touch the altar!" When we debriefed the game, I started to describe what I had witnessed. To my surprise, while telling the story, I burst into tears. My reaction showed me how devoted I am to the work of making money sacred and to my belief that we must change our relationship with money if we are to change the world.

A Second Round

In 2019, I helped start Jubilee Gift with Don Shaffer and Michelle Be Long, to reimagine money and protect what is most sacred about our humanity. Through convenings of shared inquiry, wealth holders and wisdom keepers devote themselves to reimagining money and practicing with money in new ways that support healers, wisdom keepers and sacred land return.

Also in 2019, I helped Jubilee Justice founder Konda Mason host learning journeys, which brought Black and white people together to explore land, race, money and spirit.

In the fall of 2019, Trayce and Elspeth agreed to join me to tell the Trust Web story to a group of 30 convened by Jubilee Gift. One of the attendees recently told me, "When Elspeth and Trayce shared their story at the 2019 Jubilee Gift gathering, I thought 'YEAH — that's what I have been wanting to do!'" She had also attended a 2019 Jubilee Justice gathering that, in her words, "lit this fire that didn't have a path." She said, "Those two gatherings were like a floodgate that opened with permission to work with money in a different way." And, like Elspeth, she didn't want to make decisions by herself.

This woman set aside $10 million of her inheritance to distribute along with a mixed-race, mixed-class group of five people, starting in 2024. Each participant would receive $1 million to keep or distribute as they wished. This was the initial amount she had gotten at the age of 21, and she liked the idea of giving them that same amount. No strings attached. This group is still in a process together to figure out how to distribute the remaining $5 million.

In 2021, the original Trust Web engaged in storytelling internally, during the pandemic. Eventually, the group agreed that they were ready to share more publicly. We began with a few webinars to tell the story to some people who work in the field of donor organizing, including Mijo Lee. We wanted to spread the model and even support others who may be interested. Later, Mijo was at a gathering with Charlie Spears, an inheritor of a Greek shipping fortune, who was in the process of breaking the trusts he'd inherited so that he could do a comprehensive wealth redistribution with his wife, Ava Keating. They were interested in giving organizers money rather than going through traditional philanthropy channels. Mijo gave him information about the Trust Web, and Charlie found his way to Elspeth. In 2024, Elspeth, Trayce and I supported Charlie and Ava in creating a trust web of their own design through a series of retreats and Zoom meetings.

After a nine-month process, they decided to expand the idea of a trust web to work in closer collaboration with an existing network of organizers. They innovated on what we had done by deciding to, in Charlie's words, "dig deep with an existing network of organizers, rather than inviting a mix of folks from different backgrounds that would only know each other through Ava's or my relationship with them." In early 2025, Charlie and Ava initially allocated a multimillion-dollar donation to the People's Network for Land and Liberation (PNLL) as a no-strings-attached donation.

They then pitched the trust web idea to the leadership layer of PNLL, referencing the design that emerged from the successful experiment with Elspeth's inheritance. After numerous discussions, PNLL opted into a trust web process with a portion of the donation.

We look forward to continuing to tell the story and support people like Charlie and Ava, who are inspired by this cross-class, dendritic distribution model.

Reflections

The majority of the original Trust Web members continue to work together to make meaning of our experiences, tell the story more broadly of this approach to wealth distribution, support others on the path and experiment in the Trust Web community as we continue to transform our relationship with money, ourselves and each other.

It was clear from the outset that this experiment would provide transformation for Elspeth, releasing this money and "sharing the burden" of giving it among the Trust Web. But more of a surprise to me are Alex's comments:

> **The transformation goes both ways. It's not just about changing rich people, but changing our relationship to capital by practicing a new way of being. It is a full transformation of society. Being in the nonprofit industrial complex as an executive director, hustling and being told "No" for 20-plus years, there is a dominant framework under capitalism: power over. The Trust Web was a healing transformation and showed me that a different path is not only possible but necessary.**

Elspeth added:

> We all need healing and transformation. The Trust Web
> has been about being in it together, across race and class.
> The relationships we're building are critical in this time of
> cancel culture, climate change and threats to democracy and
> organizations. We have to build the muscle to be in it with
> each other through all the shit, particularly around money
> and class, because our relationships are the foundation for
> everything that we can imagine and build together.

Trayce added,

> I was taught, and I believe, that sharing is caring. If people are
> honest and open and paying attention, there is abundance
> around us. If we give and are generous, the sense of
> abundance expands. Not only for recipients — but for the
> giver, too.

Ana Maria Vasquez, a Colombian woman who is part of the group
of 12 that we call the original Trust Web, said:

> Money is a resource like the water and the air. It is all for
> everyone. I always have this image of the heart that is
> pumping. When the heart cannot pump, these resources are
> stuck. You get a heart attack. This flow is needed, just like the
> water is needed, just like the air is needed. And the resources
> are not meant to be kept, to cause a heart attack. No, they
> are meant to move so that life can happen. Trust is important,
> because we cannot see the whole thing. We just trust the
> little strand that each is holding. We move these strands and
> know that whatever it is, we make this beautiful weaving
> together. In this beautiful earth, we have created terrible
> things to make life very complicated. But like a young woman
> one time said, we made this happen; we have the power to
> undo it. We have the power to take these stumbling blocks
> that we have created so that nothing flows; we can take them
> down and make it flow.

It has been more than 10 years since Elspeth first invited me to

Art by Trust Web member Ana-Maria Vasquez shows a choice: "When we touch our hearts and say 'I can open it up. I don't have to die' then comes abundance. We can give out constantly all the time every day as the earth does." (Courtesy of Trust Web)

provide coaching for her as she imagined a new way to be with the giving of her inheritance. Ten years of listening, following the thread, supporting movement toward the possibilities expressed, first by Elspeth; then by Trayce Elspeth and Sonia; and, ultimately, by all 12. We could NEVER have imagined this at the beginning.

For me, it has been an affirmation of having faith in my fellow humans and the possibility of transformation — even in the belly of the capitalist beast, where money has been a tool of such division and destruction. As I write, I am reminded of a moment in 2007, when I participated in a yearlong training called Art of Change. I was in a conversation with a peer coach named Jeff. Jeff asked me how I would explain the work I do. I responded, "Leaning on faith: make sure everything is in order, set the tone, hold the space, keep things moving, weave the story. All of that infused with a little secret — understanding the power of love."

At the center of the Trust Web experiment was a task to redistribute money.

These brilliant, imaginative, powerful and faithful humans all said YES, as did I. It is safe to say that every single participant had a complex, if not fraught, relationship with money, whether having too much or too little or not liking how and where it usually moves. Many held money as the most toxic substance of all. There is so much trauma embedded in each of our money stories.

That's why this storytelling about the Trust Web is focused more on the *how* of the distribution than the *what*. The *process,* in my view, is where the potency and possibility of social change is underexamined. I am hopeful that this Trust Web story shows you that we can increase our intimacy and understanding of money and stay open to changing our story about money, while deepening trust in relationships across differences to channel the flow of money — so that it can go on new pathways, further into the places and people who need it.

Free the People to Free the Money to Free the People.

At the end of the summer of 2024, with the world-changing election still in the future, 11 of us gathered again at Elspeth's family's farm. We came together to plan our next moves; what is the story we want to tell? How do we want to change the dominant narrative of money and for whom? What have we learned? In a session designed to help us articulate our shared purpose, we broke into small groups to describe the Trust Web experience so far.

I was delighted to land in a group that included a Trust Web member who is a musician. Because he writes songs, as I do, I hoped our report back to the group could be in song. Our small group generated, in rapid fire, phrases to capture what the experience had been for us. For me, remembering the beginning with Elspeth, alone with her yearning; then the early, not-yet-trust-filled process with Elspeth, Trayce and Sonia; and then looking around at the vitality, intimacy and excitement embodied in these kindreds who want to share with the world the transformation they've experienced, I blurted, "It's a fucking miracle!" "There's our chorus!" they said. Minutes later, with guitar accompaniment, we sang our new song to the group:

It was suddenly possible in this circle of trust.
The power of relationships, the liberation of all of us.
Healing from trauma and pain. Investigate and process class.
Explore Big Money — Why me? Why not me? Transformation.
It's a fucking miracle. It's a fucking miracle,
Dreams coming true... ∎

Trayce Peterson, Marian Moore and Alex Tom sport their "Fucking Miracle" T-shirts at the Solidaire National Conference, 2024 (Courtesy of Trust Web)

JO SAUNDERS

Michael Gast

A version of this piece originally appeared on the Organize the Rich Substack in November 2023.

When I was 28 years old, 5 years after I got involved with Resource Generation, I went to my first owning-class workshop led by Jo Saunders.[1]

At that time, she already was an old woman, small in stature, her long gray hair tied in a ponytail, with a string of pearls around her neck. She had grown up in an owning-class English family during World War II when, like many children, she was sent off to live with her relatives in the countryside. She had lived through a lot.

There were 40-50 of us there, coming to learn how we could regain and reclaim our minds from the patterns of greed, arrogance and indifference (to name a few) we had taken on as owning-class people.

1 These were peer-counseling workshops as part of Re-evaluation Counseling (RC), where participants learn to trade time listening to each other tell our stories and let go of the painful emotions that hold us back. Some of you might have heard about RC and have your own experiences with or reactions to the theory and practice. It is one of many healing practices that I have seen be useful in addressing the difficult experiences and harmful messages that limit our lives. Regardless of whether you know of RC or not, I think there is something to learn from what Jo put forward. I certainly have.

As we arrived at the main room of the conference center, she walked around and greeted each of us personally. I remember her small, strong, bony hands reaching out to hold mine. I remember her looking into my eyes and welcoming me warmly, with a kind and piercing gaze. She worked hard to communicate to each of us that it was good we had made it to the workshop, and that we were wanted and belonged with her that weekend.

The opening evening of the workshop she led us all in a round of introductions: "What's your name? How much money do you have? And where does it come from?"

Her tone was light and firm. As we went around the room, every once in a while, she would stop and tease us about our embarrassment and slipperiness around saying numbers and being honest about where the money came from. As people would share their numbers, she would warmly ask, "Soooo, have you lied yet?" We laughed uncomfortably and knowingly at our collective predilection to underestimate the money in our control.

She knew us and our patterns well. She spent many decades leading and counseling owning-class people all around the world, to regain our integrity, return our stolen wealth and back the working class in ending all oppressions.

As people would share their numbers, she would warmly ask, "Soooo, have you lied yet?"

Jo was my mentor and teacher — one more leader in this work that I want you to know. Over more than a decade, I attended many of her workshops, met with her regularly, relied on her counsel and became quite close to her.

Here are a few of the lessons I take from her that I want to share with you today.

1. "Show me a monster, and I'll show you a child with a broken heart"

Jo was unflinching in her ability to look at what the owning class had done. She knew the details of what her English, owning-class Christian people had wrought in Britain and around the world through slavery, colonialism, native genocide, the arms trade, the sex industry and more. She studied and understood how the U.S. and Europe continued to dominate the world through military force, deeply ingrained racism, and economic exploitation. She was clear that the owning class was behind almost any human tragedy, profiting at the expense of others.

AND... she claimed all owning-class people as hers, from Trump to Musk to Qaddafi.

She was able to do that because she had a steadfast understanding of the inherent humanness and preciousness of each of us, under the crud of classism, and the accumulated confusions of our oppressive society.

She always modeled for me what it means to not blame anyone, find the good in everyone, while being steadfast in a commitment to accountability, apology and repair.

She knew how to love the person, and oppose any shitty actions that they might take. As she said many times, "Show me a monster, and I'll show you a child with a broken heart." I think that captures such a fundamental lesson in this work and in the way we orient towards ourselves and other humans as believers in collective liberation.

She knew how to love the person, and oppose any shitty actions that they might take.

2. Claim your connection to the owning class (if you have one)

Jo helped me be clear that the way towards liberation is to claim my connection to the owning class, rather than run away from it.

Instead of wealthy people separating ourselves from other owning-class people, instead of ignoring our wealth or connection to privilege, instead of distinguishing ourselves as the "good" or "better" or "more responsible" rich people, Jo encouraged us to embrace them all as "our people."

She encouraged me and many others to build relationships with every owning-class person in our lives, including those in our families. She knew that so much more would be possible if we tried to connect meaningfully with every rich person we knew, loved them as best we could, and (re)built real relationships.

Instead of denying or defending the ways I am connected to

Instead of denying or defending the ways I am connected to the owning class, Jo helped me love and appreciate myself and other owning-class people while also noticing the ways I (and we) play an oppressor role.

the owning class, Jo helped me love and appreciate myself and other owning-class people while also noticing the ways I (and we) play an oppressor role.

Jo urged us to go into owning-class spaces and bring what we know about the need for redistribution and divestment. She would say, "Put on your pearls! Put on your suits! Don't be too proud to rub shoulders with any and every single owning-class person. Get to know them. Listen to them. Show them you like them, share your thinking, and see what becomes possible."

Jo asked everyone else to claim us too. She asked poor, working- and middle-class people to consider us long-lost cousins and invite us to come home. Return the wealth and come home. A truly revolutionary idea.

3. Hurt people hurt people: The secondary patterns

Jo taught me a way of understanding the shitty behavior of wealthy people that has continued to be quite useful to me. She taught me the idea of secondary patterns.

Through her counseling of thousands of owning-class people, she showed over and over how the first thing that happens to an owning-class person, whether they are born into the owning class or as they ascend the class ladder, is a toxic mix of isolation, harshness, and often unseen or unacknowledged violence.

Those are the hurts that leave the owning class open to the secondary patterns of greed, ignorance, indifference, and pretense.

As one way to understand this, Jo explained how, because of colonialism,

The first thing that happens to an owning-class person, whether they are born into the owning class or as they ascend the class ladder, is a toxic mix of isolation, harshness, and often unseen or unacknowledged violence.

the English monarchy is at the heart of owning-class culture worldwide. The monarchy perfected the art of numbing its heirs through isolation and emotional deprivation, thereby cultivating the capacity for cruelty and detachment so necessary to maintain and justify their rule. Jo told a story about Prince Charles, as a 3-year-old, seeing his mom (Queen Elizabeth) for the first time after a three-month separation, and going to greet her by shaking hands. No warm embrace. All formality and a stiff upper lip.

As the dad of a young boy, this story hit hard. The lack of human comfort and care is heartbreaking. I think of how Charles was trained and treated as a little boy, and it makes more sense that he would grow up to justify and participate in the mistreatment of others.

In contrast, Jo taught us that laughing and crying, and generally being listened to, are time-worn strategies to help us recover from the hard things that happen in our lives. She told one workshop participant at the front of the room to try out saying, "I'd like to have integrity, but instead I'm greedy and dishonest!" Laughter rolled through the group, followed by tears at how true it was.

A key part of my work, and this project of organizing the rich, then became about seeing past the oppressive behavior (i.e., secondary patterns) in myself and others, and focusing more time and energy on healing from the initial experiences that set me and my people up to act so badly. I started to understand the importance of talking about and working through feelings connected to this damage, including the hard things that happened to me as well as the intergenerational traumas I carry. I now know that when I am acting controlling, I am most likely scared and feeling alone, like I was when I was little, and it's time to ask for help or call a friend. This knowledge doesn't always make the behavior easier for me or others to handle, but it does help me name what's happening and better assess what I can do about it.

This emotional work can feel trivial in the face of the many compounding crises we face. And I've found that my organizing and leadership has been profoundly strengthened by attending to the deeper wounds I carry.

4. Give it back!

Jo was clear that we won't be able to end oppression by emotional healing alone, she was adamant that every owning-class person give back the stolen wealth that has ended up in our bank accounts. She knew that there was no way to have the money and not accumulate the "better than"/separate/entitled attitudes of the rich. If any of us, as owning-class people, want to regain our full integrity, she made clear we needed to give back the wealth and give up the justifications for it. This meant ALL of the inherited wealth and whatever excess wealth we accumulated through work or investments.

> If any of us, as owning-class people, want to regain our full integrity, she made clear we needed to give back the wealth and give up the justifications for it.

I loved her clarity, even as I've struggled with the specifics of how and how much to give back in my own life. This idea, of divestment and redistribution, shapes my hopes for every wealthy person I interact with. I want for all of us to give back what our people have stolen, while making sure we simultaneously build the relationships and communities we need to support ourselves and live big, full lives.[2]

5. Big vision

By the time I met Jo, I already was highly invested in and excited about organizing wealthy people towards justice. And yet, I had never met anyone with as big a vision as Jo had for owning-class people. She was unflagging in her insistence that we give back inherited and excess wealth. She was steadfast in her belief that we could look at the exploitation and violence we had profited

---

2 Jo was clear, and so am I, that divestment needs to go hand in hand with the concerted attention and effort being given toward the financial stability, health and well-being of the wealthy people involved. Divestment should not be about martyrdom or be done quickly for the sake of alleviating guilt and shame. While personal divestment is different from a foundation spending down its assets, I loved seeing this article that was recently published by dear colleagues — Ash-Lee Woodward Henderson and Farhad Ebrahimi, "We Need a Strategy for Spending Down," *Stanford Social Innovation Review*, Winter 2024 — and think they pose some useful and relevant questions.

from and then work to end it. She came up with statements to guide us. They remain some of the most inspired thinking I've seen in this work.

These two statements are particularly powerful to me:

> **"Imagine a world where the owning class are so sure of their own goodness that they can face unflinchingly the genocide, slavery, and oppression that they have engineered and profited from for centuries and commit to backing those that can end it."**

> **"I promise always to remember that I and my people are completely good, and I need never pretend again. No matter how frightening it feels, I will give up the control of wealth and the justifications for it. And I will come home and humbly take my own place with working-class people in setting the world completely to right."**

It was so reassuring to meet Jo and have her share a vision that treated my people with love and respect, while demanding the big changes I knew were necessary.

6. Antisemitism as the glue of our class society

Jo was one of the most dedicated and powerful allies to Jews I've ever met. She deeply knew how antisemitism, this thousand-year-old oppression, was key to maintaining the power of the owning class. She taught so many, including me, about how antisemitism was used over and over by the rich and ruling classes as a deflection and pressure-release valve when the masses started organizing against them.[3] She saw clearly how owning-class Jews are used as convenient scapegoats by the gentile owning class, and, over and over, she would remind Jews and gentiles alike about antisemitism's horrific

She deeply knew how antisemitism, this thousand-year-old oppression, was key to maintaining the power of the owning class.

---

3 See Erik K. Ward, "Skin in the Game: How Antisemitism Animates White Nationalism," *The Public Eye*, Juen 29, 2017.

costs. She knew that if we were ever to end classism and racism, we would need to end antisemitism and she was unapologetic about creating a kind and protected space for Jews within this work for owning-class liberation.[4]

She was always looking out for chances at her workshops to notice and call out antisemitism. She was delighted to be told about her mistakes and the mistakes of other gentiles. Once, she asked for volunteers to talk about their oppressor patterns, the justifications and behaviors that lead people to treat others badly and hoard their wealth. A friend, a young Jewish woman, raised her hand. No one else did. She was about to call on my friend when a Jewish leader in the room pointed out that the only volunteer was a Jew. Jo said, "Thank you" and then talked passionately about the need for the many white gentiles at the workshop to contradict their patterns of silence, fear and freezing. She made clear the importance of not letting Jews be on their own taking risks, but instead, to raise their hands, be vulnerable and join Jews in taking courageous action. It was such a very small thing, and the fact that she took it seriously was everything.

Jo left me with a deep desire to see an independent non-Jewish movement to end antisemitism, a clear conviction that it's possible, and a steadfast confidence that it's just what's needed to counter the divide, conquer strategies of the right, and unlock the full power of poor and working-class organizing efforts. She, more than anyone I've ever met, knew how to take full responsibility, as a white owning-class gentile, for antisemitism and its impact, and because of her, the bar is forever raised in my mind.

7. Owning-class liberation

Jo showed me that this work is not just about moving money or organizing to support working-class movements. This is about my liberation. This is about me getting free, me and my owning-class siblings reclaiming our integrity and intelligence and having the biggest, boldest, most connected lives we can. This idea, of

---

4 April Rosenblum's 2007 zine "The Past Didn't Go Anywhere: Making Resistance to Antisemitism Part of All of Our Movements" is a great resource.

owning-class liberation, has galvanized my life ever since. This project is about freeing my people from the horrible roles we play in capitalism and our class society. This is for me.

* * *

I feel so lucky to have known Jo. She was always thrilled to hear about my activism and organizing efforts. She cheered me on and delighted in knowing the details of what I was up to. She reminded me of my Jewish grandma in so many ways. Strong willed, determined, a bossy and big-hearted older woman who loved me deeply. I will always carry Jo in my heart and in my mind. And, when I need a laugh or a bit of courage, I will hear her voice asking me, "Are you lying yet?!" ∎

> **I will always carry Jo in my heart and in my mind.**

"IMAGINE A WORLD WHERE THE OWNING CLASS ARE SO SURE OF THEIR OWN GOODNESS THAT THEY CAN FACE UNFLINCHINGLY THE GENOCIDE, SLAVERY, AND OPPRESSION THAT THEY HAVE ENGINEERED AND PROFITED FROM FOR CENTURIES AND COMMIT TO BACKING THOSE THAT CAN END IT."

Jo Saunders

WHAT'S NEXT?

Rajasvini Bhansali

Editor's Note (MG): I couldn't think of a better person to close out this first-ever Organize the Rich anthology than Rajasvini "Vini" Bhansali. Early on in this project, Vini challenged me. She said some version of "You've played the role of the 'nice white guy.' What does being more bold and courageous look like for you?" I loved the agitation and challenge. It is one of the many reasons I have taken on this Organize the Rich project.

Vini is a visionary. She is a leader in building cross-class coalitions. She knows what it means to engage wealthy people with kindness and high expectations. She models a dynamic, fun and ruthlessly strategic leadership we can all learn from. It feels just right to have her bring our first anthology to a close.

When we think about building movements for long-term transformation, we must understand the lineage of what came before us. Knowing our history is both about honoring what has been done and evolving it to meet the conditions we face today. Without this historical grounding, we repeat the same mistakes rather than making new ones and learning from them.

We stand on the shoulders of people who never saw a reality without racial exploitation. We stand on the shoulders of people who never saw significant numbers of wealthy people working to end wealth inequality. I'm thinking of my mentors — June Jordan, Raúl Salinas, Ana Sisnett and so many others who spent their lifetimes imagining and working toward a truly equitable and multiracial democracy. It is our job to bring that work to completion.

Even as we meet the present with all its constraints and challenges, we're seeding what will blossom into the work of future generations. My nephews' and nieces' children — my grandkids — will start from where we leave off and take it further.

Looking toward the future, here are seven reflections to help guide this work forward.

1. Expanding Beyond the Margins

Over the past 50 years, we've done a remarkable job pulling together something of a Bad News Bears team of rich people. We've been very good at organizing the black sheep of wealthy families, the radical ones, the ones who have been pushed to the margins — and we've made something significant. Yet we still struggle to reach the heart of the owning class, where much of the power and wealth lies.

We need to see ALL people, including wealthy people, not as empty vessels but as agents of change already enacting their own version of transformation.

To move beyond the margins, *we must be willing to listen.* We need to see ALL people, including wealthy people, not as empty vessels but as agents of change already enacting their own version of transformation. We have something to learn from them.

We often veer toward people we find easy to talk to — it's comfortable to jam on ideas with like-minded folks. But if we're going to adopt an organizer mindset, we must engage people who challenge or irritate us and support their transformation while learning from them.

Our listening skills in this work are often poor. We're not building a broader base because we don't act like we fundamentally care what some people have to say. We're always working to convince others that our point of view is precious.

I've experienced this firsthand with donors who don't fit our prototype. One such person told me, "I just hate the word *organizing.* "Organize the rich" doesn't work for me. It feels like my agency is stripped away." In the past, I would have preached about frameworks and tried to sound smart, which would only have alienated her further. Instead, I simply said, "Tell me more" and listened as she talked herself out of her own argument.

2. Scaling our Impact

When we look at organizations like Resource Generation and Solidaire, we keep growing beyond our capacity, primarily by word of mouth and through personal relationships. Every

305

conservative shift in the U.S. floods our organizations with people seeking alternatives. It's a good problem to have.

A few years ago, when Solidaire grew from 100 to 200 members, some were concerned: "We need to stop growing. Let's stay small. I'll miss the intimacy of knowing every person." But that's not what this political project is about. How do we create conditions for intimacy, mutual learning and community building, while understanding that we must be much larger than 500 members to organize all the wealth needed for social change?

This isn't just a domestic question. Capital is everywhere. Capitalism is everywhere. And our members are international — they're moving and making money here and abroad. The internationalization of this work is happening, whether we like it or not. The question is how we help it grow and adapt while finding the space and time to do it well.

3. Developing Leadership

We need to see our members' full capacity and potential leadership and develop it, adapting the tactics that we've learned from effective frontline movements. We don't just need more staff to meet rising demands — we need to organize and strengthen a movement-aligned base of donor members. This means investing in donors not simply as sources of funding, but as essential actors in movements for justice.

This means investing in donors not simply as sources of funding, but as essential actors in movements for justice.

At Solidaire, we've learned that developing donor and funder leadership requires political education, organizing skill-building and clear expectations for what it means to be a member in solidarity with movements. We must grow from offering short-term, reactive solutions to being long-haul actors who understand how movements evolve over time and who are ready to show up with integrity, humility and consistency. This includes creating value-aligned giving plans, committing to multiyear movement funding and being responsive to emergent needs without losing strategic focus. Trustees and foundation staff have a critical role to play in organizing their peers and institutions around a shared vision — one that increases giving, supports policies that serve communities, transforms grantmaking practices to meet the needs of movements and shifts the sector from wealth hoarding to collective investment in a liberatory future.

The whole ecosystem needs to switch from a service approach to an organizing mindset.

Beyond individual organizations, the progressive donor network movement must align on this approach. Currently, donors can pick and choose: "If I go to this donor network, I'll get treated like a queen bee. If I go there, I'll actually have to work and show I'm capable of organizing others." It becomes too easy to pick the path of least resistance. The whole ecosystem needs to switch from a service approach to an organizing mindset.

4. Building Coalitions

In my experience, coalitions are great to theorize about but hard to sustain in practice. Sometimes you just have to start experimenting with two like-minded organizations rather than trying to build unity among 50. Successful coalitions require follow-through, smart facilitation, meaningful roles for participants and actionable items between meetings. They need leaders who keep people focused and goal-oriented, avoiding the tendency to muddy the waters with random funding requests that destroy fragile trust. The in-between follow-through that many leaders neglect is critical for making people feel valued and respected for their time and energy.

One example of this in practice is the Block and Build Funder Coalition, which emerged in response to a call to action from movement leaders in the summer of 2024, sounding the alarm about escalating repression. It grew from a strong alignment between Women Donors Network Action and Solidaire Action, as we leveraged our distinct social and political capital to bring the right people together at the right time. We've now grown to 240 members,[1] including donors, funders and philanthropy-serving

---

1 As of May 8, 2025.

organizations, working to build solidarity across philanthropy, coordinate strategic defense of movements and build long-term solutions to protect our civil liberties.

5. Navigating Emotions and Relationships

The emotional terrain within us — the childhood stuff we're always grappling with — profoundly affects our leadership. The class trauma we all carry in different ways holds us back from integrity and effectiveness. There are no shortcuts in addressing this. We all need consistent practice to know ourselves — not a workshop once a year, but a regular practice that helps us notice what old feelings are coming up, see where we're getting hooked by the conditions

We all need consistent practice to know ourselves — not a workshop once a year, but a regular practice.

around us and do what's needed to regain clarity and perspective. For me, that practice includes daily yoga and meditation, grounded in my Jain spiritual tradition, which helps me return to stillness, humility and discernment in the face of complexity.

As a woman of color working in the primarily white and wealthy world of philanthropy and leading a primarily white and wealthy base, I've learned the importance of relationship building as fuel for continued creativity for myself and as a way to break through stereotypes that others may have about me. I still do many one-on-ones, even though our team of organizers has expanded. I talk to our members, trustee-level people and their peers of color. I try to be available to people who want support, advice or just someone to vent to. Our organizing and community building is all relational work. There are no shortcuts.

I also hold clear boundaries about what I'm available for: sophisticated, difficult, strategic and relational conversations, yes; obligatory networking, no. I'm becoming better at drawing those boundaries while still respecting people's humanity. I want to value other people's time as much as I value my own.

6. Preparing for Victory and Backlash

History shows us that when the working class wins governing power and the possibility of redistributive policies, there's often a short-term victory followed by fierce pushback from wealthy people — more angry and organized than before. We saw this in Chile after Salvador Allende won, in the U.S. after the New Deal and in countless other examples.

In the U.S., with disproportionate power in the hands of a few, we don't have a choice but to bring rich people along. That's our challenge. If we leave rich people disenfranchised and alienated, they will cause more harm than good. We have no choice but to engage wealthy people, because left disorganized and feeling like they have no role in social reconstruction, they will undermine our progress. It's not just a strategic choice, but a principled one. In the world we want, every life is sacred.

> We have no choice but to engage wealthy people, because left disorganized and feeling like they have no role in social reconstruction, they will undermine our progress.

This requires long-arc work and skill-building that we don't yet have. All of us doing our part to lead social change need laboratories for practice where we can try things at a scale where failure is possible. For those of us in the U.S. and other Western contexts, we've been shaped by systems that have colonized our imaginations, sanitized our desires and led us to internalize a false sense of superiority. The myth of meritocracy lives in our bones.

Divesting from these internal systems is long-term transformational work. We must give people room to test their skills, fail miserably, pick themselves up and try again — not canceling them for their mistakes or giving up on them, but holding them in a network of deep care.

7. Developing a Long-Term Vision

Class societies have been around for thousands of years. Let's not be naive. If we are serious about building an equitable and just society — where access to resources is organized around collective well-being rather than wealth and social status — we must think in terms of generations, not grant cycles.

Social movements have long taught us to dream beyond the limits of the present. A winning strategy for the philanthropic sector must include a multigenerational vision — one that stretches across the next 150 years. This kind of long-term thinking is core to many Indigenous worldviews, where ancestors and descendants alike shape present-day choices. As someone whose own lineage carries the legacy of caste-oppressed people who have resisted systems of domination for over 3,000 years, I know that enduring struggle also gives rise to enduring imagination.

As we look forward, we must ask: What do we want to figure out together over the next six generations? If our efforts are successful, what will our communities look and feel like? How will we relate to work, to land, to money — and to one another?

Developing a bold and hopeful vision for a world beyond racial capitalism, settler colonialism and authoritarianism will be key to mobilizing more people, including those with wealth, into meaningful long-term participation. If the best vision the left can offer wealthy people is to become "really great donors," we have not pushed far enough. The opportunity — and responsibility — is to engage people with access to resources as full participants in a collective process of transformation, helping them shift from wealth hoarding to wealth redistribution, from control to collaboration, from fear to shared purpose.

If the best vision the left can offer wealthy people is to become "really great donors," we have not pushed far enough.

Donor and funder organizers must take seriously the role they can play in building this future. Philanthropy must recognize itself not as the answer, but as a tool — and only a temporary one — in service of a much broader liberatory project. Our task is to act with both urgency and patience, planting seeds today that can grow into a future rooted in dignity, self-determination and shared abundance.

310

Conclusion

The work of organizing wealth toward justice is still fledgling in many ways, but it's growing beyond what many of us once imagined. At Solidaire, I've had the deep privilege of working alongside extraordinary members, trusted allies and movement leaders who are driving bold experiments in justice — building new systems, forging unlikely coalitions and reimagining power across race, class, gender and geography. They remind me every day that this work isn't just about moving money — it's about transforming ourselves and the systems that created inequality in the first place. By honoring our lineages, building courageous leadership, nurturing coalitions and committing to personal and political practice, we are planting the seeds for generational transformation.

Rajasvini Bhansali
Executive Director, Solidaire ∎

"THIS WORK ISN'T JUST ABOUT MOVING MONEY — IT'S ABOUT TRANSFORMING OURSELVES AND THE SYSTEMS THAT CREATED INEQUALITY IN THE FIRST PLACE."

Rajasvini Bhansali

ACKNOWLEDGMENTS

There are so many that made this anthology possible.

Thank you to Patricia Francisco for all the coaching, support, large and small edits, perspective and confidence you gave to each of us in this process. So much of this book would not be possible without your help. Thank you to Cynthia Williams for your detailed and tireless copy editing.

Thank you to Dio Cramer, our talented designer who brought skillful, artful insight and a depth of experience to the job. It was a delight to work with you. Everything you, the reader, love about the look and feel of this book has been made possible by Dio.

Thank you to Allison Harrison for your diligent work on the end notes and so many of the details that went into this Anthology.

Thank you to the team at Smart Set for printing the book on a tight timeline.

Thanks to Jamie and Angela Schwesnedl and Moon Palace Books for distributing this book for us and answering lots of our questions.

Thank you to the advisory committee of Organize the Rich: Erin Heaney, Elspeth Gilmore, Yahya Alazrak, Taj James, Iimay Ho, Braeden Lentz, Rajasvini Bhansali, Chuck Collins. Your confidence and support made all of this possible.

Thank you to the Solidaire Network team for being such committed partners, cheerleaders, advisors, and supporters of Organize the Rich. Your generosity and confidence has given this project wings.

Thank you to all the contributors and interviewees for your willingness to share your story and hard-earned perspective: Winona LaDuke, Rajasvini Bhansali, Iimay Ho, Braeden Lentz, Linda Burnham, Max Elbaum, Nina Luo, Billy Wimsatt, Chuck Collins, Nigel Charles, Leah Hunt Hendrix, and Mijo Lee.

Thank you to the many many peers and colleagues whose advice, insights, edits, comments and encouragement were invaluable: Allison Budschalow, Adam Roberts, Barni Qaasim, Bronwyn Walls, Chad Jones, Chris Westcott, Anne Ellinger, Christopher Ellinger, Emily Lee, Ethan Kerr, Farhad Ebrahimi, Garrett Neiman, Hez Norton, Iris Brilliant, Isaac Lev Szmonko, Jason Franklin, Jenny Ladd, Joanna Levitt Cea, John Poore, Karen Pittelman, Laura Wernick, Mario Lugay, Nicole Lewis, Rachel Sherman, Rye Young, Taij Moteelall, and Terry Odendahl.

Thank you to the financial support of Working Families Party, Solidaire Network, Resource Generation, Jenny Ladd, Elspeth Gilmore, Katrina Schaffer, and Molly Hein.

In addition to those already mentioned,

From Michael: I would like to thank Ariel Luckey, Christian Leahy, David Basior, Gila Lyons, Ginger Hintz, Joseph Phelan, Josh Healey, Liz Sullivan, Raphael Cohen, and Zoe Levitt for their support along the way.

I also want to give a special shout out and so much love to everyone I met, learned from and organized with at Resource Generation. You developed me into who I am today. Thank you.

I would also like to give a huge, tremendous thank you to my mom, Lea Park. You are many things to me, including my favorite editor in the world. This project has been so much more fun and enjoyable because of your support. I love reading through and editing my writing with you. I love how smart and supportive you are, and how you always challenge me to cut down on my tendency towards lefty jargon. Yes! Working with you on this has been one of my favorite parts of this project.

Lastly, thanks to my family and particularly my wife and son, Rachel and Leo, whom I love so much and who had to deal with me while I was a distracted stressball and an insecure mess while working on this project. You make my life so full of joy and fun.

From Marian: I want to thank the Donuts who opened the door into this extraordinary work and world that has shaped all of who I am. Thank you to my Jubilee Gift, Jubilee Justice and Trust Web circles, where spiritual community, reimagination, trust and practice has enabled new ways of being with money and each other across culture, race and class. For the writing part, thanks to the "Writing Arms" of Ain Bailey, Rachel Bagby and Sage Wheeler for reflecting so exquisitely what you hear in my writing. And always thanks to my children, Jamie, Eamon and Maeve, for your unconditional love and support!

From Alex: I would like to thank the Chinese Progressive Association San Francisco and Center for Empowered Politics family for the trust and embracing my many ideas and leadership, especially Shaw San Liu, Le Tim Ly, Emily Lee, J Ishida, Linda Lee and Joyce Lam. Thank you to the Trust Web for the support, encouragement and showing me the possibilities of building a cross-class space centered on trust, relationship and liberation. And much love to my partner and wife, Mychi Nguyen and my awesome and autistic son, Collin Tom.

WELCOME HOME: AN ORGANIZE THE RICH CHEAT SHEET

HOW DO I FIND COMMUNITY, SUPPORT AND A POLITICAL HOME BASE AS A WEALTH HOLDER WHO CARES ABOUT EQUITY AND JUSTICE?

A cheat sheet written by Michael Gast. These are Michael's completely biased opinions only. The groups listed are almost all based in the United States.

Want a cross-class crew of intergenerational donor organizers?

- Solidaire

Want a crew of young radicals with wealth, 18-35?

- Resource Generation if you live in the US
- Resource Movement if you live in Canada
- Resource Justice if you live in the UK
- Resource Transformation if you live in Germany or Austria
- Resource Generation Australia

Want to join a team of progressive wealthy women?

- Women Donors Network
- Women Moving Millions
- Ms. Foundation
- Freedom School For Philanthropy
- A regional or local member of the Women's Funding Network

Want a multi-racial crew of donors of color?

- Donors of Color Network

Want to join a community of wealthy white women addressing the racial wealth gap?

- Impact Collective

Want to tax the rich? I know I do!

- Patriotic Millionaires
- Millionaires for Humanity

Looking for a home for progressive political givers from around the US?

- Way to Win
- Movement Voter Project
- Democracy Alliance

Want a community of international donors?

- Thousand Currents
- Grassroots International
- Global Fund for Women

Want a home for political givers in your state or region?

- Committee on States is a network of progressive state donor alliances around the U.S. To get connected to a state based group of donors supporting progressive electoral organizing and long-term power building, email them at info@committeeonstates.org.

Want to be part of a political party with a vision and plan to win multiracial working-class governing power? I sure do!

- Working Families Party
- Connect with their development team, Braeden Lentz and Colette Henderson, development@workingfamilies.org

Want a home for giving in your local community?

- Check out social justice aligned public foundations or community foundations in your area: https://tr.ee/sjintermediaries

Want to join a crew of employers of domestic workers, organizing for domestic worker rights?

- Hand in Hand

Want a community of philanthropic leaders committed to rebuilding the labor movement?

- Democracy Takes Work https://tr.ee/democracytakeswork

Want to be part of a community of business owners who care about the collective good?

- Main Street Alliance
- Small Business Rising
- Aspen Business Roundtable on Organized Labor

Want to become a social justice aligned investor?

- Center for Economic Democracy's Social Movement Investing Report
- Justice Funder's Just Transition Investment Framework
- The Transformative 25 by Collective Action for Just Finance
- Find a financial advisor using Values Advisor
- Look into the RG Financial Professionals Database https://tr.ee/ rgfinancialprofessionals

Want to support reparations and decolonize your relationship to wealth?

- Decolonizing Wealth and their donor community, Liberated Capital

Want to be part of a multi-generational community of wealthy people integrating collective giving and personal transformation?

- Threshold Foundation

Want to join a community of donors on any range of important issues?

- Check out these justice aligned philanthropic interemediaries: https://tr.ee/sjintermediaries

Want help making and managing a social justice giving plan?

- Find a donor advisor https://tr.ee/sjdonoradvisors

Want to do transformative personal work around your relationship to money?

- Wisdom and Money Network
- Jubilee Gift
- Hire a money coach https://tr.ee/sjdonoradvisors

What to join a community of financial activists shifting the flow of capital and power?

- Apply to Just Economy Institute

These are just some of the groups ready and able to engage and organize the rich. There are surely great groups and individuals missing. This is a living document, kept updated on the Organize the Rich substack, send us your thoughts and suggestions at cheatsheet@organizetherich.com.

ORGANIZATION LIST BY DECADE

This is a list of all the key organizations named in Free the People to Free the Money to Free the People, organized by decade. It is not a comprehensive timeline of this ecosystem or organizing lineage. It is meant as a helpful reference tool as you read through this anthology. All organizations are ongoing unless listed with an ending date.

1900-1960s
- 1917-1948 **Rosenwald Foundation**
- 1961-1986 **Stern Fund**

1970s
- 1971-1988 **Movement for a New Society**
- 1972-2011 **Vanguard Public Foundation**
- 1973 **Ms. Foundation for Women**
- 1976 **Faith and Money Network** (formerly Ministry of Money)
- 1974-1976 **Amalgamated Rich Folks** (ARF)
- 1976-1979 **Conference on National Priorities**
- 1974 **Haymarket People's Fund**
- 1977 **Astraea Lesbian Foundation for Justice**
- 1977 **Bread and Roses Community Fund**
- 1978-2005 **Funding Exchange**
- 1978 **North Star Fund**
- 1979 **Women's Foundation of California**
- 1976 **Liberty Hill Foundation**
- 1976 **Tides Foundation**

1980s
- 1980-2007 **National Network of Grantmakers**
- 1980 **Schumacher Center for a New Economics**
- 1980 **Social Justice Fund Northwest** (formerly A Territory Resource)
- 1981-2008 **Grassroots Fundraising Journal** (merged with Grassroots Institute for Fundraising)
- 1981 **Peace Development Fund**
- 1981 **Threshold Foundation**

- 1981 **Crossroads Fund**
- 1983 **Grassroots International**
- 1983 **Mama Cash**
- 1983-1990 **Rainbow Coalition**
- 1984 **Boston Women's Fund**
- 1984 **Headwaters Foundation for Justice**
- 1984 **RSF Social Finance**
- 1985 **Thousand Currents** (formerly IDEX)
- 1987 **Chinook Fund**
- 1987 **Global Fund for Women**
- 1987 **Social Venture Network**
- 1988 **The Sister Fund** (became HLH Family Foundation)
- 1988 **Common Counsel Foundation**

1990s

- 1990 **Women's Funding Network**
- 1991-1992 **The Impact Project**
- 1992 **Be Present Inc**
- 1992 **Investors Circle**
- 1992 **Business for Social Responsibility** (BSR)
- 1993 **Global Greengrants Fund**
- 1993 **Joint Affinity Groups** (now CHANGE Philanthropy)
- 1993-2006 *More Than Money* **Journal** (from The Impact Project)
- 1995 **Harvest Time**
- 1995 **United for a Fair Economy**
- 1996-2020 **Grassroots Institute for Fundraising**
- 1997 **Responsible Wealth**
- 1997 **Third Wave Foundation**
- 1997 **Tides Advocacy** (formerly The Advocacy Fund)
- 1998-2008 **Changemakers**
- 1998 **Resource Generation** (originally Comfort Zone)
- 1998 **Working Families Party** (formerly The New Party)
- 1998 **Southern Partners Fund**
- 1999 **EDGE Funders Alliance** (originally Funders Network on Trade and Globalization)
- 1999 **Rachel's Network**

2000s
- 2001 **American Independent Business Alliance**
- 2001 **Common Future** (formerly BALLE)
- 2002 **Women Donors Network** (formerly Resourceful Women)
- 2004 **Democracy Alliance**
- 2004-2018 **Play BIG**
- 2004 **Yes! Leveraging Privilege Jams**
- 2004 **Working World**
- 2006 **Women Moving Millions**
- 2008 **Main Street Alliance**
- 2007-2016 **Bolder Giving**
- 2007 **Committee on States**
- 2009 **Justice Funders**
- 2009 **Slow Money**
- 2009 **Voices for Progress**
- 2009 **California Donor Table**

2010s
- 2010 **Giving Pledge**
- 2010 **Giving Projects Network aka The Giving Project**
- 2010 **Hand in Hand**
- 2010 **New Media Ventures**
- 2010 **Patriotic Millionaires**
- 2012 **Center for Economic Democracy**
- 2012 **Center for Popular Democracy**
- 2012 **Local Progress**
- 2012 **New Economy Coalition**
- 2013 **Movement for Black Lives**
- 2013 **Solidaire**
- 2014 **The Trust Web**
- 2015 **Groundswell Fund**
- 2015 **Movement Voter Project**
- 2016-2019 **Lead with Land**
- 2018 **Resource Justice** (UK)
- 2015 **Resource Movement** (Canada)
- 2015 **Resource Transformation** (German-speaking countries)
- 2016 **Donors of Color Network**

- 2017 **Wisdom and Money** (formerly Harvest Time)
- 2017 **Just Economy Institute**
- 2018 **Decolonizing Wealth**
- 2018 **Community-Centric Fundraising**
- 2018 **NDN Collective**
- 2018 **Way to Win**
- 2019 **Jubilee Gift**
- 2019 **Jubilee Justice and Ancestral Journey Program**
- 2019 **Wealth Reclamation Academy of Practitioners**

2020s

- 2020 **Donor Intro to Grounded Giving** (DIGG)
- 2020 **LandBack campaign**
- 2020 **Seed the Vote**
- 2020 **Securing the Roots**
- 2020 **Impact Collective**
- 2021 **Millionaires for Humanity**
- 2021 **Resource Organizing Project** (of Movement Sustainability Commons)
- 2021 **Small Business Rising**
- 2021 **Good Ancestor Movement**
- 2021 **Ancestors & Money**
- 2023 **Perennial Sunflower Project**
- 2023 **Freedom School for Philanthropy**
- 2025 **Resource Generation Australia**

BIBLIOGRAPHY

Books referenced or relied on by the editors in creating this anthology.

Abichandani, Dimple. *A New Era of Philanthropy: Building Equity into Giving.* New York: Routledge, 2022.

Bai, Matt. *The Argument: Inside the Battle to Remake Democratic Politics.* New York: Penguin Publishing Group, 2008.

Bofu-Tawamba, Ndana, Ruby Bright, Stephanie Clohesy, Christine Grumm, Musimbi Kanyoro, Helen LaKelly Hunt, Ana Oliveira, Laura Risimini, Jane Sloane, and Jessica Tomlin. *The Uprising of Women in Philanthropy.* New York: Routledge, 2024.

Burnham, Linda, Max Elbaum, and Maria Poblet, eds. *Power Concedes Nothing: How Grassroots Organizing Wins Elections.* New York: OR Books, 2022.

Burnham, Linda, Rachel Herzing, and Denise Perry. "Project 2050: Toward the Development of a Shared Strategic Framework on the U.S. Left." 2023. https://project2050.org.

Callahan, David. *The Givers: Money, Power, and Philanthropy in a New Gilded Age.* New York: Knopf Doubleday Publishing Group, 2017.

Collins, Chuck. *Born on Third Base: A One Percenter Makes the Case for Tackling Inequality, Bringing Wealth Home, and Committing to the Common Good.* White River Junction, VT: Chelsea Green Publishing, 2016.

Collins, Chuck. *The Wealth Hoarders: How Billionaires Pay Millions to Hide Trillions.* Cambridge, UK: Polity Press, 2021.

Collins, Chuck, Pam Rogers, and Joan P. Garner. *Robin Hood Was Right: A Guide to Giving Your Money for Social Change.* New York: W.W. Norton, 2000.

Daniels, Vanessa. *Unrig the Game: How to Fix Our Broken Democracy.* New York: One World, 2020.

Dreier, Peter, and Chuck Collins. "Traitors to Their Class." *New Labor Forum* 21, no. 1 (Winter 2012): 86-91. https://doi.org/10.4179/NLF.211.0000014.

Ellinger, Christopher, and Anne Ellinger, eds. *More Than Money Journal.* Impact Publishers, 1991-2010.

Garza, Alicia. *The Purpose of Power: How We Come Together When We Fall Apart.* New York: One World, 2020.

Gast, Michael. "Organize the Rich." Substack newsletter, 2022-present. https://organizetherich.substack.com.

Gerber, Lynne, and Tracy Hewat. "Money Talks. So Can We. Resources for People in their 20's Compiled by the Comfort Zone." Organize the Rich Public Archives under Resource Generation/RG Publications, 1997. https://organizetherich.substack.com/p/resources.

Giridharadas, Anand. *Winners Take All: The Elite Charade of Changing the World*. New York: Knopf Doubleday Publishing Group, 2018.

Goldberg, Alison, Karen Pittelman, and Resource Generation. *Creating Change Through Family Philanthropy: The Next Generation*. New York: Soft Skull Press, 2007.

hooks, bell. *Where We Stand: Class Matters*. New York: Routledge, 2000.

Hunt-Hendrix, Leah, and Astra Taylor. *Solidarity: The Past, Present, and Future of a World-Changing Idea*. New York: Pantheon Books, 2024.

Kivel, Paul. *Living in the Shadow of the Cross: Understanding and Resisting the Power and Privilege of Christian Hegemony*. Gabriola Island, BC: New Society Publishers, 2013.

Kivel, Paul. *You Call This a Democracy? Who Benefits, Who Pays, and Who Really Decides*. New York: Apex Press, 2004.

Leondar-Wright, Betsy. *Class Matters: Cross-class Alliance Building for Middle-class Activists*. Gabriola Island, BC: New Society Publishers, 2005.

Lurie, Theodora. "Change Not Charity: The Story of the Funding Exchange." 2016. https://www.fex.org/.

Mayer, Jane. *Dark Money: The Hidden History of the Billionaires Behind the Rise of the Radical Right*. New York: Knopf Doubleday Publishing Group, 2016.

McGhee, Heather. *The Sum of Us: What Racism Costs Everyone and How We Can Prosper Together*. New York: One World, 2021.

Mogil, Christopher [now Christopher Ellinger], and Anne Slepian [now Anne Ellinger]. *We Gave Away a Fortune: Stories of People who Have Devoted Themselves and Their Wealth to Peace, Justice, and the Environment*. Gabriola Island, BC: New Society Publishers, 1992.

Neiman, Garrett. *Rich White Men: What It Takes to Uproot the Old Boys' Club and Transform America*. New York: Beacon Press, 2023.

Odendahl, Teresa J. *Charity Begins At Home: Generosity And Self-interest Among The Philanthropic Elite*. New York: Basic Books, 1991.

Ostrander, Susan A. *Money for Change: Social Movement Philanthropy at Haymarket People's Fund*. Philadelphia: Temple University Press, 1995.

Pearl, Morris, Erica Payne, and The Patriotic Millionaires. *Tax the Rich! How Lies, Loopholes, and Lobbyists Make the Rich Even Richer*. New York: New Press, 2021.

Phillips, Steve. *How We Win the Civil War: Securing a Multiracial Democracy and Ending White Supremacy for Good*. New York: New Press, 2022.

Pittelman, Karen, and Resource Generation. *Classified: How to Stop Hiding Your Privilege and Use It for Social Change!* Brooklyn, NY: Catapult, 2005.

Rabinowitz, Alan. *Social Change Philanthropy in America*. Westport, CT: Praeger, 1990.

Rashid, Jasmin. *The Financial Activist Playbook: 8 Strategies for Everyday People to Reclaim Wealth and Collective Well-Being*. New York: New World Library, 2021.

Resource Generation. *Social Change Financial Planning Notebook*. New York: Resource Generation, 2014. https://tr.ee/rgfinancialplanningnotebook.

Risher, Jen. *We Need to Talk: A Memoir About Wealth*. Seattle: Sasquatch Books, 2021.

Sherman, Rachel. *Uneasy Street: The Anxieties of Affluence*. Princeton, NJ: Princeton University Press, 2017.

Solomon, Joel. *The Clean Money Revolution: Reinventing Power, Purpose, and Capitalism*. Gabriola Island, BC: New Society Publishers, 2018.

Taylor, Astra. *The Age of Insecurity: Coming Together as Things Fall Apart*. New York: House of Anansi Press, 2023.

Villanueva, Edgar. *Decolonizing Wealth: Indigenous Wisdom to Heal Divides and Restore Balance*. Oakland, CA: Berrett-Koehler Publishers, 2018.

Wernick, Laura J. "Critical Consciousness Development Impact on Social Justice Movement Giving among Wealthy Activists." *Social Work Research* 40, no. 3 (2016): 159-169.

Wernick, Laura J. "Leveraging Privilege: Organizing Young People with Wealth to Support Social Justice." PhD diss., University of Michigan, 2009.

Wernick, Laura J. "Leveraging Privilege: Organizing Young People with Wealth to Support Social Justice." *Social Service Review* 86, no. 2 (2012): 323-345.

Wernick, Laura J., Daniela R. Jimenez, Mica Nimkarn, Blythe L. Robbins, and Derek Brian Tice-Brown. "Moving Money to Support Social Justice Movements: A Spiritual Practice." *Journal of Community Psychology* 53, no. 1 (2025). https://doi.org/10.1002/jcop.23157.

Wimsatt, William Upski. *Bomb the Suburbs*. New York: Soft Skull Press, 2008.

Wimsatt, William Upski. *No More Prisons*. New York: Soft Skull Press, 1999.